TEACHING A DIVERSE PRIMARY ART CURRICULUM

Other titles from Bloomsbury Education

100 Ideas for Primary Teachers: Art by Adele Darlington

Art Shaped: 50 sustainable art projects to kickstart children's creativity by Darrell Wakelam

Bloomsbury Curriculum Basics: Teaching Primary Art and Design by Emily Gopaul

The Arts in Primary Education: Breathing life, colour and culture into the curriculum by Ghislaine Kenyon

Time to Shake Up the Primary Curriculum: A step-by-step guide to creating a global, diverse and inclusive school by Sarah Wordlaw

TEACHING A DIVERSE PRIMARY ART CURRICULUM

A practical guide

KAYTIE HOLDSTOCK

BLOOMSBURY EDUCATION
LONDON OXFORD NEW YORK NEW DELHI SYDNEY

BLOOMSBURY EDUCATION
Bloomsbury Publishing Plc
50 Bedford Square, London, WC1B 3DP, UK
29 Earlsfort Terrace, Dublin 2, Ireland

BLOOMSBURY, BLOOMSBURY EDUCATION and the Diana logo are trademarks of Bloomsbury Publishing Plc

First published in Great Britain, 2024 by Bloomsbury Publishing Plc

A catalogue record for this book is available from the British Library

ISBN: PB: 978-1-8019-9353-1; ePDF: 978-1-8019-9354-8; ePub: 978-1-8019-9351-7

2 4 6 8 10 9 7 5 3 1 (paperback)

Typeset by Newgen KnowledgeWorks Pvt. Ltd., Chennai, India
Printed and bound in the UK by CPI Group (UK) Ltd., Croydon, CR0 4YY

Evolve

Contents

Enjoy!

Experiment

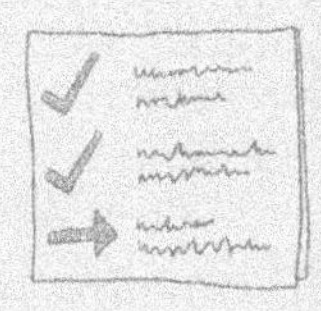

Evaluate

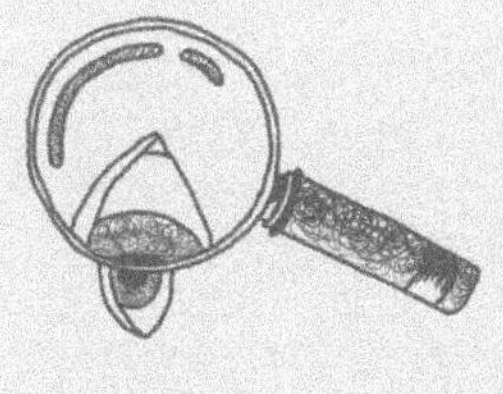

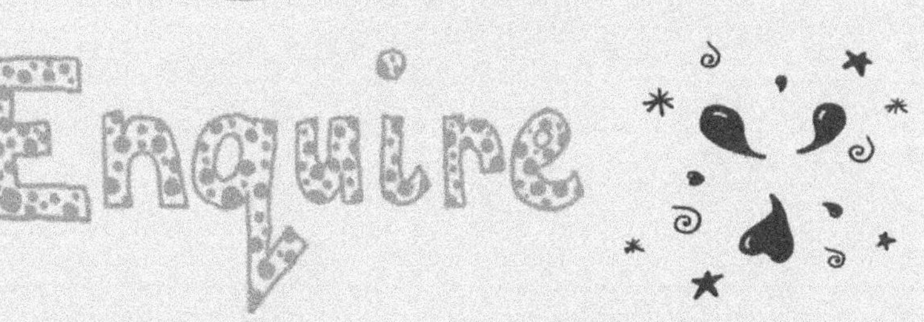

Acknowledgements

It still does not feel real to have written an actual book! I'm so grateful to everyone who encouraged me on this path and as I'm sure you can imagine, there are so many people to thank.

This journey began when I emailed Bloomsbury in a spur of the moment act of spontaneity one afternoon with a rough idea that had been bouncing around my head for a while. I didn't expect a reply, I certainly didn't expect that email to set the wheels in motion that would bring me here. I knew there was a huge need for a book like this, but it never really crossed my mind that anyone would think that I was the one to write it. So my first thank you goes to Emily Evans, Commissioning Editor of Bloomsbury Education. From the word go, your positivity and belief in me as an author has been unwavering. I'm so grateful it was you that picked up that email that day!

It turns out that writing a book is pretty time-consuming! So enormous thanks has to go to my mum and dad, who, as always stepped in with whatever was needed: from entertaining the children to walking The Beast... I know how lucky we are to have you on our team.

To Ophelia, Artemis and Azraea, our gorgeous girls. Thank you for your invaluable help with the artwork for this book. I will forgive you for trashing my art supplies because you have never stopped reminding me that, 'It's so cool that Mummy wrote a book!'. I love you very much and I hope you know how grateful I am for our little family.

I would finally like to thank Tom, on whom everything depends. You are my fiercest advocate and my strongest supporter. Without your encouragement, I would never have even have considered this book could be a possibility. You are the glue that holds everything together.

To everyone else who has been part of my life along the way, I'm grateful for everything, even the tough bits. It turns out everything really does happen for a reason!

Enjoy the book,

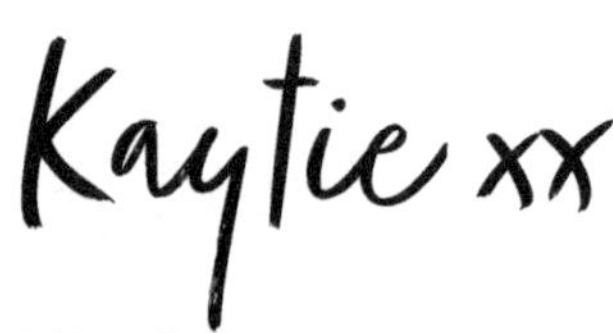

Introduction

The rationale behind this book is a difficult one to put into words. During my 20 years' teaching in the primary classroom, I've evaluated and re-evaluated my practice time and again but one thing has remained a constant: art.

Creativity has always been at the heart of what I've tried to do in the classroom. As a teacher, as an arts advisor for the local authority and now, as an art lecturer for primary trainee teachers, I genuinely believe that creative thinking puts the magic back into learning. This isn't just because of the impact that I believe art can have on a child's holistic development, but because offering a creative curriculum puts the fun back into teaching and helps you remember why you went into education in the first place.

Despite the ever-changing landscape of teaching shaped by trends in government policy, I can honestly say that the only approach I have never questioned is the power of art in a child's education. Not because I have tested it empirically or because the research agrees (it does!) but because I have seen it first-hand.

By giving children exciting and open-ended tasks, art can reach everyone. Making space in the week where children take the lead in their learning has an incredibly empowering effect and develops thinking skills that can translate to further engagement throughout the curriculum. Maybe it will be the quiet child who hasn't found their voice yet, or the academic child just waiting to be released from their pigeonhole. The pupil whose confidence is rock bottom or even the child that just can't sit still; art brings out the best in everyone. An arts-based curriculum boosts self-esteem and encourages children to think outside the box. After all, these are key attributes that chalk up to a successful, healthy life – not top marks in a maths test.

However, prioritising creativity in some schools is a challenge for even the most passionate teacher. I have worked for headteachers who have fully encouraged my drive to instill the arts into the children's daily lives. I have also worked for those that haven't. My hope is that this book will make you stand firm in your commitment to the power of art and reassure you that children's development is definitely enhanced by more art, not less. The evidence for this is explored in the next chapter.

But why a diverse primary art curriculum? In some ways, this book is my cathartic attempt to remedy the mistakes of my own teaching past. I am ashamedly aware that for the majority of my education I never once questioned why every single artist I learned about was a White man. I bought into the idea that these were just the most significant artists in art history and foolishly regurgitated this verbatim to the children in my classes. It is only more recently, through my own personal study, that I have begun to uncover the corruption and whitewashing in which art history has been complicit.

Art history, like history itself, has been written by the winners. The majority of the traditional artists we study in school were the elite establishment. They were White, European men born into affluent families with the resources, the social standing and the access to education that enabled them to launch full-time careers as artists. If you dig deeper and explore art's rich and diverse 'hidden' histories, that is where the real inspiration can be found. That is when you uncover the rule breakers, the rebels, the social activists and the artists that overcame all odds to pursue their passions. For me, these artists encapsulate what I want for my young people. To dream big, be themselves and fight for what they believe in.

Despite this, it is not fair to say that historically, no women, people of colour, disabled people or LGBTQ+ people have succeeded as artists. In fact, quite the opposite is true. Many of the incredible artists featured in this book did actually experience financial recognition and worldwide renown within their lifetimes. What I mean to say is that after their deaths, an establishment that had a clear idea of what an artist should look like obliterated their legacy. Yet in reality, an authentic art history draws its influences from all ages, abilities, genders and orientations.

Even worse, there is evidence throughout history of White men stealing and appropriating the ideas of artists who did not fit the traditional canon. Take Duchamp's infamous urinal, which was probably originally submitted by Baroness Elsa von Freytag-Loringhoven; Lee Miller's development of solarisation, first attributed to Man Ray; and Lucas Samara's mirrored room that opened to great acclaim just months after Yayoi Kusama's installation of almost exactly the same name.

This is why art has so much to teach us. The stories of the artists in this book are often as inspirational as the artwork they produce. And this is why it is important to share these stories with children. We want our young people to grow up with a strong moral compass, to challenge the status quo and act as champions for what they believe in. The only way for us to move forward is to learn from the mistakes of our past and view our histories with a critical eye.

The purpose of the primary art curriculum is not for children to paint pretty pictures. It is not a break from more academic subjects. Primary art is a vehicle through which children can be encouraged to express themselves freely and openly. To respond creatively in an environment with no barriers or restrictions. Where they can learn about themselves and others without judgement. These are not skills that are easily developed through an increasingly narrow curriculum, making art not an option, but a necessity.

For you as a teacher, primary art is an area where you have freedom and autonomy. The National Curriculum is sparse and the guidance is limited. You are free to develop starting points that will inspire and create an environment where your children will thrive. You have the space to prioritise engagement and fun. Remember, the things you do in your art lessons are the things your children will remember for the rest of their lives. Make it count!

Chapter 1

How to teach a diverse primary art curriculum

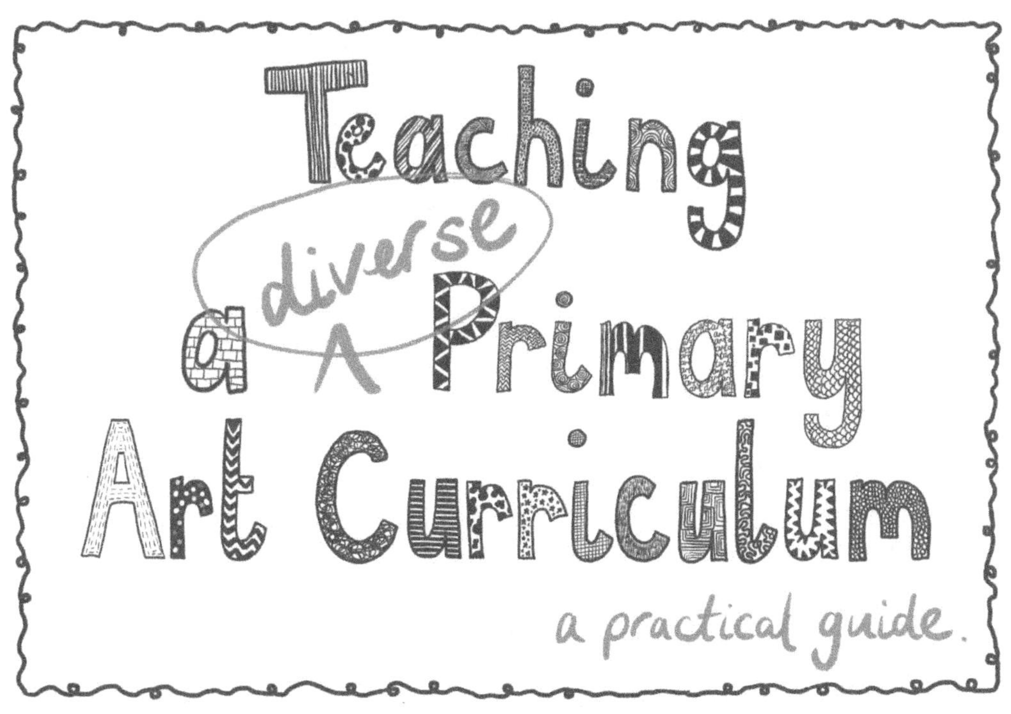

An outstanding art curriculum is nothing without diversity at its heart. The two cannot exist without each other. But how do we ensure that all our children are getting the best possible opportunities in art? How do we get our schools on board? Let's start at the beginning.

Why is art important?

If you are working in primary education, you will already know that many teachers with a passion for art find themselves in the position of having to fight for their subject. Perceptions that art is both expendable and easy to teach are embedded throughout primary education, leading to the gradual erosion of time, resources and attitudes towards the subject (The All-Party Parliamentary Group for Art, Craft and Design in Education, 2023). Even the most recent Ofsted Research Review in Art and Design (Ofsted, 2023) acknowledges these challenges. So, if you are a passionate art educator wanting to put diversity at the heart of your curriculum, your first step is often to convince those around you of the incredible value and importance of art in primary education. Only then can you truly begin to advocate for change.

Let's start with the proven benefits of the arts.

There are so many reasons why art is essential for children's holistic development. The Cultural Learning Alliance (CLA), in their 2017 report 'The Case for Cultural Learning', present the significant key benefits of an arts-rich education that would make even the most resistant educators pay attention.

The arts can make you **CLEVERER** (by up to 17 per cent in fact!):

As well as this increase in cognitive function, participation in the arts improves children's attainment in reading and maths. Arts-based learning also impacts the skills and behaviour that lead to children doing better in school. Based on this evidence alone, we could improve our children's academic outcomes by doing more art, not less.

The arts can make you **HEALTHIER**:

Incredibly, people who take part in regular arts activity report themselves to be 38 per cent healthier. People who prioritise opportunities for creativity are happier, healthier and more fulfilled. Why would we deny children the chance to develop healthy habits with such powerful, long-term benefits?

The arts can make you **MORE SUCCESSFUL**:

Studying arts subjects means you are more likely to find and keep employment. Quite the opposite of the myth that many secondary schools profess when it comes to choosing GCSEs. The arts also have a significant impact on social mobility, with children from low-income households who study arts subjects at university more likely to get a degree and become engaged citizens that volunteer or vote.

This is compelling evidence. Once we convince schools that art matters, only then can we convince schools that art matters for *everyone*.

Why do we need to change our approach to art?

Which artists did you learn about at school? The answer to this question will differ from person to person but I am sure that there would be some similarities. Maybe you studied Monet's calm and tranquil waterlilies, his smudges merging and combining to create a garden filled with movement and texture. Or maybe you remember the beautiful concentric circles of Kandinsky, swirling and spiraling in all their rainbow glory? And who could forget the deep and emotional work of van Gogh, with his dynamic brushstrokes and vibrant contrasts of colour (and the ear story of course, a guaranteed hit in every primary classroom!).

There may be some variation in the list of artists that are studied in primary schools, but there is one very predictable consistency. All the artists will be men, most of the artists will be White and many of the artists will also be dead. This 'perfect three' ensures that Picasso, Warhol, Matisse and Klee also regularly make the cut.

There is nothing wrong with these artists being celebrated in school. In fact, it is wonderful that children can be inspired by such incredible artistic visionaries. This book does not advocate for the removal of these artists, or the degradation of their undeniable impact on the world of art. Instead, this book calls for the inclusion of equally inspirational artists who were contemporaries of the great masters, yet whose contributions have been consigned to the past because they did not fit the face of art at the time. It also advocates for a diverse range of living artists, who will inspire children to see art as something that is achievable for everyone. With the UK creative industries growing at a staggering rate, art is not only a legitimate career path, but also a creative skill set on which this country is fiercely reliant.

This book is not designed to make you as an educator feel guilty. Like you, my art education was grounded in the same, limited selection of artists, and for much of my career I have taught children in the same way without ever thinking to question why. But as my passion for art education has grown, so has my realisation that I have been missing out on so much. My knowledge of art and artists has been so incredibly limited by the narrow lens through which I was taught to observe the history of art.

What this means for all of us is that there is important work to be done. Ofsted's latest art and design research review reinforces this in no uncertain terms:

> "Subject leaders and curriculum designers should think carefully about the examples and case studies they include in the curriculum to illustrate the variety of established, contested and neglected stories of art. High-quality art curriculums will give examples of the diversity of art in different areas of making..."
>
> **(Ofsted, 2023)**

Change is long overdue. Children in our primary art classes deserve an art curriculum that is as richly diverse as they are. It is imperative that children see themselves represented in the art that we teach. It is essential that our curriculum is designed so that children truly believe that art is for everyone and everyone can be an artist.

How do we choose who to study?

There is nothing in the National Curriculum that tells us which artists we should study. The only statutory advice we are given is that children should be taught:

> **Key Stage 1:** 'about the work of a range of artists, craft makers and designers, describing the differences and similarities between different practices and disciplines, and making links to their own work.'
>
> **Key Stage 2:** 'about great artists, architects and designers in history.'
>
> **(Department for Education (DfE), 2014)**

This gives enormous freedom for art teachers to design a curriculum that meets the needs of our diverse world. It is also a wonderful opportunity for teachers to choose artists whose artworks really inspire them as educators and will connect with the pupils that they teach. Your enthusiasm is the most valuable tool in engaging your class with art, so choose art and artists that evoke a genuine passion in you, and this in itself will light up your delivery and inspire the children to want to know more.

Diversifying your art curriculum is not about replacing the White, dead men. It is more about showing children the multiple ways that art can exist. Instead of removing the action paintings of Jackson Pollock from your curriculum, why not hold his powerful dynamic work up against the way that Frank Bowling experiments by moving and tilting the canvas beneath pouring paint? Both artists celebrate the way that paint moves, splashes and flows, and children will learn more about their own painting from engaging with these different approaches together than they ever could from studying just one artist in isolation.

If children are going to truly meet the aims of the National Curriculum, they need to be 'describing the differences and similarities between different practices and disciplines' (DFE, 2014). And for this comparison to be authentic, these links need to be made explicit so that children can talk with confidence about their observations.

Another powerful way to open children's minds to a broader spectrum of art is to compare artists by theme. A study of abstraction inspired by Kandinsky's circles would be greatly enhanced by a comparison to the work of Sonia Delaunay; just as children will get a greater understanding of portraiture by looking at the work of Alice Neel and Amy Sherald alongside Pablo Picasso. These artists exist in different times and have contrasting, but equally brilliant, ideas of what a portrait should look like. It also raises opportunities to engage children in social activism and reflect on what we can all learn from art about society and ourselves. This diversity of stimuli is encouraging for children. It makes them look at their own work in new ways and recognise that there are infinite ways of achieving the same objective. By celebrating our own unique perspective, somewhere amongst this wealth of inspiration, children will find their own artistic paths.

There are also opportunities to improve the diversity of the primary art curriculum in the genres of art that we choose to teach. Craft, the act of making things by hand, has traditionally been considered a lesser art form, with many crafts historically being consigned to the domain of women. Textile disciplines such as sewing, weaving and embroidery are often labelled 'homecrafts', whilst 'fine art' such as painting and sculpture have been reserved for the men in the art elite. In 1886, Harriet Powers, a Black American woman born into slavery, produced her 'Bible quilt' the same year that Paul Cézanne painted his 'Still Life with Cherries and Peaches'. Both these pieces of art are now considered masterpieces, but there is a reason why you are more likely to have heard of one than the other. We need to bring back these crafts that are so intertwined with our origins and ensure that the children we teach feel a connection and pride in the art of their ancestors. Only then are we giving a true reflection of the artists, craft makers and designers who have worked throughout history.

How do we engage children in artists' work?

The principles of engaging children with artists' work are the same whether you are introducing children to a new, exciting artist from your diverse curriculum, or studying the traditional favourites. Either way, there is nothing to gain from children copying an artist's work. Putting an image of Vincent van Gogh's sunflowers on the whiteboard to copy is the quickest way to tell children that they are failing as an artist. In the same way that we would not ask children to copy swathes of text from a Michael Morpurgo book for them to develop as authors, copying someone else's art is nothing but a mundane task to be completed. There is an assumption that all art is creative, but this is an example of how wrong this can be.

Aside from imitation, there is so much that children can learn from artists' work that can be translated into their own ideas.

Paula Briggs, art champion and founder of incredible visual art charity AccessArt, encourages teachers to start each lesson with a question (Briggs, 2022). This idea is the perfect foundation for encouraging children to dive right into truly creative art lessons. When engaging children with the work of other artists, this tiny shift in the way you frame your learning objectives could have a powerful impact on the quality of children's responses. Instead of fixed ideas or 'I can' statements that are outcome-based, reframe your intention to open up a wider range of possibilities.

Outcome-based learning objective	Open question / starting point
I can paint in the style of van Gogh	How did van Gogh create movement with paint?
I understand that pointillism uses dots to create a picture	What happens when dots are combined?
I can paint a still life	When you really look, what can you see that you didn't see before?

You will still know what you are hoping children will find out. You will also know what inspiration you will share to move children forward with their thinking. But where the journey will lead, that's for you and your class to find out together. That is the magic and uniqueness of art.

Reframing your input will also generate art lessons that encourage choice. Although modelling a new skill or a new technique is vitally important, too much modelling can be restrictive. So many subjects in the primary curriculum require children to conform to a specific set of rules or a required standard. Art is the opposite. There are no WAGOLLs

(What a good one looks like) in art and design. The 'here's one I made earlier' approach instantly shuts down children's creative thinking because they will assume that the gold standard of work will be to create something that looks exactly like yours.

The best way to model creative thinking is for you to go on the journey with the children. Sit down, open your sketchbook and join in. Model your thought processes out loud, try new things, celebrate your successes and show how you manage the disappointment when things don't look the way you imagined. It won't take long for the children to follow.

Structuring your lessons

> "The arts' position in the school curriculum symbolizes to the young what adults believe is important."
>
> **(Elliot Eisner, 2002)**

This statement needs to be at the heart of your diverse art curriculum. Make time to do art properly. Even if you can't do it every week; when you do it, do it well. This shows children that art matters. And if it matters to you, it will matter to them.

The art expedition

Each art expedition included in this book follows the same structure. The art expedition is a scaffold developed to encourage a truly creative approach and to allow children to take ownership of their art whilst maintaining a clear learning intention.

The expedition is also designed to incorporate the three domains of knowledge categorised by the Ofsted Research Review: practical, theoretical and disciplinary (Ofsted, 2023):

- Children will develop practical skills by learning new techniques and processes that they will practise and perfect.
- They will gain theoretical knowledge by studying different movements of art, the lives of artists, and bringing these neglected histories to life by making connections between makers and craftspeople they already know and artists they are about to discover.
- And finally, their theoretical knowledge will be encouraged by asking and answering 'big' questions through art, forming and justifying opinions, and evaluating their own ideas against what has come before.

Here is an example of how an art expedition is structured:

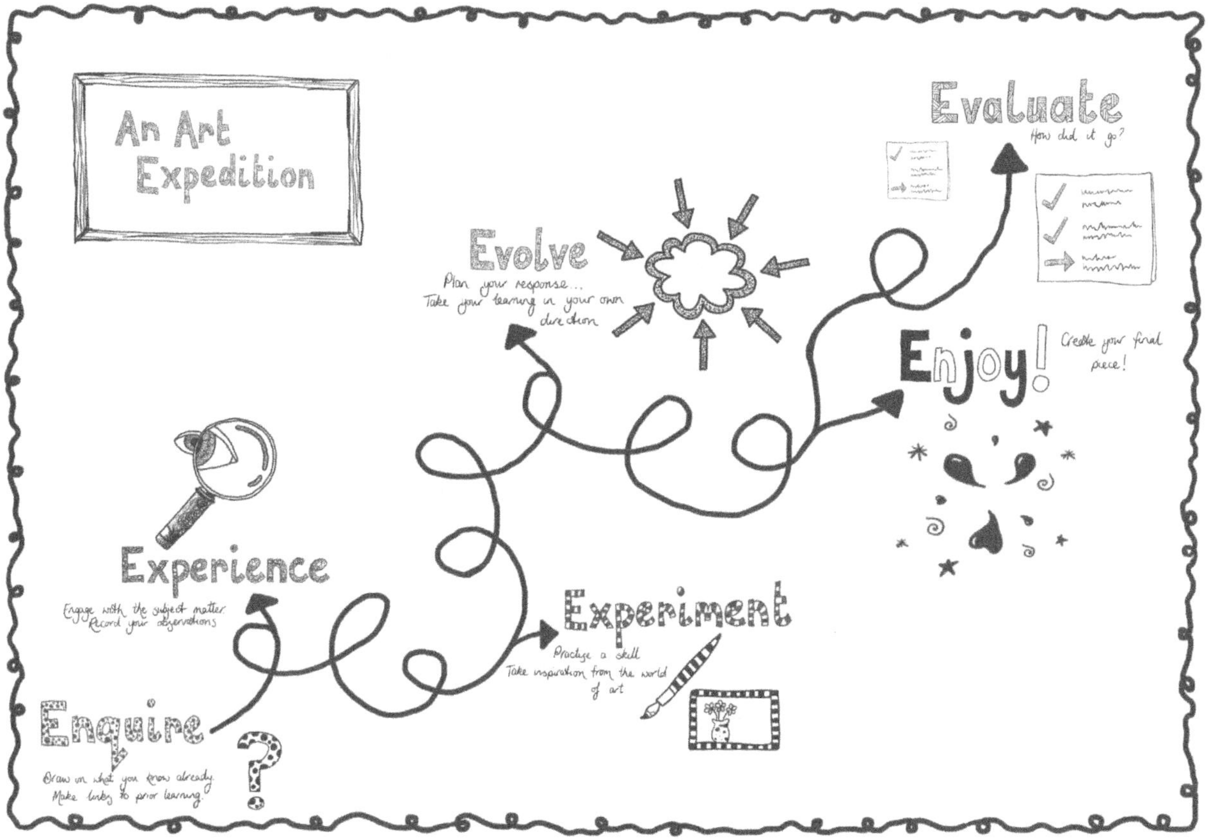

An Art Expedition

Enquire
Draw on what you know already
Make links to prior learning

Experience
Engage with the subject matter
Record your observations

Experiment
Practise a skill
Take inspiration from the world of art

Evolve
Plan your response...
Take your learning in your own direction

Enjoy!
Create your final piece!

Evaluate
How did it go?

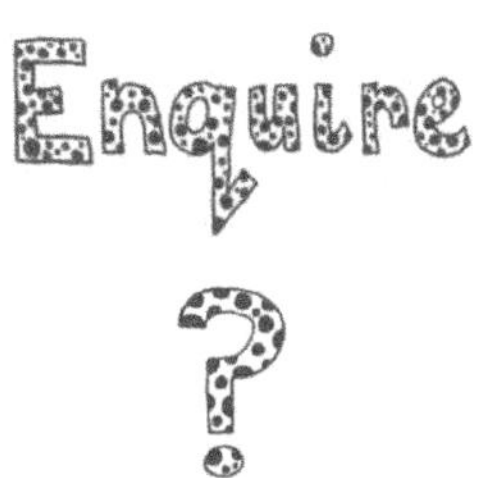

Draw on what you know already; make links to prior learning.

Share the question (see the table on page 12 outlining different questions you could use at Key Stage 1 and 2) and start your expedition with open discussion, where children can share their thoughts and make links to their own experiences. What have they done in previous lessons that might inform their thinking?

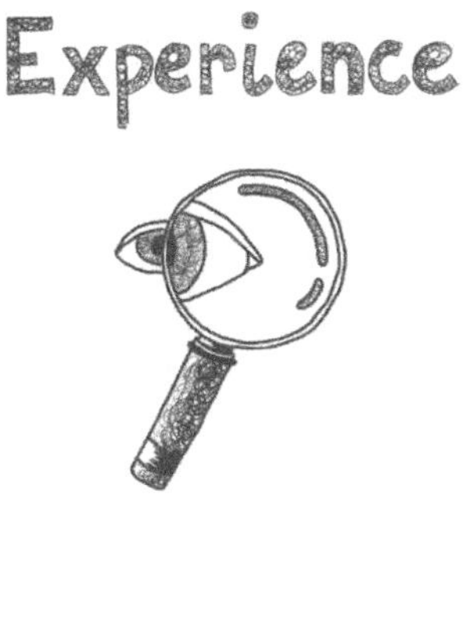

Experience

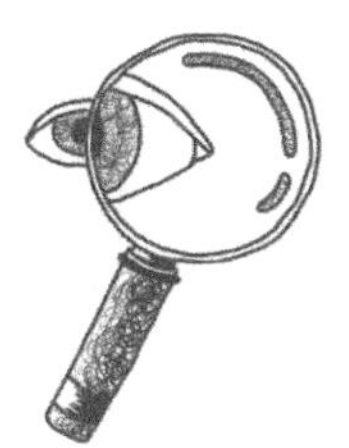

Engage with the subject matter; record your observations.

Put the question in the middle of a page and give children as much opportunity as possible to explore it independently, recording their observations in their sketchbooks. Allow access to choices of media and ask children to sketch, take rubbings, photograph, find pictures in magazines, mix colours; whatever inspires them. Encourage children to use their senses by looking closely, feeling for texture, listening, smelling; whatever helps them to learn more.

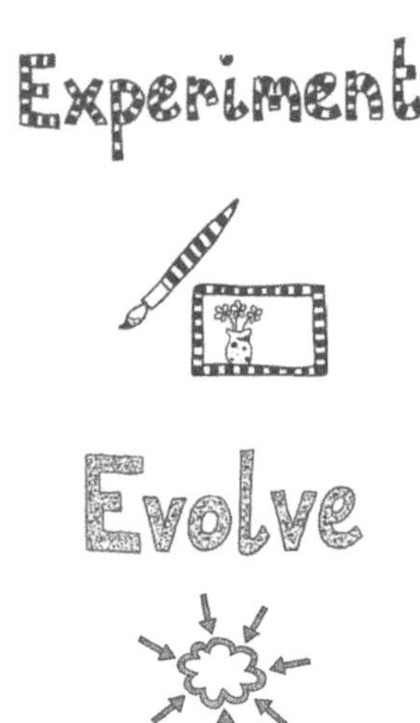

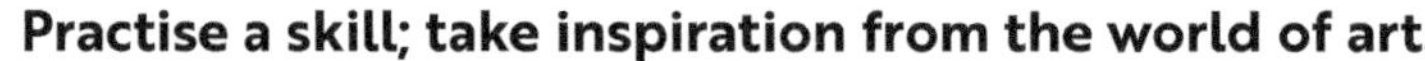

Practise a skill; take inspiration from the world of art.

Introduce something new. Maybe it will be inspiration from a new artist or a new skill to learn. Try out these new techniques. We don't copy the work of other artists, but we might ask questions about how they work and try to emulate those techniques for ourselves to develop our own understanding of how a medium can be used.

Plan your response; take your learning in your own direction.

Children need time to design their final response. How will they use the new technique or knowledge to create their own personal reflection on the question? This is the planning stage where children practise the skills they will need to realise their idea. Encourage children to make mistakes as part of the learning process. Much of the frustration children experience around art is as a result of diving into a final piece without the opportunity to practise and find out what works beforehand. This sketchbook page, where all the ideas for the final piece are collated, might look like a mood board, a sketch or something entirely different.

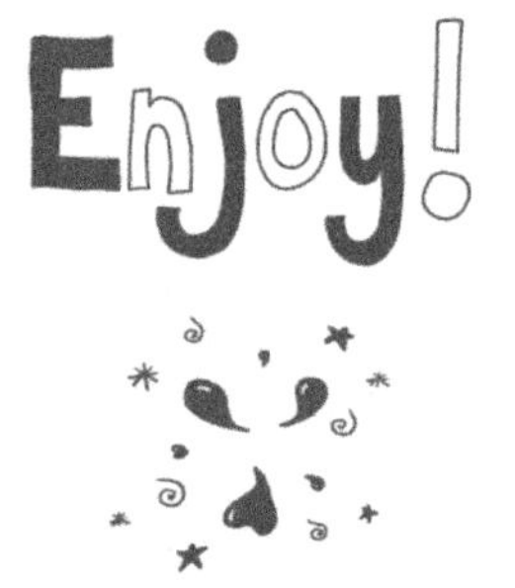

Create your final piece.

This is when children create their own personal response to the question, using the skills or techniques they have learnt. This has been carefully planned but we should still encourage children to stray into new territory as they adapt to the progress of their artwork. The sketchbook practice and planning stages will empower children to create individual and authentic responses with clear intentions. They have had the opportunity to try things out and will have developed a clear idea of what they want to create.

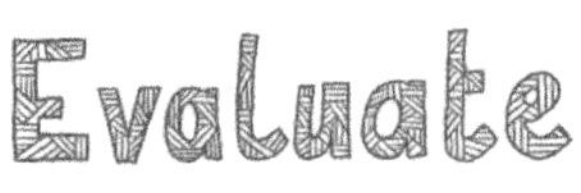

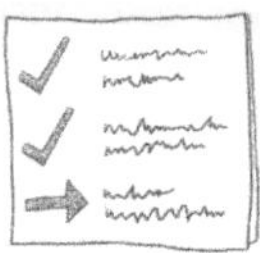

How did it go?

It is important for children to have the opportunity to reflect on their artwork. Encourage children to celebrate their successes and think proactively about how they could develop their thinking. Ask children to consider where they could have taken the project further.

There is purposely no time allocation for each of these sections. Different projects will provoke different responses, so move along the expedition together at your own pace. You may move through several sections within the space of one lesson; some sections may take more than one lesson to explore fully. Allow yourself and the children the freedom to get the most out of the journey and, most importantly, enjoy the expedition!

A whole school curriculum

Look at your school's curriculum as a whole. If you are the art lead, you either have the privilege of rolling out a brand-new art curriculum with diversity at its heart, or take a softer approach and make links between the 'perfect three' artists (White, male, dead!) already being studied, and complement their work with artists who represent a more accurate and holistic view of art history.

Within this book I will try to offer solutions to both approaches. Although my priority is to introduce you to artists who may have been overlooked by the historical canon of 'what an artist is', I have also made suggestions of how these artists could be incorporated alongside those more traditionally taught. There is also space deliberately left in each year group for artistic skills and processes to be taught in isolation.

Within your curriculum overview, children should have the opportunity to refine and develop different art styles and processes. Giving children the opportunity to work with clay in Year 2 does not mean that children have 'done clay'. They can only really become proficient in an art process if they are given opportunities to rehearse and revisit the skills they are learning.

Remember, the age groups suggested for each artist are very rough guidelines. You know your children and this will put you in the best place to decide which projects will be most suitable for your class. Your children will also access the initial questions in their own ways and will explore the subjects from the position they are in on their own artistic journey. As a result, all of these projects can be easily adapted for any age group.

The table on page 12 illustrates the artists and learning expeditions outlined in the rest of this book. Choosing just 23 artists was indeed a challenge! My hope is that this structure will empower you to create your own adventures in art underpinned by the amazing, diverse artists that mean something to you.

Key Stage 1	Lower Key Stage 2	Upper Key Stage 2
Drawing		
Zaha Hadid What is a line? **Jean-Michel Basquiat** Who is your hero?	**Stephen Wiltshire** How do you draw a journey?	**Kenturah Davis** What can a portrait say about us?
Painting		
Hilma af Klint How do you paint a feeling?	**Sarah Biffin** How do artists use paint? **Jacob Lawrence** Can art tell a story?	**Kehinde Wiley** How is power depicted in art?
Sculpture		
Cecilia Vicuña What is a sculpture?	**Ai Weiwei** What does it mean to be individual?	**Lubaina Himid** What do we remember?
Collage		
Deborah Roberts How are we different? How are we the same?	**Moses Williams** Can shadows be art?	**Chila Kumari Singh Burman** How does food connect us?
Photography		
Mitchel Wu What do toys do when we aren't there?	**Cindy Sherman** Who do I want to be?	**Victoria Villasana** Why is water important?
Printing		
Utagawa Hiroshige What can we learn about trees?	**Favianna Rodriguez** How do colours work together?	**Elizabeth Catlett** What does it mean to be free?
Textiles		
El Anatsui Can rubbish be beautiful?	**Judith Scott** What can you do with a thread?	**Hew Locke** Why do we come together?
Inspiring children to understand the world of art Many ideas to celebrate the traditional, modern and contemporary art that has evolved from cultures all around the globe.		

How do we assess pupil progress in art and design?

The answer to assessment in art is not specific to a diverse art curriculum, but the answer does in fact lie in diversity. This is because learning in art is not a linear journey. Children do not pass through the same milestones in the same order. In fact, children often take completely unique paths in art and this is actually a hallmark of really good-quality art teaching. The only way you can really and truly measure progress is to compare a child against their own individual journey.

This is why sketchbooks are so important. If you keep a record of children's artistic process over time, it is actually incredibly easy to see the ways in which children have developed. It is this measure of improvement that will help you assess. Consider these aspects of each child's artistic development:

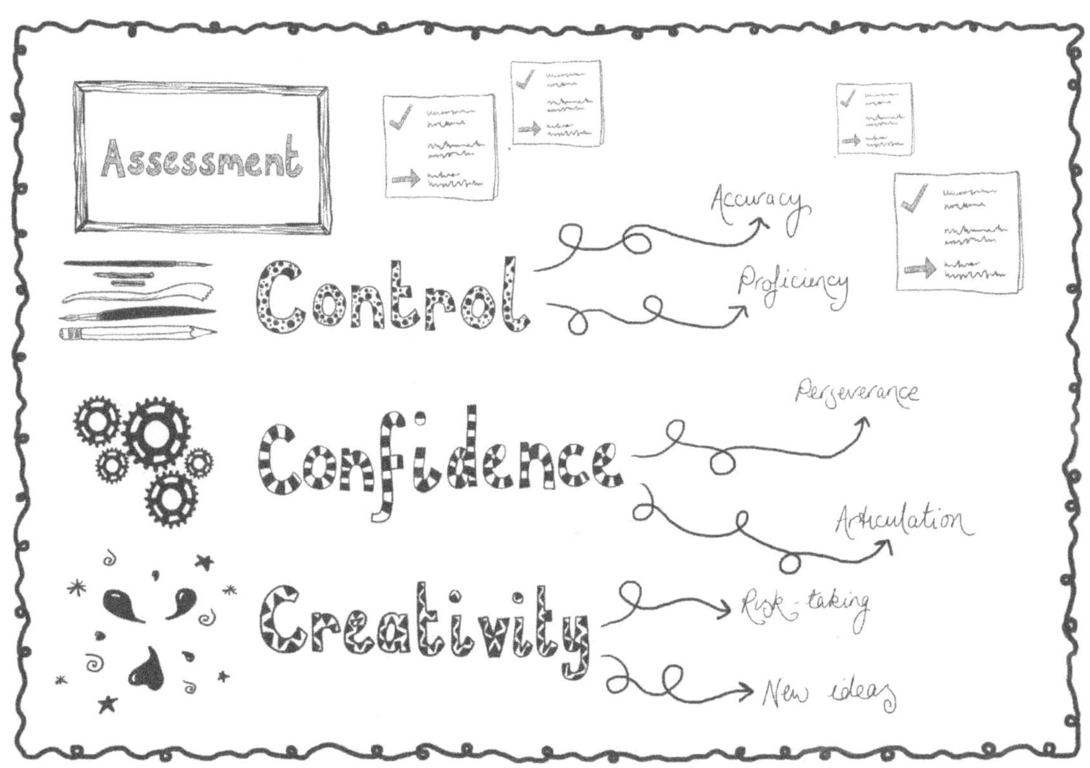

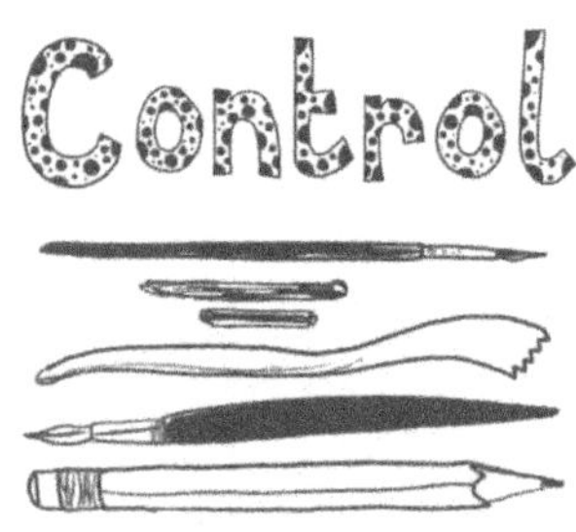

Accuracy and Proficiency

Has the child developed their control over the process you are learning?

Are they becoming more accurate in the way they attempt to achieve their intentions?

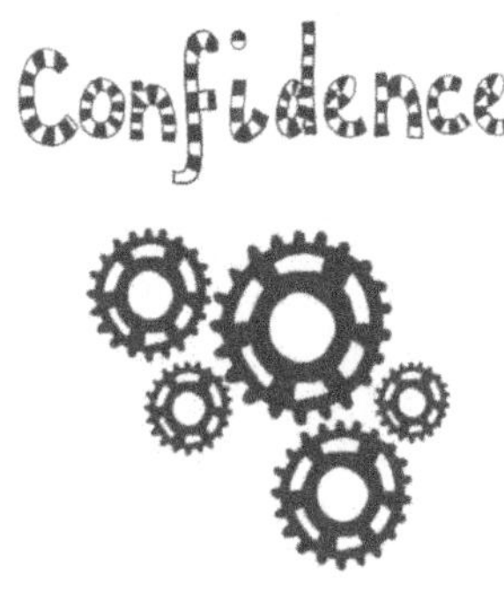

Perseverance and Articulation

Can the child articulate what they are doing?

Do they persevere when things go wrong?

Are they developing their own preferences and styles?

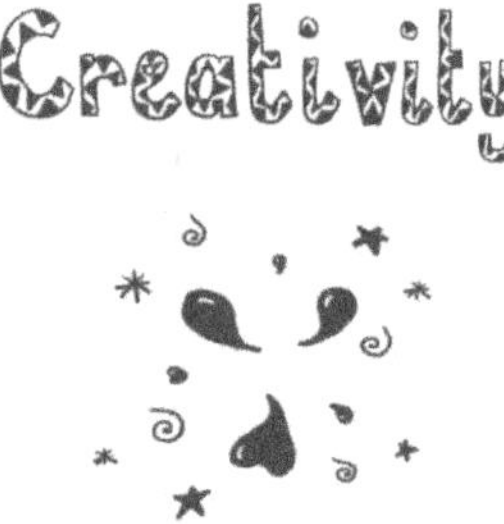

Risk-taking and New Ideas

Does the child express original ideas or do they become stuck in what they have done before?

Do they experiment and play?

Can they take their inspiration to new places or do they stay within the safety of the ideas of those around them?

Peer and self-assessment are also important tools. Many of the attributes above will become clear in children's own annotations. Encourage the sharing of peer feedback through sticky notes and ask children to respond to the comments from their classmates. Offering a structure of positively worded questions will model to children the ways that they can provide constructive feedback. Here are a few ideas:

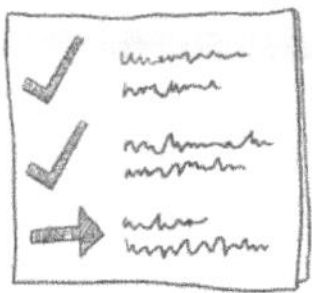

- Which ideas do you think worked best?
- Which part looks like it was tricky?
- How could this idea be taken further?

Remember, a sketchbook is a child's individual journal. Neither peers nor teachers have the right to be writing directly onto a child's personal responses. These sticky notes can be kept in a wallet stapled to the inside cover of the sketchbook, or paperclipped to the page for children to refer to.

We do not have the right to say whose art is 'best'. If children are engaged in truly creative art, it should be impossible to look at 30 final pieces and rank them in order of quality. Only the process will reveal if the children are developing the skills they need to become authentic and fluent artists. After all, what is a diverse art curriculum without the celebration of the diversity of its artists at its heart?

Chapter 2

Drawing

Introduction to drawing

Drawing can often be a child's biggest barrier to accessing and enjoying the art curriculum. If you teach in Key Stage 2, you will already be familiar with the groans that accompany getting out the pencils along with the protests of 'But I'm rubbish at drawing!'.

The problem is that we have been educated into thinking that observational drawing is all that there is. Drawing is actually a fun, dynamic and playful exercise where the marks being made on the page outweigh the importance of the meaning attached to them. Your job will be to show children all that drawing can be, so they reframe their perceptions and start to engage with the process and fall back in love with drawing again.

Imagine a toddler clutching a crayon. That child is going to draw, just you try and stop them! They don't care what you think their squiggles are supposed to be, what surface they do it on or whether you like what they've drawn at the end. They just want to make marks and experience the joy of creating something new. We ruin drawing for children when we insist that they draw 'things' and then make unfavourable comparisons between the real thing and the marks the child has made. Very few children get past the disappointment of not being able to create a life-like image, so they soon give up.

Remind your class of what drawing really is: the deliberate or unintentional marks made on a surface. It doesn't have to be a pencil, it doesn't have to be paper. You can draw with anything: sticks, charcoal, objects, paint, pastels; the list is endless! You can also draw on anything and on any scale. Once you take away the idea that drawing is always with a pencil on a piece of white, A4 paper, a whole new world of artistic possibilities can emerge.

Ways of reimagining drawing

Here are some practical ways that drawing can be reimagined.

Sensory drawing

This is when children use their senses to engage with an experience or an object and make marks to represent what they discover. This could be drawing to represent what can be heard when the traffic drives past or making marks to demonstrate the way that the bark of a tree feels. It could be mark making to music or drawing patterns to represent an emotion.

Continuous line drawings

Encourage children to form images from one continuous line. A good entry point into this is to give children a ball of string and see if they can create images from one continuous strand. The beauty of this strategy is that children can rework, adjust and make changes without starting their image again. Continuous lines are also effective because they encourage children to work quickly, embrace the ambiguity of their work and tolerate mistakes when they are made. This shows children that realism is not the mark of a 'good' drawing and that you as the teacher are excited by the variety of outcomes.

Blind drawing

If you have ever watched children draw, half of the battle is getting them to really look at what they are supposed to be observing. Children can all too easily become entrenched in what they 'think' an object looks like, rather than being able to really look closely and challenge their initial ideas. You carefully arrange objects for children to observe, only for the whole class to spend the entire lesson with their heads down, furiously drawing what they have already decided their picture should look like. One way to approach this is to make a hole in a paper plate and pop it on top of the child's pencil so they can no longer see the paper. Although the outcome will now be very abstract, once the child cannot see their paper, they will focus their attention on the object. This means that once the paper plate has been removed, then the children will have a much better idea of the way the subject looks on their next attempt.

Gestural drawing

It is important for children to recognise that drawing is not always about fine, accurate details but often about capturing the 'essence' of the subject. Encourage children to use dynamic marks to create the feeling of movement or to roughly mark out the shape or form of a subject. Using coloured sugar paper allows children to use the colour of the surface as the mid-tone, upon which they can then use chalk and charcoal to accentuate the light and dark tones. Working on a large scale encourages children to draw with their whole bodies to create a sense of movement.

Drawing, like anything, is a skill that is developed through practice. There is often a perception amongst non-art specialists that a talent for drawing is something you either have or you don't. This is because most of us have grown up with a rather limited idea of what drawing can be. The reality is that anyone can develop their drawing skills – all it takes is regular and varied opportunities to practise. You do not need to be at the front of the class showing children the 'correct' way to draw. The best art facilitators are those that immerse themselves in the process and learn alongside the children.

Lesson plans

These lesson plans aim to encourage different types of drawing based on the varied but equally significant work of Zaha Hadid, Jean-Michel Basquiat, Stephen Wiltshire and Kenturah Davis. During your art expedition, try some (or all!) of the above strategies to encourage children to use their mark making to further their understanding of the starting point.

Lesson plan Key Stage 1: What is a line?

Artist biography

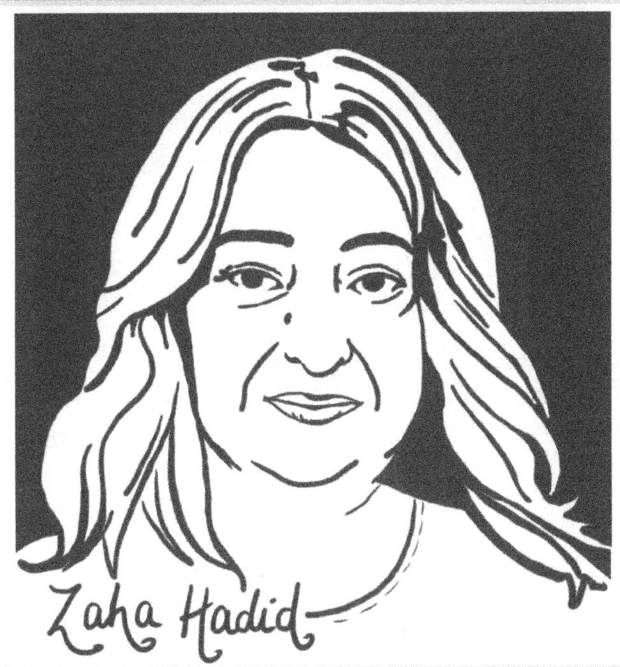

Dame Zaha Hadid

Born:	1950
Died:	2016
Birthplace:	Baghdad, Iraq
Discipline:	Architectural design

Zaha Hadid was a pioneering architect who pushed the boundaries of what buildings could be. In fact, for a long time, people did not believe that her designs could even be built. But Zaha was determined to prove them wrong.

Zaha was born in Iraq in 1950 and began her career studying mathematics. It was whilst learning geometry that she discovered her passion for architecture. Zaha's sketches show how she used drawing to experiment and innovate using quick, gestural marks. This lightness of touch is evident in many of her buildings that, despite their size, seem to float on air as if weightless. Zaha's sketchbooks are filled with quick, dynamic line drawings, which although abstract, carry the very essence of her designs.

Zaha designed and created almost 1000 buildings, from the London Aquatics Centre to the Riverside Museum in Glasgow. Her aspiration was to create buildings with no 90 degree angles. This is encapsulated in her design for the 2017 Brit award; you will definitely recognise her signature style that earned her the nickname of 'The Queen of the Curve'.

In 2004, Zaha Hadid became the first woman to be awarded the prestigious Pritzker Architecture prize and she went on to receive the UK's top architectural prize, the Stirling Prize, two years in a row.

Despite her death in 2016, Zaha's iconic designs are still inspiring artists all around the world to push the boundaries of what a building can be.

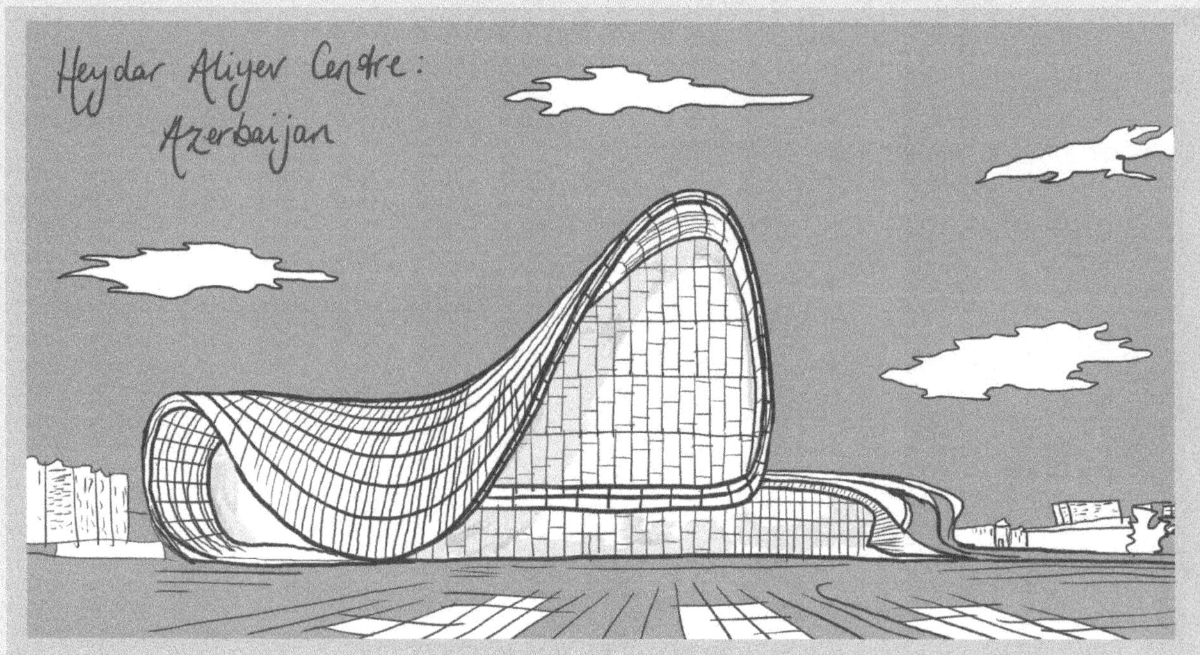

Find out more

Sketches: www.archdaily.com/868315/the-creative-energy-of-zahas-sketches

Early paintings and drawings: https://artsandculture.google.com/story/5QWxo3d3KMjuLQ?hl=en

Images to inspire

Enjoy Zaha Hadid's sketches online. Look at examples of her sketchbooks to show children examples of her initial continuous line drawings that inspired her architectural forms. See if they can spot any of the shapes and patterns in her finished buildings.

Other artist links

Edvard Munch: Look at Edvard's lino cuts of 'The Scream'. His images show how he has incorporated line into his landscapes.

Christa Rijneveld: Christa uses lines and mark making to create amazing images of mountains.

Henry Moore: Look at Henry's sketches where the images appear to emerge from his scribbles and marks.

'I don't mind being on the edge, actually. It's a good place to be.'

Zaha Hadid (Graham, n.d.)

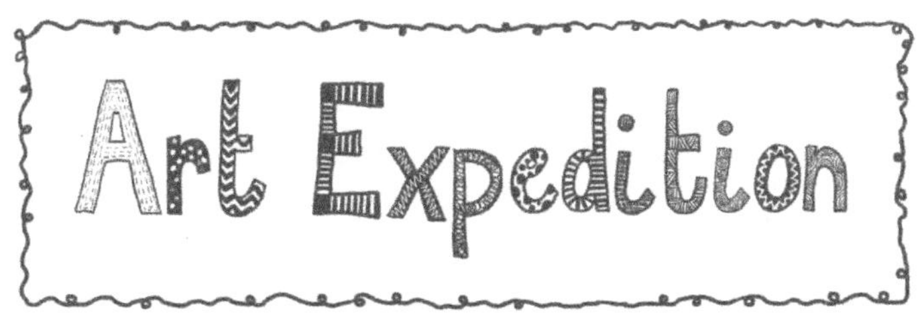

Zaha Hadid • Key Stage 1 • What is a line?

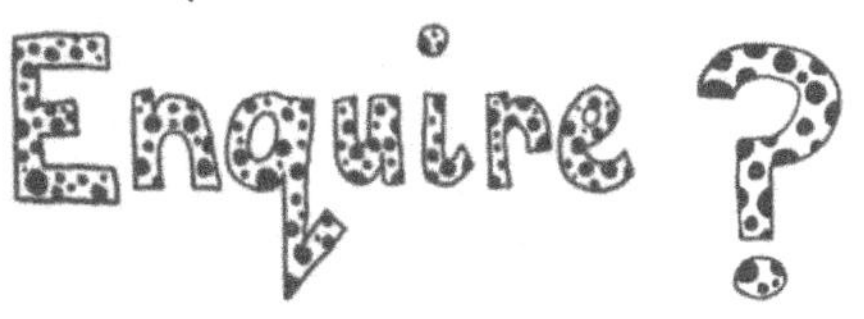

Ask the question and encourage children to discuss in groups. How many lines can they see around the classroom? Can they describe their similarities and differences?

Signpost: Through this project, we will be drawing and mark making, inspired by the buildings around us.

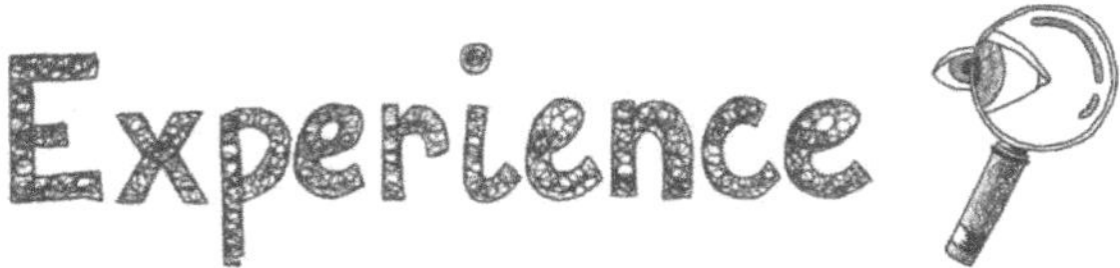

Give children a chance to experience lines using physical materials. What shapes can they make?

Remind children of the question. What can a line be?

Give children access to string, wool, cotton and wire. Work on the floor to see what shapes they can make. Do some materials create certain shapes more easily than others? You might give children prompts to ensure they try lots of different things:

- Can you create a zig zag?
- Can you create curves?
- What happens when you make loops?
- Can you create a spiral?
- What shapes are created when the material is dropped?
- When you make small changes to a shape, what new shapes can you make?

Then encourage children to make smaller examples from the different materials that can be stuck in or photographed for sketchbooks. Annotate (or discuss) how the different shapes or lines were created and how easy or hard it was to manipulate the materials.

Experiment

Play with a variety of media to collect different kinds of lines and patterns.

Introduce Zaha Hadid and her sketches. Show the children some buildings designed by Zaha so that they can make the connection between the fluid design process and the style of architecture she is famous for. Ask children to look for ways that Zaha uses the art element 'line' in her drawings. The speed of Zaha's movements and the continuous line where her pen does not leave the page are all part of her dynamic drawing style. What kinds of line can they see in Zaha's work? Encourage children to describe different lines and shapes to see the variation that can exist.

Give children a range of drawing tools. How many different kinds of lines, patterns and marks can they create? Fill a sketchbook page with different marks in different media using pictures of Zaha Hadid's sketches for inspiration. Children can come up with unique names for their lines and patterns (verbally or written), thinking about the properties of the marks they have created.

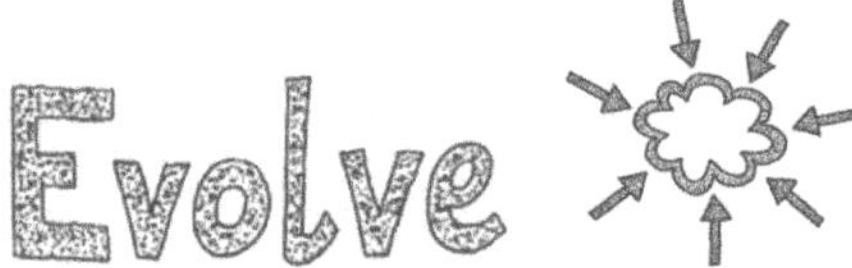

Use photos as well as direct observation to create continuous line drawings of different environments.

Remind children of the different lines they have created in their sketchbooks. Using these, ask children to create continuous line drawings of different landscapes. Go outside and draw the playground or the school, but also use photos of the beach, a forest or a cityscape to encourage children to think about the different lines that each environment would require. Experiment with different tools: felt pens, gel pens, markers, pencils, charcoal, and let the images overlap and blend together to make an exciting sketchbook page. Pens work well for this because it takes away the urge to rub out! Provide just a couple of minutes for each drawing but make sure children have plenty of time for self-reflection in between opportunities. We want the children to produce quick, dynamic lines that create an essence of the landscape. Some drawings will work well and others not so well, but all will have incredible value as the children learn more about the tools they are using. Encourage children to look for areas of light and dark, and fill the gaps with patterns and shading inspired by the lines they created during the experiment phase.

Another fun way to engage children in this activity is to tape plastic document wallets to the classroom windows and let children trace continuous line drawings of the landscape they can see through the plastic. You can do this with a whiteboard pen or a sharpie if you want to keep the results!

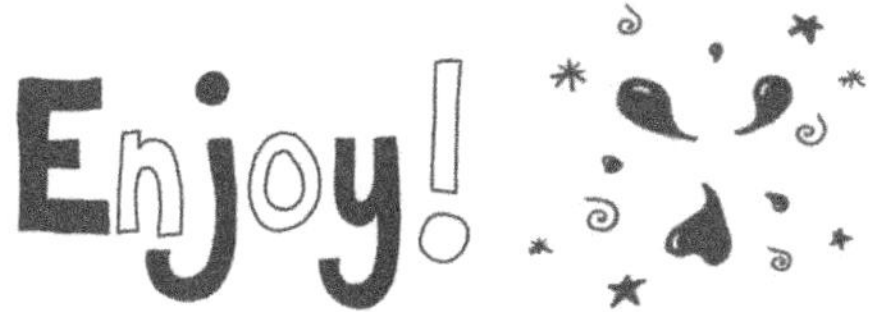

Create a final piece – a line drawing of your chosen environment.

Children choose one of their landscapes to work up into their final continuous line drawing full of patterns created from their unique mark making.

Do this on a large scale so that children can use their whole bodies to create dynamic lines. Allow children to choose the medium they most enjoyed working with (or move between different media), basing this on their preferences during previous stages of the art expedition. Encourage children to add marks to add texture and movement into their image. Keep a photo of the landscape that inspired the lines so that you can see how the children's thinking has developed!

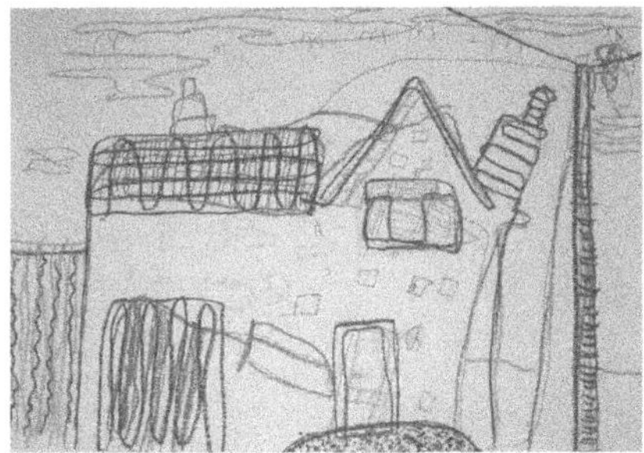

This child has used felt pens, crayons and pastels to create a continuous line drawing of their house. They have then worked into the drawing, looking for different patterns and lines to add textural details.

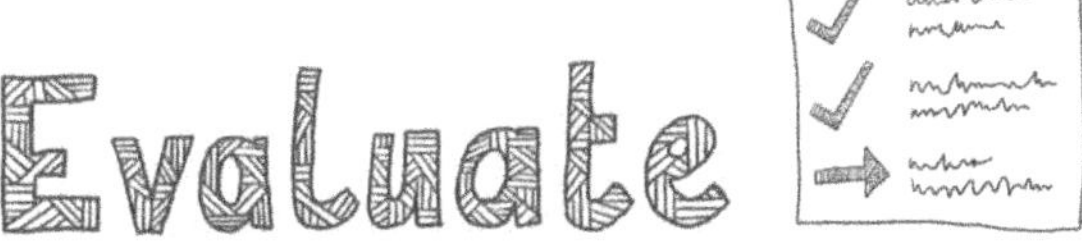

How did it go? Peer and self-assessment

Ask children to discuss these questions in groups or pairs. They may record the responses in their sketchbooks if you feel that is appropriate, but discussion is just as valuable.

Self-evaluation

- What is your favourite line?
- Which lines did not work so well?
- What has your line become?

Peer evaluation

- Which is the most interesting line?
- What else would you add to this image?
- What kind of place do you think this is?

Lesson plan Key Stage 1: Who is your hero?

Artist biography

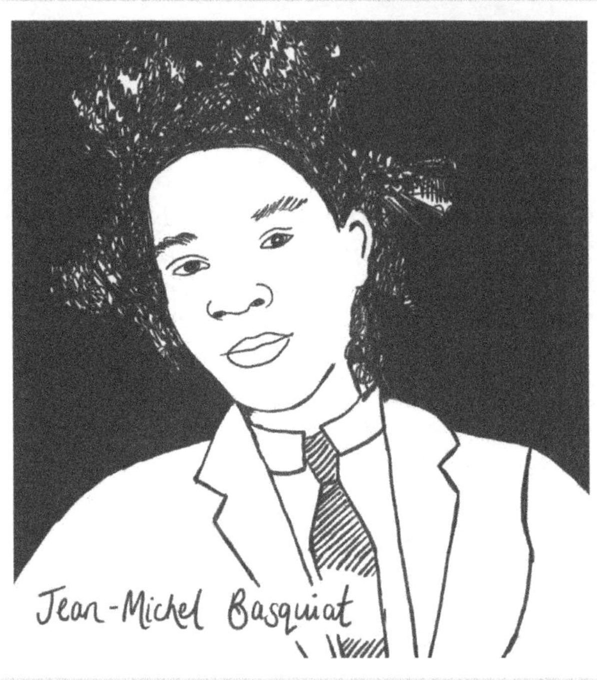

Jean-Michel Basquiat

Born:	1960
Died:	1988
Birthplace:	Brooklyn, USA
Discipline:	Drawing and painting – neo-expressionism

Jean-Michel Basquiat was born in Brooklyn, New York, where he grew up speaking French, Spanish and English. One day, when Jean-Michel was only seven years old, he was hit by a car whilst playing in the street with his friends. This accident caused internal injuries as well as a broken arm. Whilst recovering, Jean-Michel's mum brought him a textbook called *Gray's Anatomy*, full of medical drawings of the human body. That was where his obsession with the human form began.

Jean-Michel became friends with pop artist Andy Warhol and the two of them had many collaborations. The story goes that just hours after the pair met for the first time, Jean-Michel presented Andy with a painting of the two of them, the paint still wet.

In his short life, Jean-Michel created over 600 paintings and a further 1,500 drawings. Most of his images are of skeletal, graffiti-like figures painted in bold, vibrant colours with powerful, defiant brushstrokes. One of Jean-Michel's most iconic images is that of the crown. He would paint images of Black heroes and celebrate them by adding a three-point crown above their heads. The meaning of the crown is still debated but it is clear that Jean-Michel was passionate about raising the profile of both himself as an artist and others from the Black community who he felt had been similarly overlooked.

In 2017, Jean-Michel's painting 'Untitled' (1982) sold for an enormous 110.5 million dollars. This is the most ever paid for work by an American artist at auction, sealing Jean-Michel's place in history as one of the most successful artists of all time.

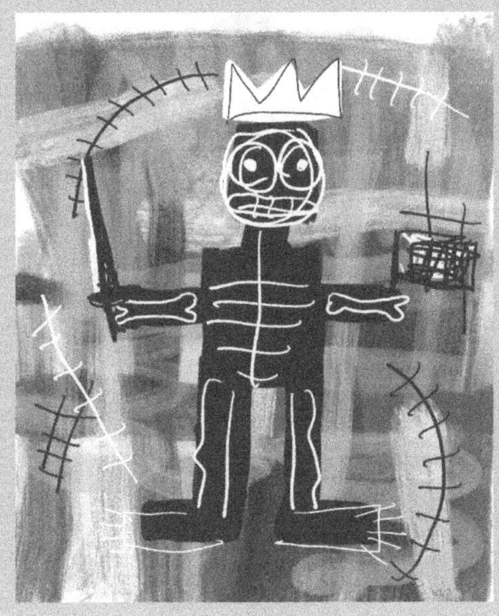

Find out more

Biography:

www.theartstory.org/artist/basquiat-jean-michel/

A brilliant book for children:

Maria Isabel Sanchez Vegara, *Little People, Big Dreams: Jean-Michel Basquiat*

Images to inspire

All of these images feature Jean-Michel Basquiat's use of the crown motif: www.incredibleart.com/basquiat-crown-meaning/

Black (1986)

Grillo (1984)

Untitled (Crown) (1982)

Red Kings (1981)

Other artist links

Noel Fielding: The Great British Bake Off presenter's art has clearly been inspired by Jean-Michel's signature style.

Genesis Tramaine: Another living artist whose artwork has many comparisons to that of Jean-Michel.

Cy Twombly: Although the subject matter is different, the use of mark making has many similarities.

Pablo Picasso: Jean-Michel listed Pablo as one of his main influences. Although their styles are very different, the deconstruction of the human form has many similarities.

'I'm not a real person, I am a legend.'

Jean-Michel Basquiat (Jean-Michel Basquiat.org, n.d.)

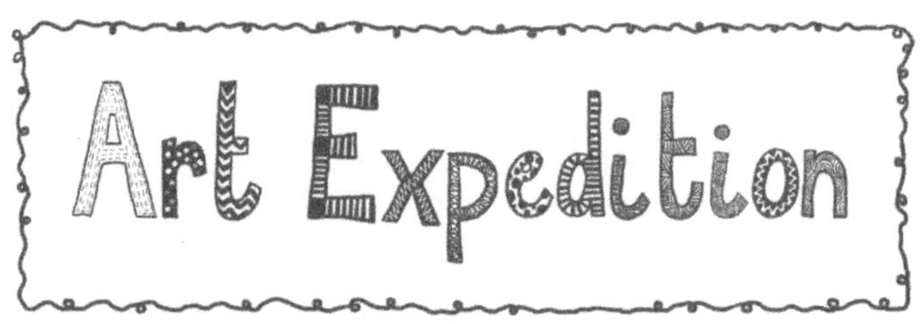

Jean-Michel Basquiat • Key Stage 1
Who is your hero?

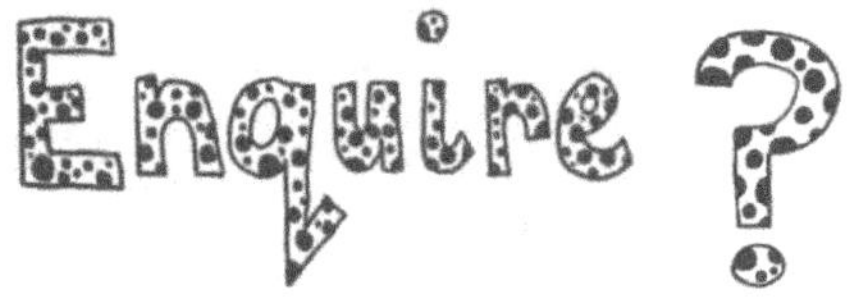

Ask children to describe what a hero is. What qualities do they have? Do they know any heroes? Who do the children consider to be heroes in their own lives?

Signpost: Through this project, we will be creating an image to celebrate the heroes in our own lives.

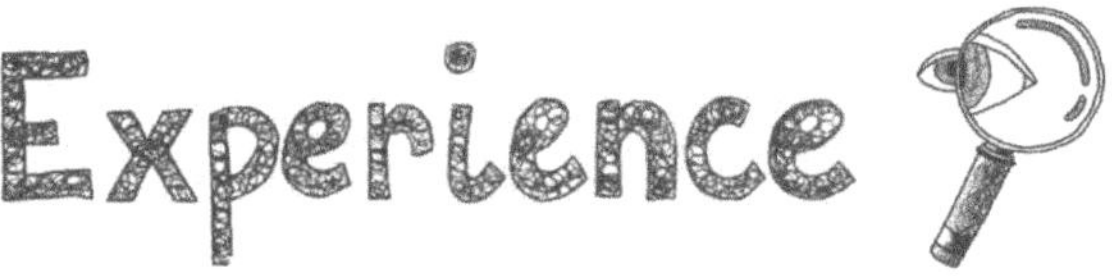

Think about your heroes... can you show me who they are?

Children will need access to:

- felt pens
- pencils
- charcoal
- crayons
- pastels
- newspapers and magazines
- scissors
- glue sticks.

Give children the chance to explore the idea of 'heroism' in their own lives. Make sure children are aware of this session in advance in case they would like to bring in images from home. There is no restriction on who this could be – it might be a parent, a best friend, a footballer or even a favourite pet!

Encourage children to sketch from direct observation, photos or from memory. Remind them to think outside the box and use all their senses. What might this person smell like? What might they say? How might their hands feel? How could we represent this through marks on the page?

To explore this idea further, children might look through newspapers and magazines and cut out images, letters or words that say something to them about the people they are thinking of. Encourage children to explore multiple ideas and find images that represent the person they have chosen. For example, if the hero is a singer, then a picture of a mouth or some musical notes might be significant. It doesn't necessarily have to be an image of the actual person. Collate all the ideas onto a busy sketchbook page.

Remember to model this experimentation by taking part! This will support children who are nervous to get started.

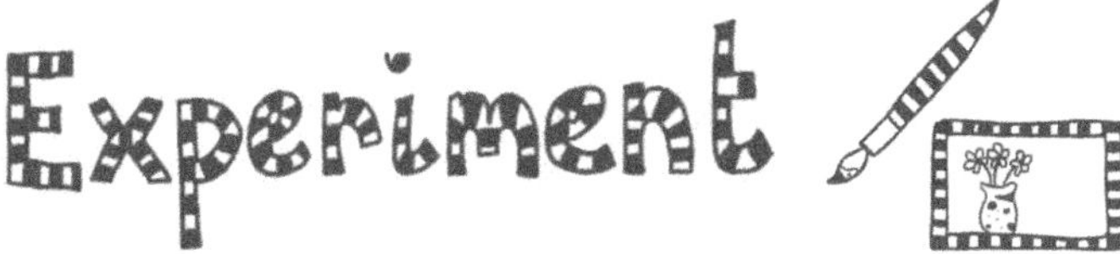

Look at Jean-Michel Basquiat's images of people. Can you draw different body parts using oil pastels?

Look at how Jean-Michel Basquiat combines collage and paint, then draws with oil pastels to create his iconic images. Also show children portraits by Noel Fielding, Genesis Tramaine, Cy Twombly or Pablo Picasso so they can compare how these abstract artists have approached portraits. Explain that Jean-Michel began his artistic journey by studying drawings of the body.

Give children oil pastels and encourage them to practise drawing parts of the human body. This could be photos but best if the children can work from direct observation. Maybe they could take turns to model for a partner whilst they use oil pastels to draw hands, faces, eyes; any part of the body that interests them. Ask the children questions to encourage their exploration of the oil pastels:

- What happens when you press lightly?
- What happens when you press hard?
- Can we blend colours together?
- What happens when we smudge?

Create a sketchbook page full of colourful representations of the human body. Make sure that children have access to Jean-Michel's images to empower them to embrace the abstract and representational nature of their drawings.

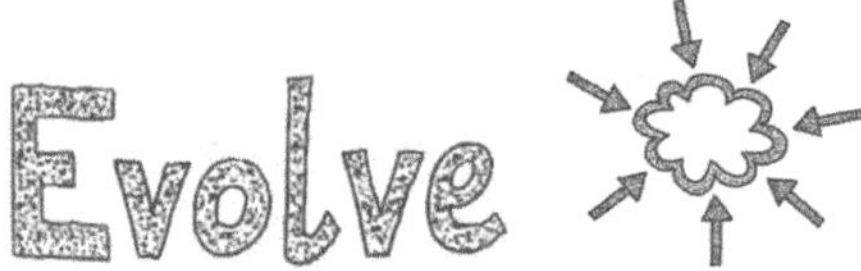

Represent your hero, thinking about the images, colours and words that might identify them.

Talk about the image of the crown and what children think it represents in Jean-Michel's work. Explain that we are going to be creating a portrait of a hero of our own using words and symbols to enhance our representation. Ask children to look within the paintings at the symbols that Jean-Michel uses to tell us more about the person in the portrait, e.g. baseball bat, sword, boxing gloves. What images could tell us more about the heroes the children have chosen?

Children start to design their finished response. How will the background look? What colour paint will they choose? What collage could be added that might provide more information about the hero? What will their hero look like in their finished piece? Which colour oil pastel will work well when drawing over the chosen colour of paint? What words or symbols will they add?

Create a mood board where children practise several compositions of their finished response and consider all the combinations of materials that they will need. This stage allows the children to make mistakes and move forward in their thinking in the safety of their sketchbook.

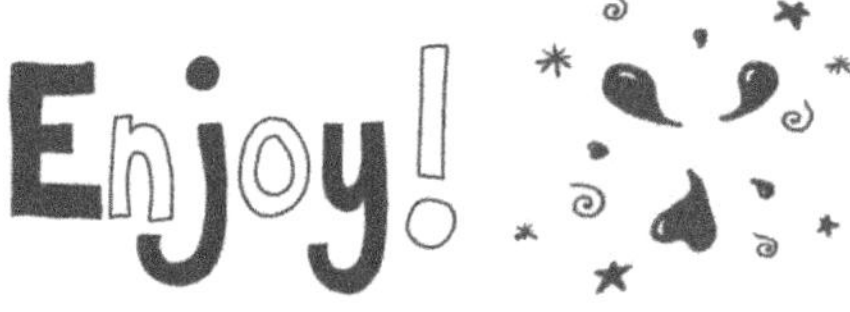

Create a final piece – a mixed media background with an oil pastel drawing of a hero.

The Enjoy stage will need to be done over two separate sessions to allow the paint to dry.

Session 1: Children create their background (I would suggest A3). They should already know which colours will work best underneath their chosen colours of oil pastels from the previous stages. Using glue and paint, children can create the background to their final piece, adding collage to create different textures, and further words and imagery if they wish.

Session 2: Children work from their design to draw the image of their hero over the top of the background, working in oil pastel. Add words and symbols to add further information about the person that has been chosen.

Don't forget to crown your hero with the all-important three-point crown!

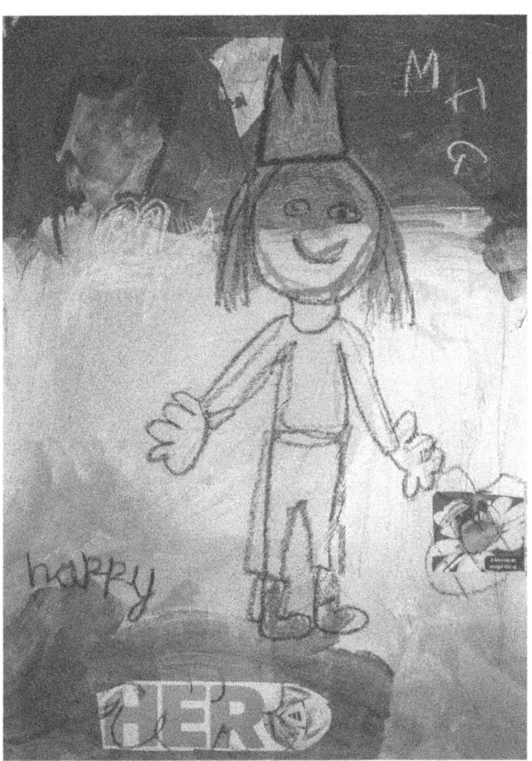

This child has chosen their best friend, Amelie, to represent as their hero! They have crowned Amelie with Basquiat's three-point crown and added images and words around the edge that represent why she is a hero.

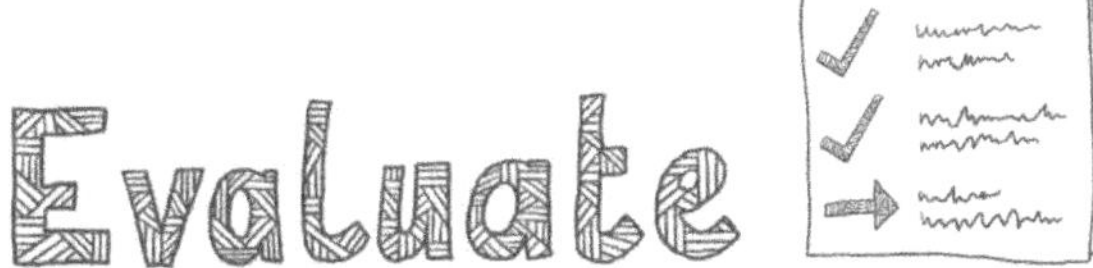

How did it go? Peer and self-assessment

Ask for volunteers to share their work. Discuss these questions as a class:

Peer evaluation

- What can you tell about this person?
- What could be added to give us more information?
- Why is this person a hero?

Then in groups, ask children to discuss these questions about their own work. If children are able, they could annotate their work with their answers, but discussion is equally valuable.

Self-evaluation

- What do you like most about your work?
- Which part did you find hard?
- Who is your hero?

Lesson plan Lower Key Stage 2: How do you draw a journey?

Artist biography

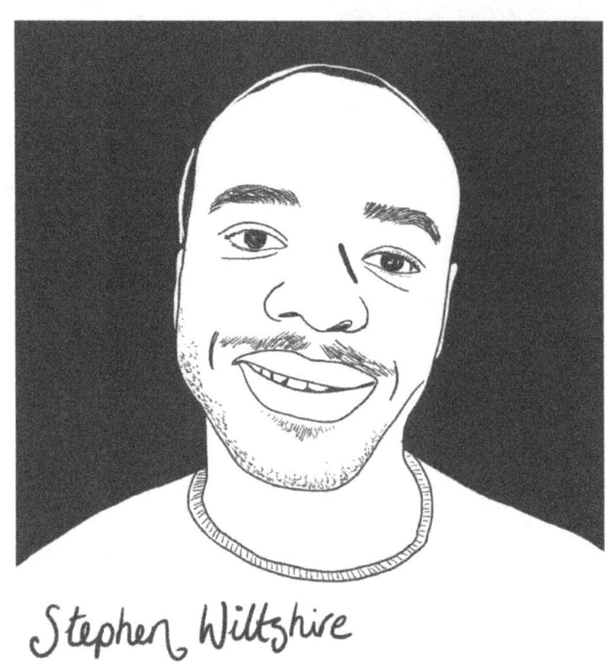

Stephen Wiltshire

Born:	24 April 1974
Died:	-
Birthplace:	London, England
Discipline:	Architectural drawing – ink pen

Stephen Wiltshire was born in London in 1974 and from an early age it was clear that there was something special about him. As a young child Stephen was mute, and even as an adult he prefers to communicate with those around him through drawing. He didn't speak his first words, 'paper' and 'pencil', until he was five years old.

Stephen has autism and has many intense fascinations with themes that occur in his drawing. Initially, Stephen was fascinated with American cars and learnt everything he could about them so that he could draw them in as much detail as he could. He also became intrigued by London landmarks, which also feature heavily in his drawing.

Stephen rose to fame when he began to draw incredibly detailed cityscapes, which he had committed to memory. Having only seen a view once, Stephen is able to draw the most incredibly detailed drawings on an enormous scale. Stephen's 19-foot-long drawing of New York City was completed after only a 20-minute helicopter ride, and the details he captured are almost unbelievable.

Stephen has worked hard to raise awareness of autism and has sold many of his drawings to raise money for autism charities. He has also been awarded an MBE for his services to art.

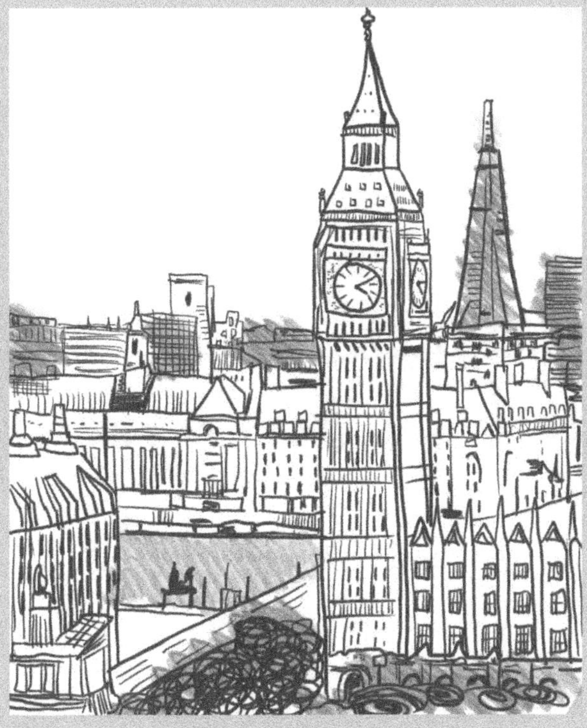

Find out more

More information: https://inspiremykids.com/stephen-wiltshire-an-autistic-artist-with-incredible-vision/

Instagram: www.instagram.com/stwiltshire/

Website: www.stephenwiltshire.co.uk/

Images to inspire

Canary Wharf Skyline (2021)

Eiffel Tower and Arc de Triomphe (2019)

Aerial view of London (2019)

London Eye and Houses of Parliament (2008)

Other artist links

Olivia Brotheridge: Olivia creates beautiful maps which feature landmarks and elements of a local area which are important to the people who live there.

Gareth Fuller: Gareth's work comprises intensely detailed aerial maps in black and white.

'Do the best you can and never stop.'

Stephen Wiltshire (Wiltshire, n.d.)

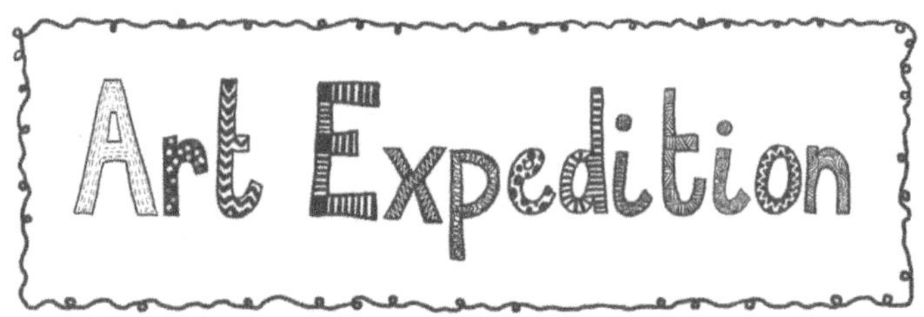

Stephen Wiltshire • Lower Key Stage 2
How do you draw a journey?

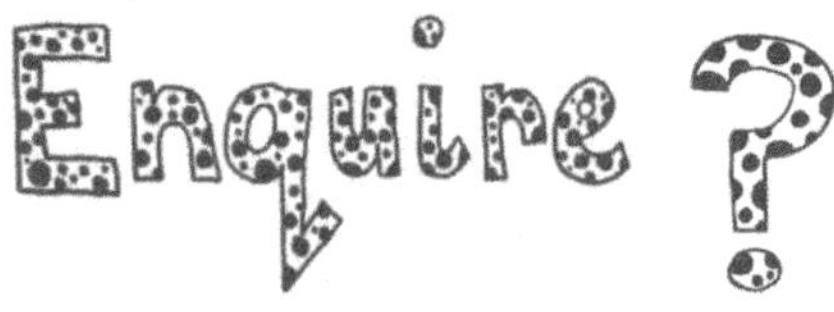

What journeys have the children been on? What landmarks do they see along the way? What do they see that tells them they are near home? Are there any journeys they go on where they see something significant as they travel?

Signpost: In this project, we will be drawing maps of our local area and thinking about the landmarks that we see every day.

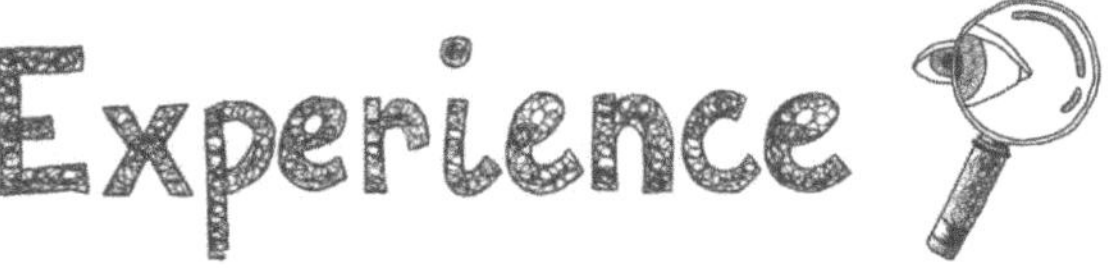

Go for a walk in your local area... draw what you see.

Take pencils and clipboards on a walk around the local area. What landmarks can the children see? Stop and draw anything of interest that you pass. Encourage children to engage in their local area by:

- Taking rubbings of interesting surfaces that you find along the way.
- Drawing the buildings on the journey and thinking about using marks to create different grades of light and dark.
- Thinking about the nature that exists in the local area. What shapes are the trees, what do their leaves look like? Are there grassy areas? What kinds of flowers or plants exist on this journey?
- Are there any other identifiable landmarks, e.g. postboxes, memorials, streetlights? Do they all look the same; are any of them different?

- Do you spot any road names on your journey? What do the signs look like? Can you take rubbings of the street signs? Investigate the fonts by copying some of the letter styles.

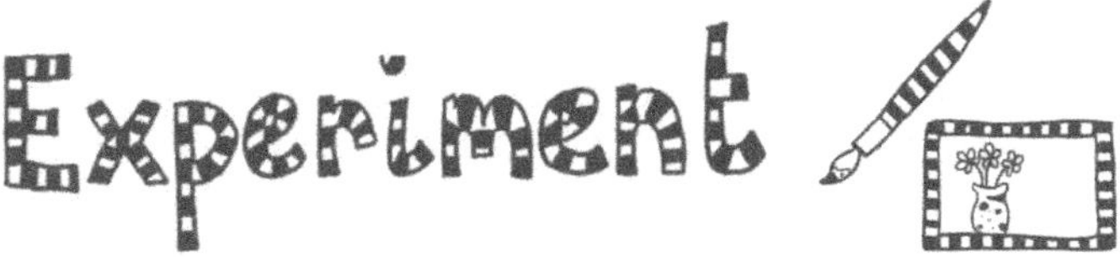

Look at Stephen Wiltshire's city plans. Draw some famous buildings of your own.

Look at the details of Stephen Wiltshire's city drawings. Can the children recognise any of the buildings? Explain how Stephen is able to draw these incredibly detailed images from memory.

Many of these images are created in black ink, with some colour added to accentuate the main features of the picture.

Give children some photos of buildings in London. Ask them to practise drawing these buildings in different ways to try to achieve Stephen's signature style. Encourage them to try:

- drawing in pencil
- drawing in fine line pen
- using dip pen and ink.

Ask children to do multiple, small drawings of different buildings to help them make decisions about which medium they prefer. Focus on areas of detail instead of the entire building so that children do not find the process too laborious and so that there is time for multiple experimentations.

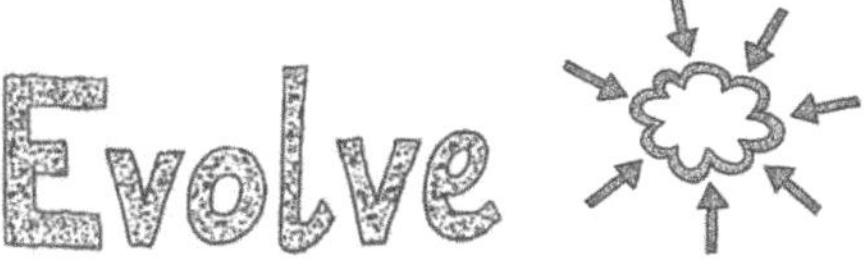

Begin to design a final piece, turning your local journey into a final piece.

You may decide to take children back out on the walk for this section to remind them of their journey, or you may feel that as Stephen produces his drawings from memory that remembering the journey is a more appropriate technique! You could introduce the illustrated map work of Olivia Brotheridge to inspire the layout of the children's maps.

To begin with, ask children to sketch a rough map of their journey, thinking about the direction that they walked and the way that the roads and paths were laid out.

Look back at the observational drawings of landmarks collected from the walk. Can children sketch in the rough locations of the things they saw? Remember, this is a rough design so children can rub out, move and edit the image as they go along to create an image that they are happy with. Work on a small scale so that children do not become too bogged down with the details.

Once the final design is complete, encourage children to decide how they will add colour. Make marks around the design in pen, ink or pencil and experiment over the top to discover which drawing medium works best with which colour medium.

For example: pen and watercolour may work well – which pen works best to ensure that the water does not cause the ink to run? Children need opportunities to find this information out before they embark on their final piece! They should also make decisions about where the colour will go to accentuate some of their landmarks. The finished sketchbook page should demonstrate the children's decision making.

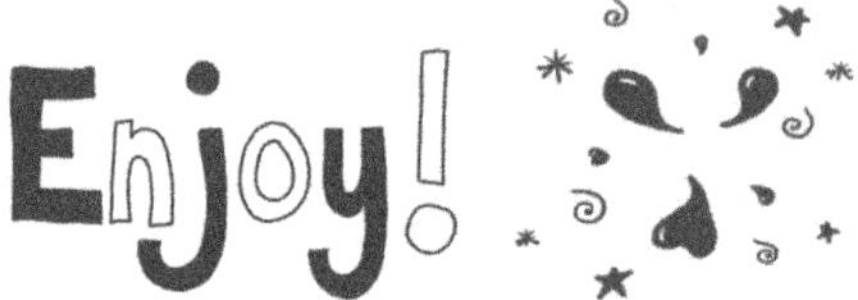

Create a final piece in black and white with accents of colour.

Turn the design into a final piece using the combination of media that the children decided upon during the Experiment stage. Children draw the map with the landmarks from their walk, using details discovered during their initial sketchbook work. Make sure that children are referring back to their sketchbook and using the information to inform their final piece.

Once the black and white image has been created, children can add loose colour to enhance their map and pick out important details.

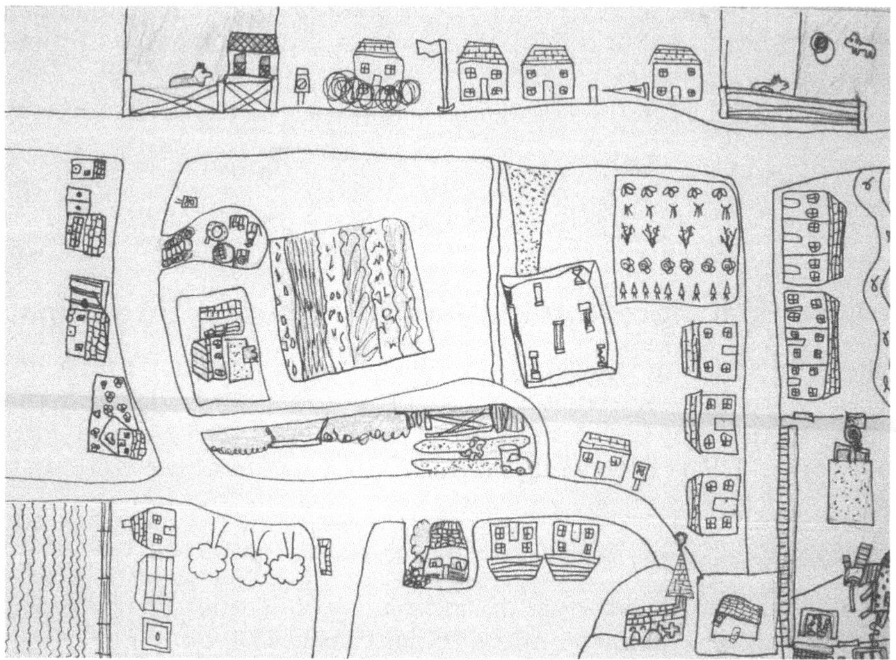

This child has collected drawings and sketches from a walk around the village and used them to inform their own overhead view of their local area.

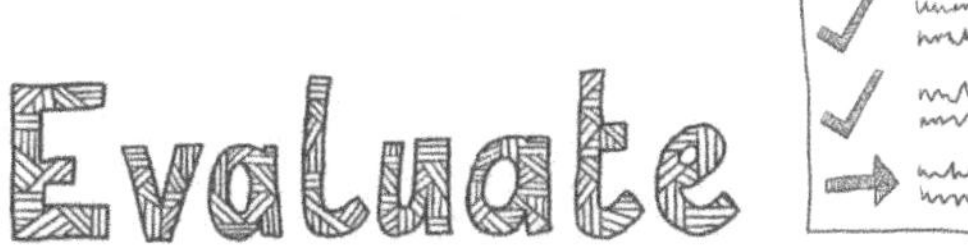

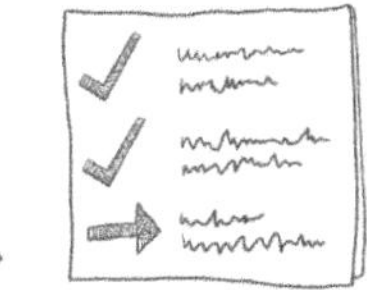

How did it go? Peer and self-assessment

Ask the children to think about these questions.

Self-evaluation

- What has been your greatest success?
- What has been your biggest challenge?
- How well did your combination of colours work?

Give children opportunities to explore each other's maps and to discuss these questions.

Peer evaluation

- Which landmarks do you recognise?
- In what ways has the drawing succeeded?
- What could be done to further develop the drawing?

Lesson plan Upper Key Stage 2: What can a portrait say about us?

Artist biography

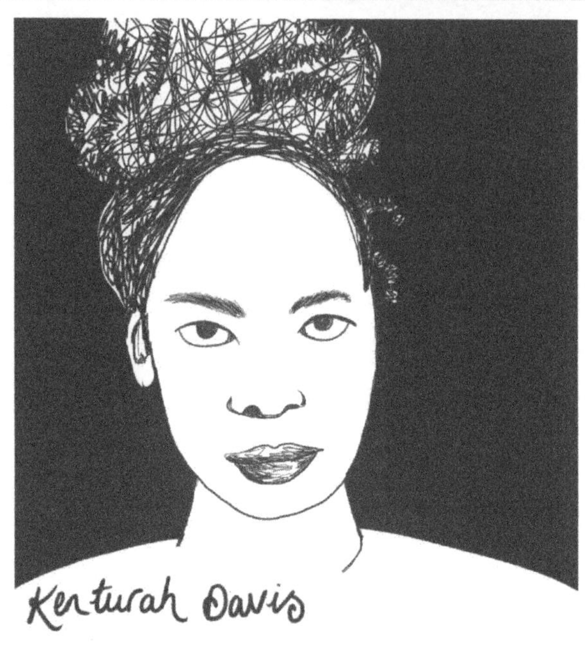

Kenturah Davis

Born:	1984
Died:	–
Birthplace:	Glendale, USA
Discipline:	Mixed media – contemporary

Kenturah Davis is an artist who works between America and Ghana, having been inspired by the rich colours and patterns of West African culture. Born to a father who was a set designer and a mother who loved to craft, Kenturah has always been surrounded by art. Kenturah has created a whole range of artwork from textiles to sculpture, but she is most famous for her large pencil drawings.

Her work is predominantly black and white and features the combination of text and mark making to create self-portraits that are often large scale. Some of her images are completed over many squares of paper which have been combined to create the finished image. Kenturah explores how language helps us to understand ourselves and the world around us by incorporating words into many of her images. Kenturah has always been fascinated with things that take time, putting hours into producing work with incredibly fine details. Some of the text that underpins her work is handwritten, some is stamped and some embossed. Meaningful phrases are written repetitively underneath the pencil portraits.

Kenturah's work celebrates the amazing women she has met in Ghana. Not famous people, but figures who have inspired her with their impact in their own communities.

Kenturah's work is filled with motion. Many of her images appear as though they have been frozen in time, in the middle of falling or dancing. Some of her pictures show her characters from multiple viewpoints as if caught in a stop motion frame as they move.

Kenturah doesn't cook, so she has turned her dining room into a studio space where she can work on her art at home.

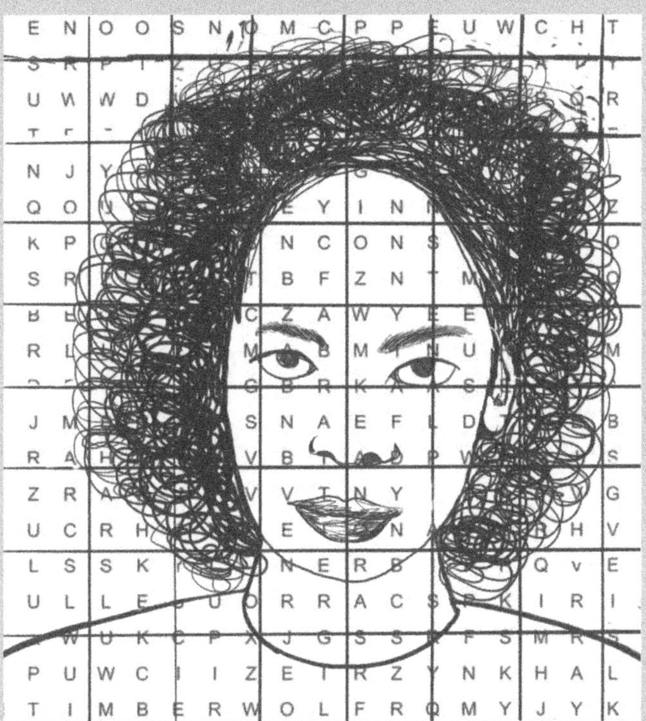

Find out more

Instagram:

www.instagram.com/kenturah/

Website:

www.kenturah.com/

Images to inspire

Fall and Recover (2021)

Tenor Drift I, II, III (2020)

Study for Entanglements (2019)

Namesake (2014)

Other artist links

Rembrandt: Have a look at some of Rembrandt's preliminary sketches and compare to his final pieces. Two very different styles of drawing.

Edgar Degas: Degas's drawings beautifully capture a moment in time and have a similar quality of movement to that of Kenturah.

Gustav Klimt: Klimt's drawings often appear to emerge out of the page with intense detail in some parts and a mere suggestion of a line in others.

'I'm interested in perception, how we perceive ourselves in the world around us.'

Kenturah Davis (Blair, 2021)

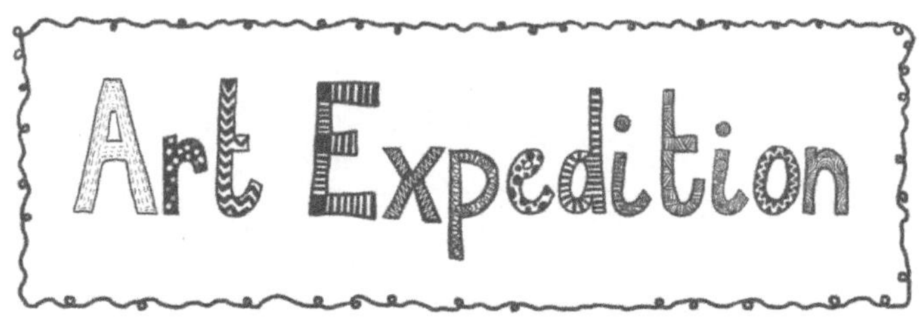

Kenturah Davis • Upper Key Stage 2
What can a portrait say about us?

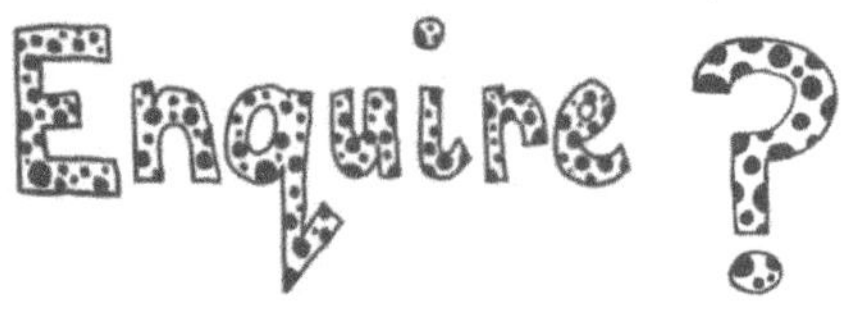

What is the purpose of painting someone's portrait? Can the children think of any famous portraits? Show children some examples on the whiteboard. What can we learn about the subject by looking at their portrait?

Signpost: Through this project, we will be exploring the relationship between text and images to create a dynamic portrait.

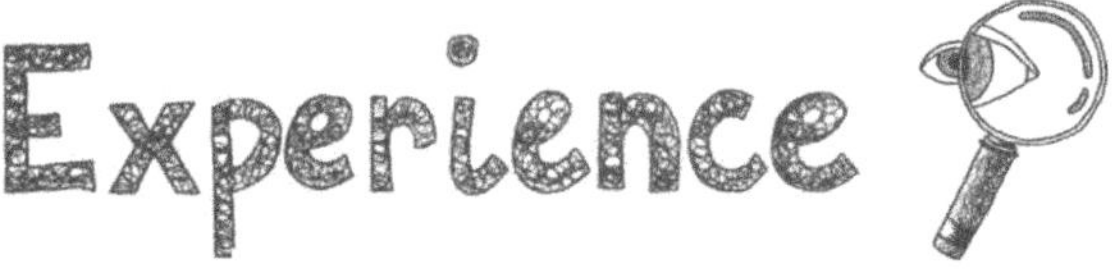

Complete a sketchbook page considering what makes the children unique.

Give children an opportunity to study their own and each other's faces to identify ways in which they are unique.

- Encourage children to draw their own faces and those around them. Ask: how do your eyes look different from your friends? How about your hair?
- The children could take photos and zoom in to really understand the detail of eyes, lips or ears.
- They could use paint to try to create their own skin tone and that of those around them.
- Ask the children to draw blindly using their other hand to feel the contours of their face.
- The children could cut out features from faces in magazines and sketch them to compare the differences and similarities.

Encourage lots of practice in different media to build children's confidence. Remember that observational drawing is only a very small part of what drawing can be. See the introduction to this chapter for more ideas!

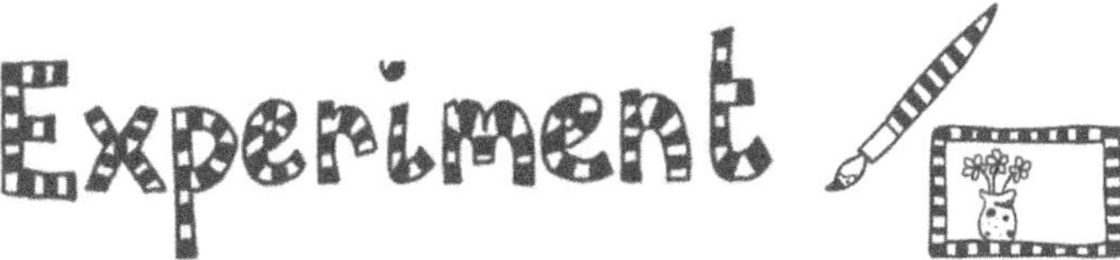

Look at the way that Kenturah Davis combines text and images.

Look at Kenturah Davis's portraits and compare them to those of Rembrandt, Degas and Klimt. How are they similar? How are they different?

Encourage children to explore the different ways that Kenturah incorporates text into her drawings. Think about why she might do this and how it might change what the portrait says about its subject. Ask children to try to recreate these text styles on small squares of paper that can be stuck in the sketchbook as a record of what worked well.

Here are some things to try.

- **Embossing**: Put two pieces of paper on top of each other. Make marks on the top layer using a biro. When you separate the paper, the indent of the pen should be visible on the bottom layer. When you shade over this, the marks will become more apparent.
- **Printing**: Children could create their own printed paper by typing words and printing them off. They could also use pre-prepared papers such as dictionary pages or text photocopied from other books. Children can draw and shade over these swatches of paper to see how effective the marks from different media are over the different surfaces.
- **Handwriting**: Try writing in different media and see how the marks they make work over the top. Which combinations work well? For example, marks made with a biro over text written in pencil might work well. What happens if the text is in biro and the marks are made in pencil? What other media could you use?

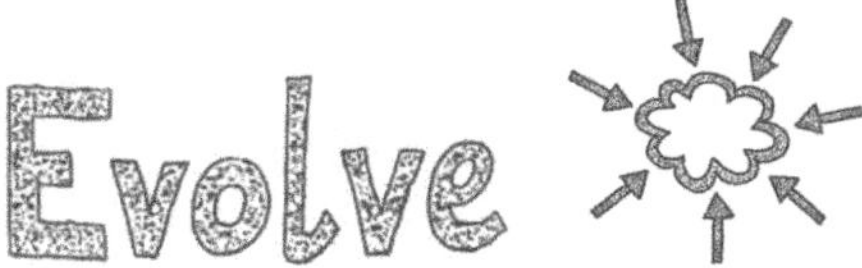

Take a photo that will be turned into a portrait. Divide it into squares which can be drawn one square at a time.

You will need a black and white photo of each child's face (I recommend A4 for this). Then, children need to divide their picture into squares (using sticky notes that can then be removed one at a time to reveal the part of the image to be drawn is a useful hack for this!).

Children can now practise drawing the content of each square in rough which will help them to orientate their drawing (think of the traditional grid method of drawing here).

These are rough sketches where children can experiment in their sketchbooks with different scales.

What text will they use to enhance the picture? It could be words to represent the person's favourite things, lines from their favourite book, a personal motto, or a lyric from a favourite song. Try these out too as children make decisions about what media, what surface and what text will be included in their final piece. Will it be the same combination for every square or will there be variation? All of this information needs to be included on the design page.

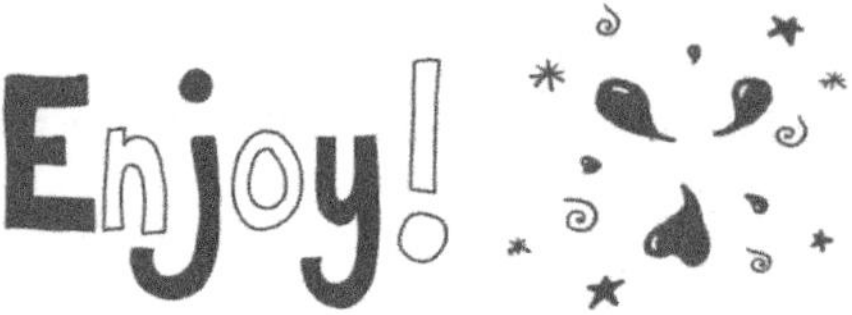

Create a final piece – a portrait, divided into squares, with text used to enhance the image.

Create the squares needed for the final piece. Children should already know how many squares they need, what they will be made out of and how the text will be added from their design. It might be worth having a template available for children to use to create their squares to ensure the image fits back together at the end! They can draw each part of the face onto each square using the media that they have chosen from their experimentation. Then combine the squares to create the final piece! Let the children decide whether to glue each square fully or just in part so that some movement remains. It is always up to the children to make these choices.

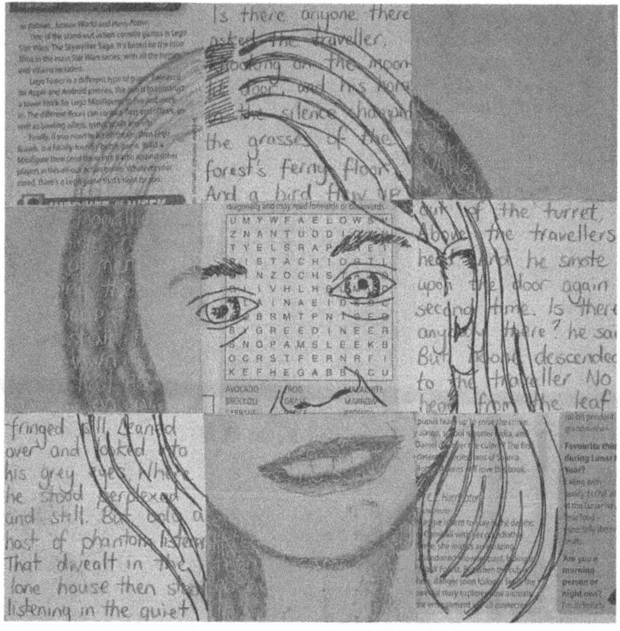

This child has used a favourite poem 'The Listeners' as the text for their portrait. If you look closely, you can see where they have embossed the paper by pressing through a layer of paper with a biro and then shading over the top.

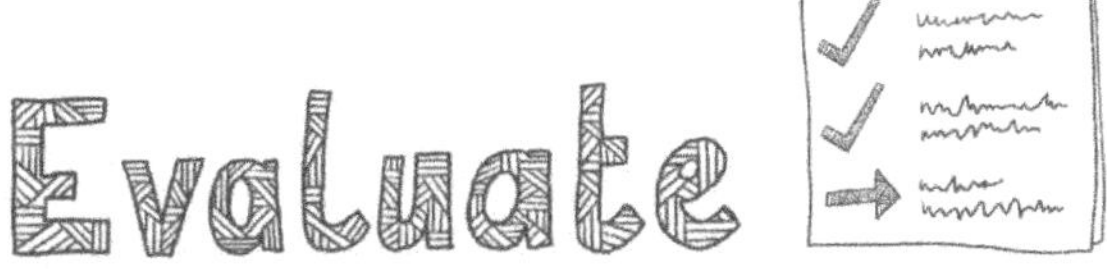

How did it go? Peer and self-assessment

Children in Upper Key Stage 2 should be given the opportunity to respond to these questions in their own way through their annotations. Peer assessment can be verbal or on a sticky note, so that children are not writing in each other's sketchbooks.

Self-evaluation

- What has been your greatest success?
- What has been your biggest challenge?
- What does your portrait say about you?

Peer evaluation

- What stands out from this work?
- What could be refined further?
- What can you tell about the subject of the portrait?

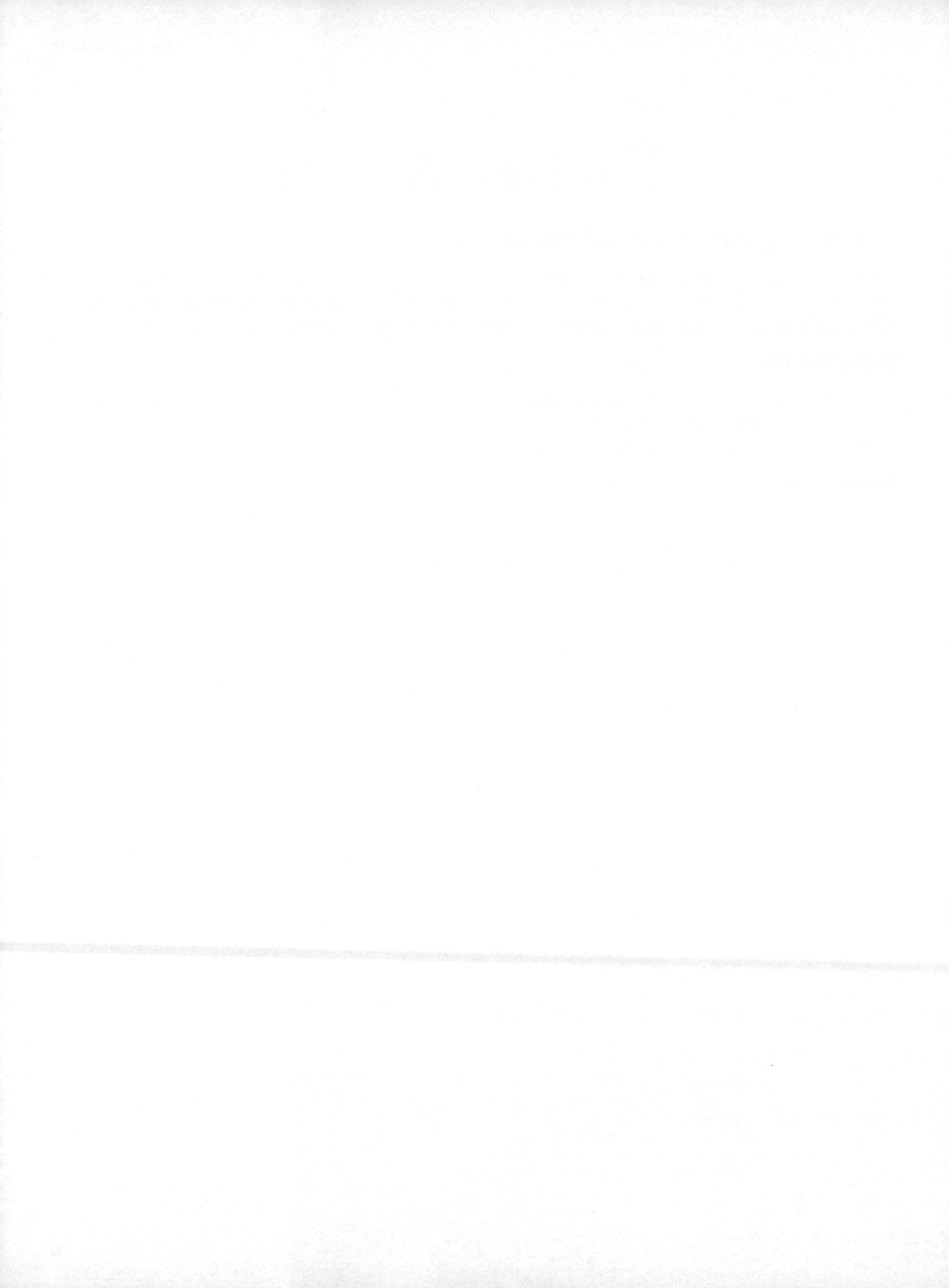

Chapter 3

Painting

Introduction to painting

When you go to get the paints out for your class, its arrival will surely be met with a resounding 'YESSSS!' So why do children love painting so much? I would suggest that a child's love of painting in school is simply because the act of painting goes against almost everything else children do during a typical school day. Painting is sensory, physical, creative, messy and most importantly, it is fun!

It is important for us as teachers to remember this when we consider how we teach painting. Although there are many skills to learn as children develop their mastery of paint, these skills cannot be explored fully if there are too many constraints. As with all art forms, experimentation and investigation really are the greatest teachers.

Colour mixing

One of the most difficult skills to master when using paint is the illusive art of colour mixing. There is so much more to understanding colour theory than just knowing the names of the secondary colours that can be mixed from the three primary colours. Colour mixing is also something that cannot be 'done' in one lesson or one unit of work; it should be a fundamental skill that is further developed every time children experience paint. This is because there are so many factors that can influence the journey to creating a desired colour. The quantity of colours added will have an obvious impact, but also the brand and type of paint can generate starkly different results. This is why children need to practise mixing colours in the early stages of every painting expedition so that when they begin a final piece, they can create predictable results enabling them to get that little bit closer to realising the idea in their head.

There is no need for 'colour mixing worksheets' or fancy colour wheels. Children just need time and freedom to explore the creation of colours. An effective strategy for this is to give children a piece of corrugated card from packaging and encourage them to use this as a palette. This can then be dried out and kept in sketchbooks alongside the child's work as a record of their artistic process. It is also a great way to avoid washing up 30 individual paint palettes!

Different types of paint

There are many different types of paint and children need a chance to experience as many of these as possible in order to understand all that painting can be. Your first session of any sequence of learning should be to allow children time to explore and play with the paint you are going to be using. This allows children a chance to experiment and make mistakes in a low-stakes environment before they attempt to use the paint to create something they are truly invested in.

Encourage children to experiment not just with the paint itself but with what happens when paint is combined with other media. For example, watercolours can produce exciting results when mixed with sea salt, masking fluid, wax crayon or when clingfilm is scrunched on top of wet paint and left to dry. Acrylic paints cling to different surfaces, which can produce interesting effects, so try painting on sandpaper, Modroc, collage or papier-mâché to turn your two-dimensional paintings into something with texture and three-dimensional form.

Poster paint is a halfway house between watercolours and acrylics, and although it has the obvious bonus of being washable, it lacks the vibrancy and flexibility of acrylic. Don't fear acrylics in primary school. Have the courage to undertake a project where children bring in old clothes and just go for it!

Tools

One of the major limitations to children discovering all that painting can be is the misconception that true painting can only be achieved with a brush. In fact, many artists use all kinds of tools to apply paint to a surface: anything from palette knives to kitchen utensils. Encourage children to make their own tools from found objects or to experiment with other items from around the classroom. Anything that delivers paint onto a surface is a painting tool, so have fun with it!

Painting frustration

Painting, like drawing, can often be a barrier to children seeing themselves as artists. This is often born from a lack of understanding of how paint really works and not being allowed the time to really achieve the best results. Drawing an image and then using paint to 'colour in' the spaces is a source of frustration as children often draw their original sketch in too much detail to be able to paint effectively. Instead, encourage children to practise their design in paint alone so they are learning how the paint will behave in their final piece. It is also important to give children time to think about the stages of their paintings. Very few artists complete a painting in a single sitting. They allow layers to dry so they can be worked and reworked until the artist is satisfied with the final image. Give children shorter time slots, but more of them, so they can develop their paintings to the best of their abilities. Many children are turned off paint when time constraints force them to paint wet paint on wet, resulting in sections bleeding together. Remember, watercolours work best working in thin washes from light to dark, whereas acrylic paint is opaque, so working from dark to light can ensure that your light colours remain vibrant and impactful.

This is another reason why I am such an advocate for acrylic paint, particularly in Key Stage 2. The option to paint over and rework areas of frustration will change the way children think about painting forever. Once children realise that paintings can be improved and developed, the fear of making mistakes can be set aside and children can embrace the process.

Lesson plans

In this chapter, we will explore the work of Hilma af Klint, Sarah Biffin, Jacob Lawrence and Kehinde Wiley. Four incredible artists, all with a very different understanding of what painting can really be.

Lesson plan Key Stage 1: How do you paint a feeling?

Artist biography

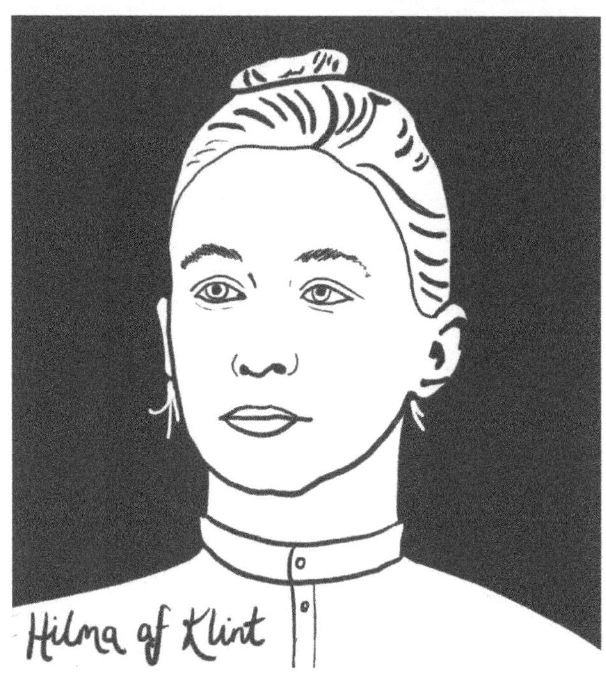

Hilma af Klint

Born:	1862
Died:	1944
Birthplace:	Stockholm, Sweden
Discipline:	Painting – naturalism, abstraction

Hilma af Klint was a skilled artist who demonstrated talent in drawing and painting from an early age. Hilma was one of the first women artists to study art at university when the Royal Academy of Fine Arts in Stockholm broke with tradition and began accepting female students. Her early career was defined by many paintings of portraits and landscapes that she sold to make money. She gained recognition for this classical style of painting but her true artistic love lay elsewhere.

When Hilma's sister died in 1880, Hilma became fascinated with the idea of spiritualism (communicating with the spirits of the dead) and this became the focus of her art. Hilma believed that she was channelling something out of her control when she painted. Her 'automatic' paintings were created 'unconsciously', and Hilma felt that they were conveying messages from another place beyond this world. It was her life's mission to use her paintings as a way of communicating with alternative dimensions.

Hilma felt that the world was not ready for her spiritualist art, so she kept it hidden away. She considered her work to be so unique and forward-thinking that she insisted that her work not be released to the public until 20 years after her death. There were 1200 paintings in the collection.

The artist Wassily Kandinsky has long been considered the first abstract artist, but it is now clear that this credit actually belongs to Hilma af Klint, who was painting abstract shapes and patterns five years earlier. Her contribution to the world of art is only recently being given full recognition.

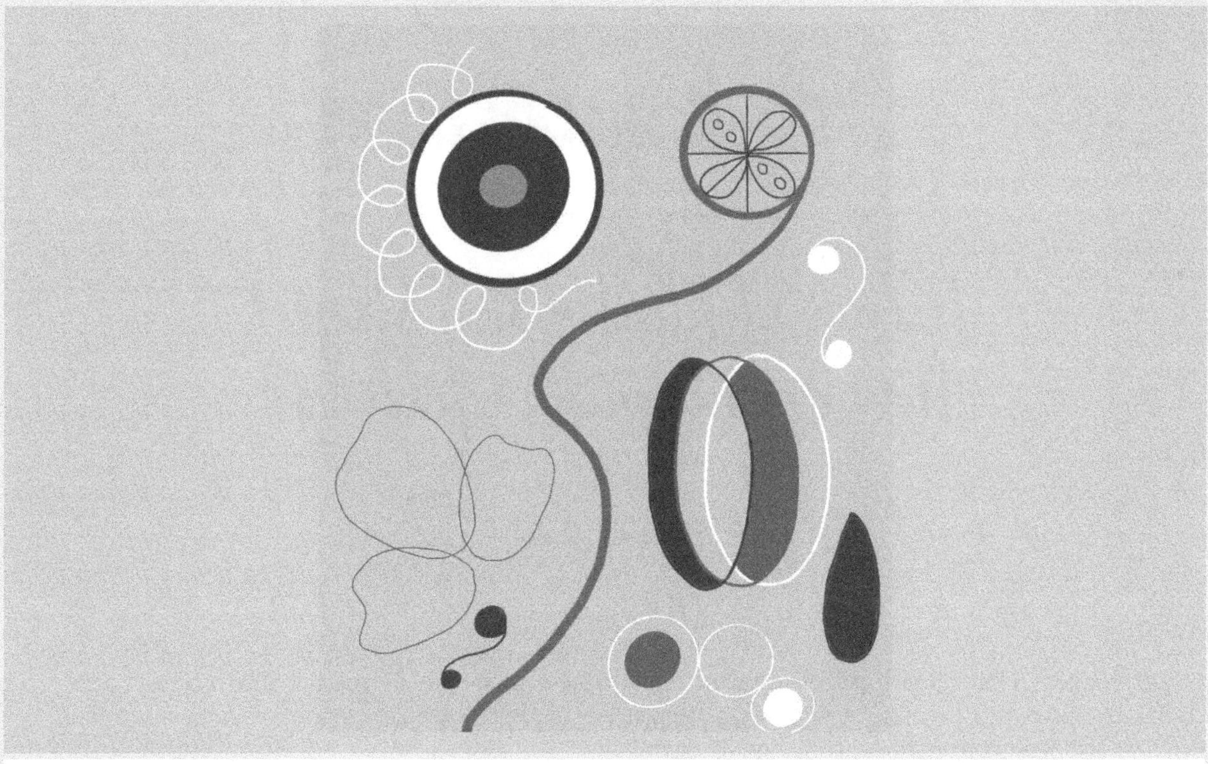

Find out more

Klint or Kandinsky?:

www.tate.org.uk/tate-etc/issue-27-spring-2013/first-abstract-artist-and-its-not-kandinsky

Website:

https://hilmaafklint.se/

Images to inspire

The Swan (No. 16) (1915)

They Tens Mainstay IV (1907)

The Ten Largest (1907)

Chaos, Nr. 2 (1906)

Other artist links

Mark Rothko: Mark Rothko purposely created combinations of colour to try to evoke an emotional reaction in his audience.

Odili Donald Odita: Odili's art style is much more organised and geometric but the use of shapes and line have many similarities.

Sonia Delaunay: The use of concentric circles exists in the work of both artists.

'I had no idea what the pictures would depict and still I worked quickly and surely without changing a single brushstroke.'

Hilma af Klint (Moderna Museet n.d.)

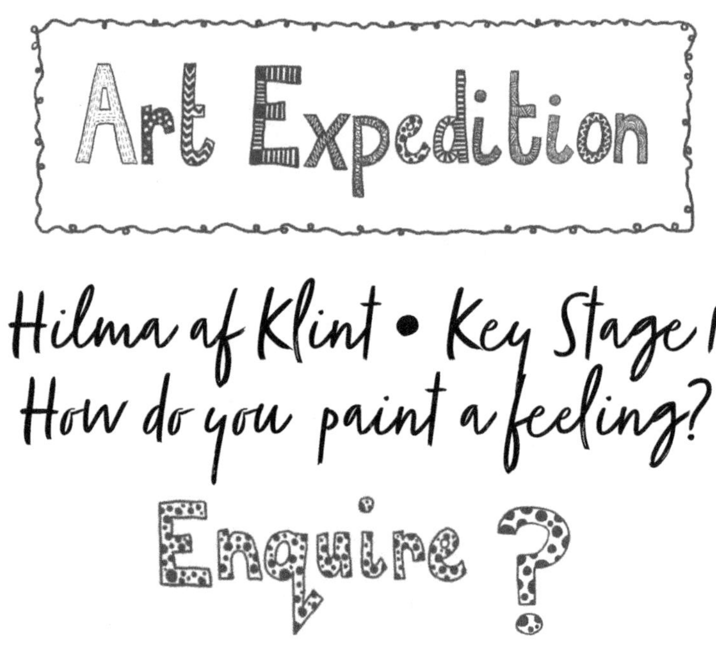

Ask children to list all the different emotions they can name. Then ask them to act out each emotion and unpick how our bodies move and change depending on how we feel. How might we create those feelings in paint?

Signpost: Through this project, we will be playing with paint, using colours and shapes to express different feelings.

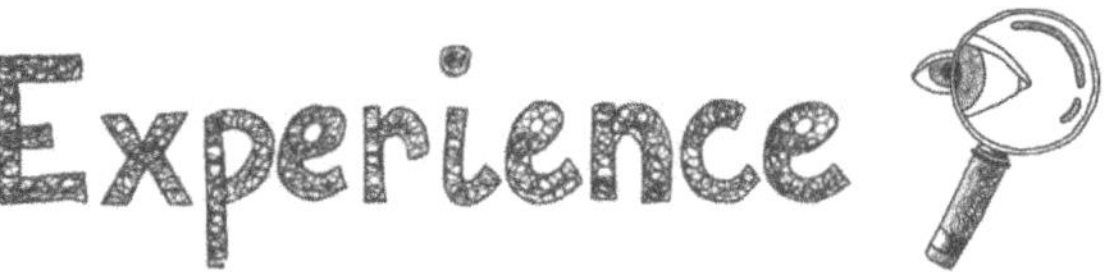

Ask children to represent different emotions using poster paint.

Children will need access to:

- poster paint (primary colours, plus black and white)
- different-sized brushes
- glue spatulas
- cotton buds
- things from which to make other tools, e.g. sticks, lolly sticks, leaves, cotton wool, j-cloths.

Think about how we can use paint to convey the way our bodies show how we feel. Children might choose to explore colours to reflect different emotions. They might also think about how the shapes and lines that they make might tell us something about how the artist is feeling.

Ask children to explore the poster paint using a range of different tools. Allow only primary colours so that children are encouraged to mix, blend and overlay colours to create new ones. Encourage children to make their own tools (or use their fingers!) to experiment moving the paint around the page in different ways. Children can annotate each example they create with words or draw a face to represent the emotions they have managed to represent with the paint.

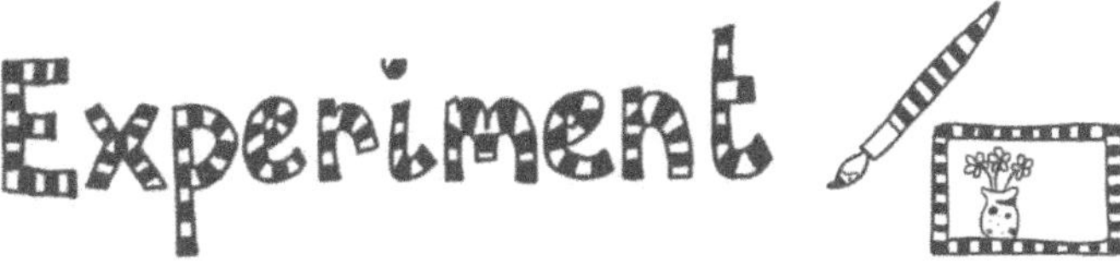

Look at Hilma af Klint's paintings. Explore the idea of 'automatic' painting.

Explain to children that Hilda af Klint painted to convey a message through her work. What might she have been trying to say? Ask children to look at the work and talk about how each painting makes them feel.

Give children some pictures of Hilma's paintings and get them to stick the images in their sketchbooks. Ask them to pick out different symbols and images from her work and recreate them using paint. Can the children find swirls, wheels, flowers, loops and other shapes and fill a sketchbook page with their own painted interpretations of these different symbols? Encourage discussion around what the children think these shapes represent. The sketchbook page should be a colourful cacophony of shapes, colours and patterns.

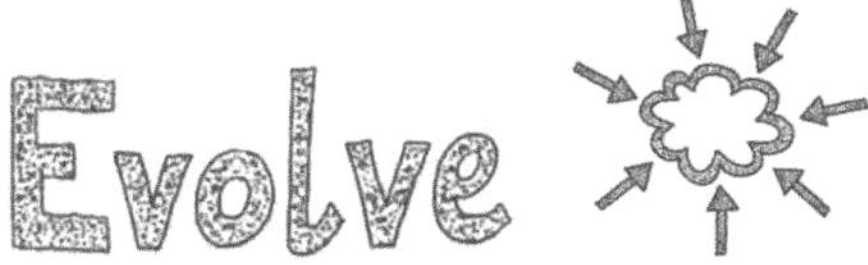

Children create their own automatic paintings using music as a starting point to inspire different moods.

Give children paint in primary colours and a selection of different tools on their tables. Play different pieces of music, each with a distinctive emotional feel, and ask children to respond to every piece on a new piece of large paper, using the paint to represent what they can hear and how it makes them feel. Remember to encourage the use of different tools and colours, the idea being that each response should convey something different from the last. Do this several times with contrasting pieces of music, each response on a new piece of paper labelled with the emotion that the child felt when listening to the music (again, for younger children this might just be represented by a face).

You could use any music you like but here are some examples of music that might generate an interesting response:

- Dire Straits: Money for Nothing (the introduction is full of suspense!)
- Pharrell Williams: Happy
- Bruce Springsteen: Streets of Philadelphia
- Christina Aguilera: Fighter.

You could be brave and do some responses blind-folded so children really use their bodies to respond and so that the images created have the feeling of the automatic nature of Hilda's own work.

Get children to discuss their results with their friends. Are there any similar patterns? Can the children tell which painting was created from each piece of music?

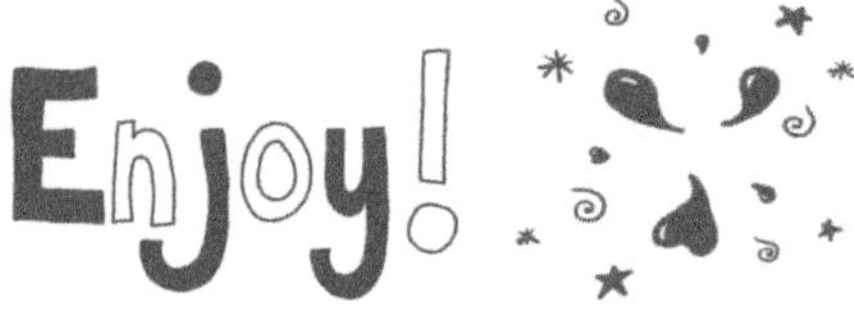

Create a final piece that uses the symbols and colours explored to represent a range of feelings and emotions.

At the beginning of the lesson, give out the dried paintings from the last session. Ask children to cut out interesting shapes or patterns that occurred in their work. Encourage children to reflect the mood of the music by the way they cut out each shape, e.g. if the music made them feel sad, maybe they could cut a tear shape, or if they felt angry, maybe a spiky shape would be more appropriate. Once the children have an exciting array of colours and shapes, ask them to arrange them onto a choice of coloured backgrounds. Let children choose but encourage them to make an informed choice. For example, 'I'm choosing blue because that will make my shapes stand out.' This arrangement of shapes can be stuck into the sketchbook and is now the design for the final piece.

Give children a blank piece of paper and poster paint and see if they can paint their design of shapes and patterns to create a finished painting that reflects a range of feelings and emotions.

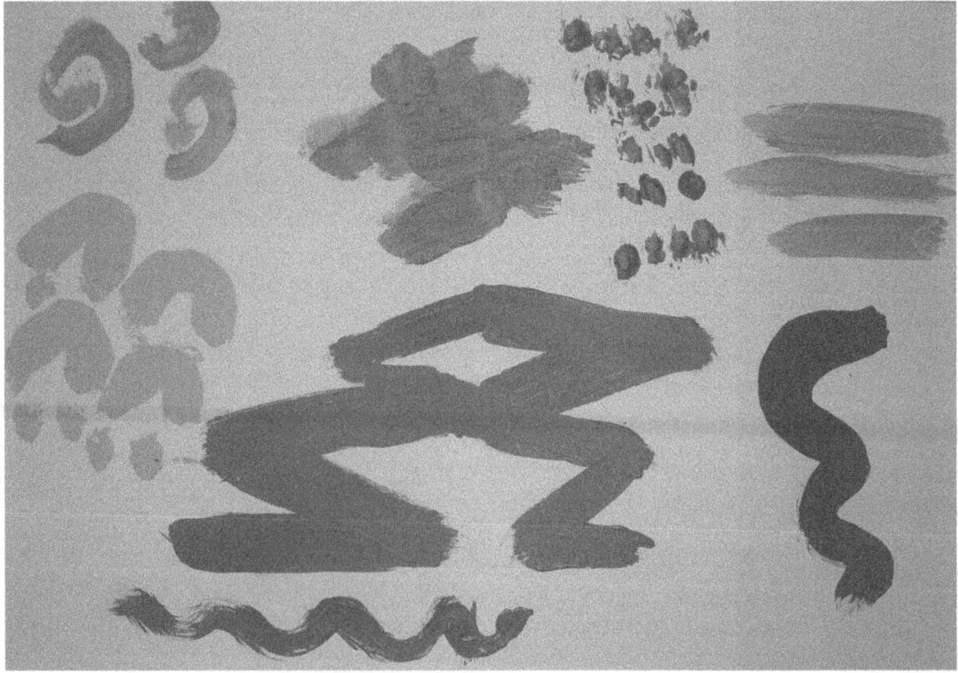

This child has used different colours and patterns to represent a range of feelings collected from their work to music. Some of the emotions are happiness, excitement, anger, boredom and sadness. I wonder if you can tell which are which!

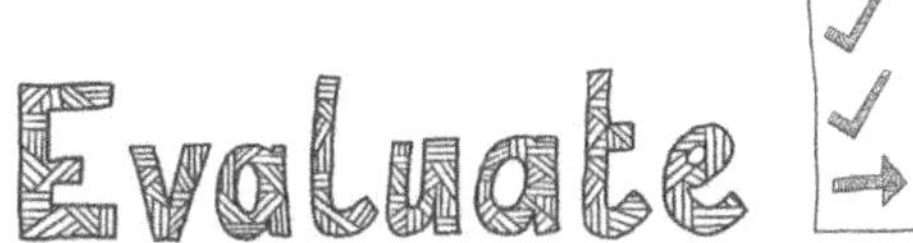

How did it go? Peer and self-assessment

Ask for volunteers to share their work.

Discuss these questions as a class.

Peer evaluation

- What is your favourite symbol?
- What do you think each symbol represents?
- What other emotions could have been included?

Then in groups, ask children to discuss these questions about their own work. If children are able, they could annotate their work with their answers, but discussion is equally valuable.

Self-evaluation

- What do you like most about your work?
- Which part did you find hard?
- How does the picture make you feel?

Lesson plan Lower Key Stage 2: How do artists use paint?

Artist biography

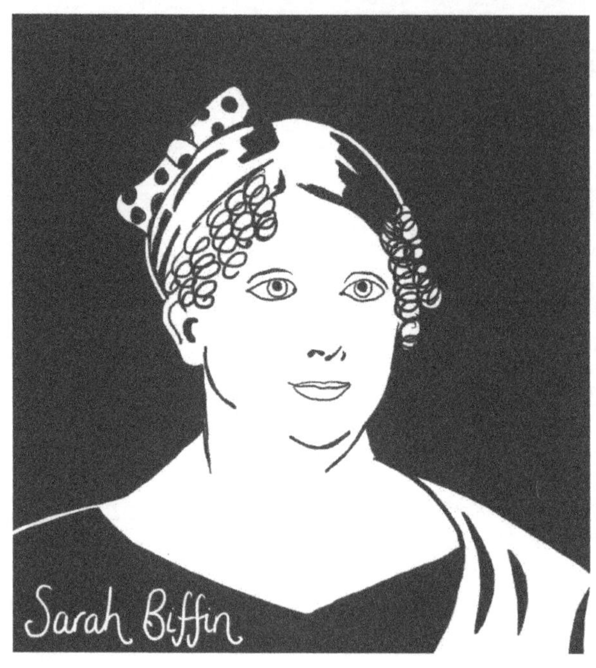

Sarah Biffin
(aka Sarah Biffen / Beffin)

Born:	1784
Died:	1850
Birthplace:	East Quantoxhead, England
Discipline:	Painting – watercolour miniatures

Sarah Biffin was born without any arms and with underdeveloped legs but despite this, she was determined to learn to paint. Holding the paintbrush in her mouth, Sarah became an accomplished artist who even had the opportunity to paint for royalty.

When she was just 13, Sarah's parents sent her to be part of a circus where she was viewed as a 'freak'. Despite her paintings selling for large sums of money, Sarah was paid a mere £5 a year. People would come from far and wide to watch her draw, paint and sew, and marvel at what she was able to accomplish with just her mouth. As her fame grew, people started to recognise her undeniable talent and the Earl of Morton took her away from the circus and paid for her to have art lessons at the Royal Academy of Art. As Sarah's painting skills developed, it became impossible to tell her paintings apart from other famous artists of the time. She became so famous, she even got a mention in Charles Dickens's book, *Nicholas Nickleby*!

Sarah is an incredibly inspirational figure. Not only did she become notorious as a woman artist in an art world dominated by men, but her talent outshone other able-bodied artists. Sarah achieved her success through sheer determination, hard work and an unwavering sense of belief in her own capabilities.

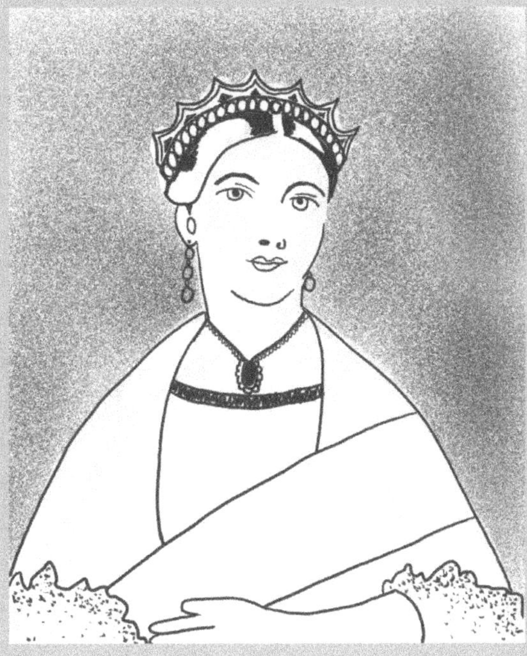

Find out more

More information:

https://artuk.org/discover/artists/biffin-sarah-17841850

Illustrated ebook:

www.rejectedprincesses.com/princesses/sarah-biffin

Images to inspire

Portrait of Victoria (1819–1901), Queen of Great Britain (1837–1901) (1848)

Portrait miniature of a lady, in a puce dress (1846)

H.R.H. Princess Mary, Duchess of Gloucester (1834)

Study of feathers (1812)

Other artist links

Tom Yendell: Tom was born with no arms and has developed incredible painting skills using just his feet.

Saranjit Birdi: An able-bodied artist who taught himself to draw with his feet while teaching people with disabilities to engage with art.

Franz Xaver Winterhalter: Another artist who painted Queen Victoria – it is good for children to see Sarah's work against that of an able-bodied artist and see that there is no distinction in skill!

'I do not regret my situation; I thank God that he has been pleased to make me as I am.'

Sarah Biffin (Hunt, 2023)

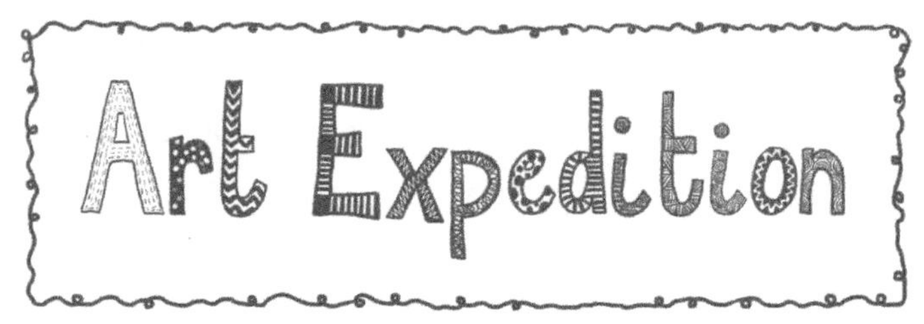

Sarah Biffin • Lower Key Stage 2
How do artists use paint?

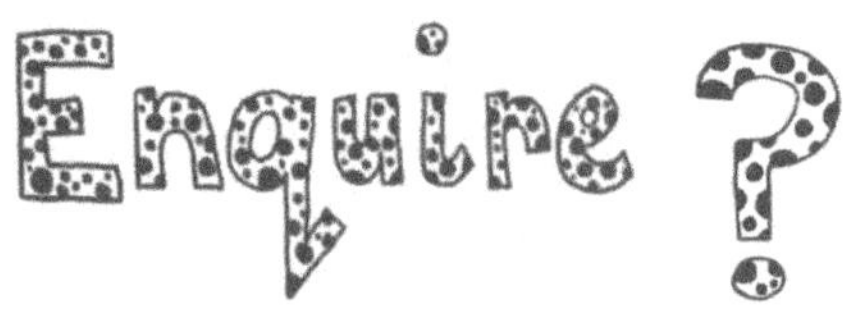

Ask children to think about what paint can be used for. How is it used in daily life, how is it used by artists? Explore the children's prior experience of using this medium.

Signpost: Through this project, we will be thinking about the different ways that paint can be used by experimenting with different tools and the ways that we can use them to create art.

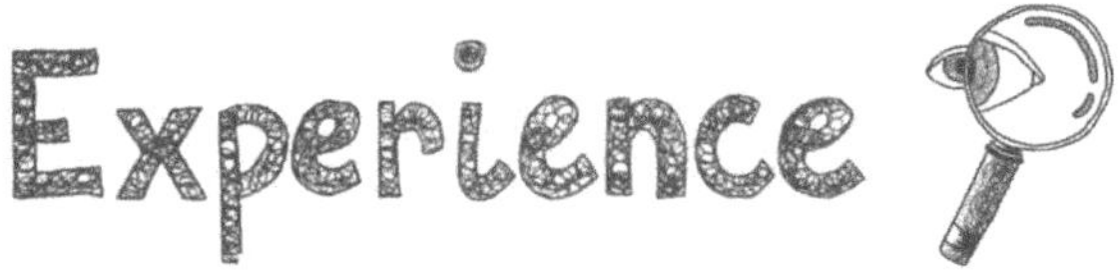

How many ways can you use paint?

Give children access to poster paint. Giving the children only primary colours will encourage more mixing and experimentation. You might also want to use cardboard or old packaging as palettes. Keeping the palettes once they have dried out so that they can be stuck into sketchbooks is an excellent way to demonstrate the artistic thinking children have undergone. It also saves on washing up!

Remind children of the question. We are not looking for a picture, or any representational marks. What we want is for children to see how many ways they can use the paint itself.

Encourage children to think about the tools that they could use to achieve this:

- fingers
- lolly sticks
- glue spatulas
- bits of fabric or cloth
- forks
- homemade tools from found objects

- leaves
- feathers.

The list is endless! Encourage children to annotate as they go, so they can remember how they made each mark.

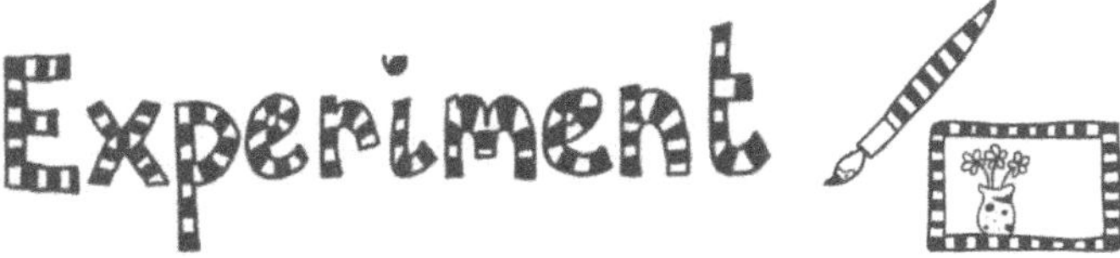

Look at Sarah Biffin's work – paint with different parts of the body.

Introduce the work of Sarah Biffin (do not mention her method of painting at this point). Look at some of her famous portraits and ask children to make observations about the paintings. What can they deduce about the artist from their work? Once children have explored Sarah's paintings, reveal that all the paintings they observed were painted by Sarah holding the paintbrush in her mouth. It is also worth flagging that many of Sarah Biffin's paintings were tiny! What do the children think about the paintings now? Show the children the two portraits of Queen Victoria by Sarah Biffin and Franz Xaver Winterhalter side by side. Can they tell which one is which?

The important thing for children to understand is that Sarah's paintings weren't just incredible for someone painting holding the paintbrush in their mouth; they are comparable in standard to the work of the most accomplished artists painting with their hands.

Does this information add to our understanding of how we can use paint?

Give children time to experiment using paint without their hands. They could hold the paintbrush in their mouths, elbows or toes. What kinds of marks can the children make? Are there any shapes that are easier or harder to create?

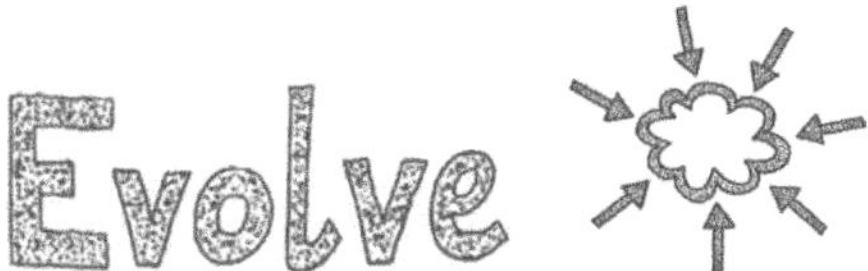

Children directly observe feathers and create their own studies, using different body parts to hold the paintbrush.

Show children 'Study of Feathers' by Sarah Biffin. Stick an image of the painting into sketchbooks. Around the edge, see if children can recreate the marks, colours and patterns that Sarah captures in her paintings without using their hands. This is an opportunity for children to make decisions about the part of their body they feel most confident in using to create their finished painting.

Collect different feathers or give children photos of real-life feathers to observe. Add these to the sketchbook and see if children can recreate them using their chosen body part to hold the paintbrush. Paint directly onto the pages without drawing first so children understand how the paint will work in their final piece.

Encourage children to make lots of quick paintings. The purpose of this is for children to build their confidence in this style of painting. Although they may find it hard to produce an image they are happy with initially, they will quickly become more decisive with their mark making as they practise. Celebrate the interesting outcomes that evolve out of this process!

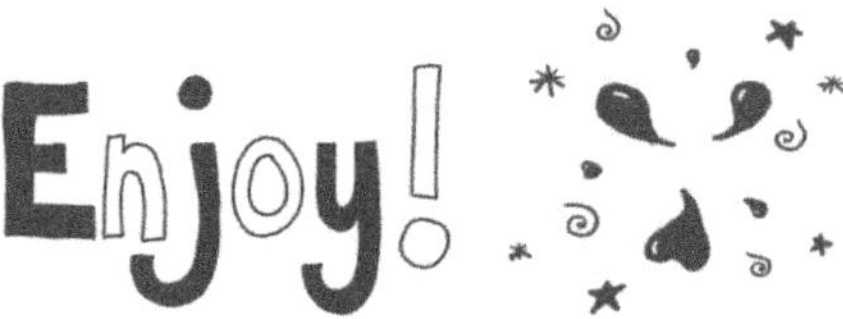

Create a 'Study of Feathers' without hands, using sketchbook work to make artistic choices.

Ask children to look back at the different images of feathers that evolved from their sketchbook work. Encourage them to turn their practice paintings into a final piece by selecting the most successful feathers from last time and recreating them, without hands, to produce their own 'study of feathers' in the style of Sarah Biffin.

Remind children to embrace the dynamic, colourful marks they make rather than attempting to create realism. Remember, Sarah Biffin perfected her incredible talent over many years and we are developing a new art skill over just a few weeks.

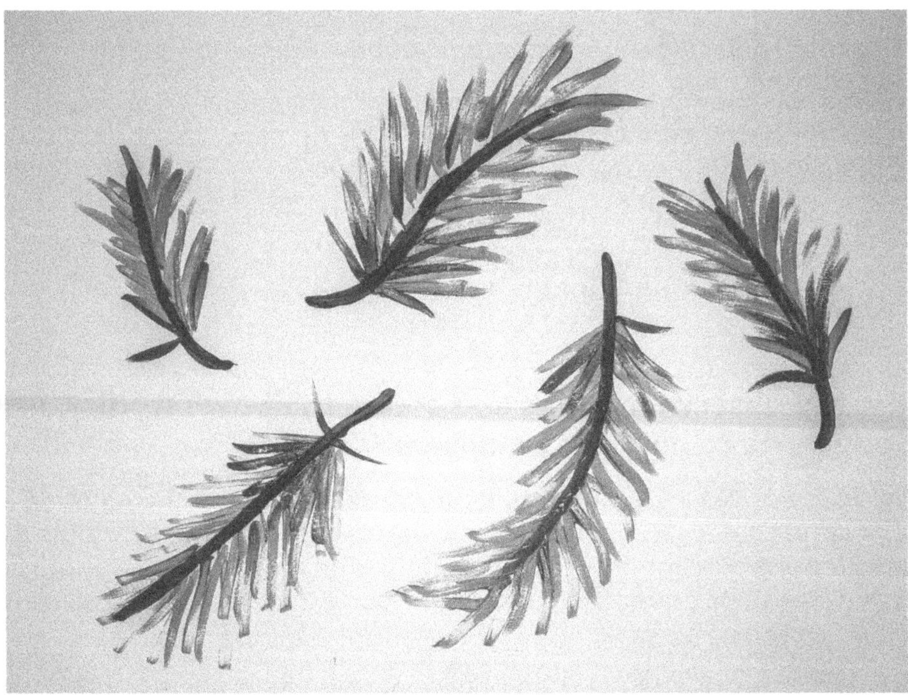

This painting may look simple, but the child has made all of these marks using their feet, which demonstrates amazing control of both the paint and the brush!

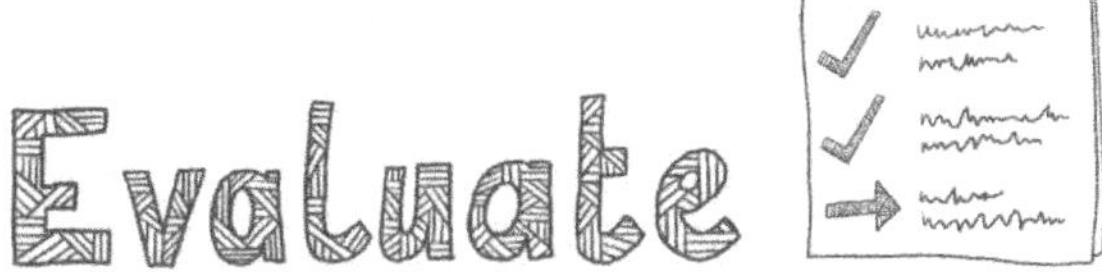

How did it go? Peer and self-assessment

Peer evaluation

Encourage your pupils to enjoy each other's work in a positive and celebratory way! Here are some questions that might promote discussion.

- Which is your favourite feather? Why?
- How has painting without hands created interesting results?
- Look at the sketchbook work. How have the artist's skills improved?

Self-evaluation

Encourage your artists to think deeply about what they have achieved. Although it is important for children to think about how they could improve and what they have learned for next time, ensure that they are kind to themselves and acknowledge their many successes! Here are some questions to get your class thinking critically about their own work:

- How did it feel to be painting without hands?
- What part of your painting are you proudest of?
- How has your understanding of paint changed?

Lesson plan Lower Key Stage 2: Can art tell a story?

Artist biography

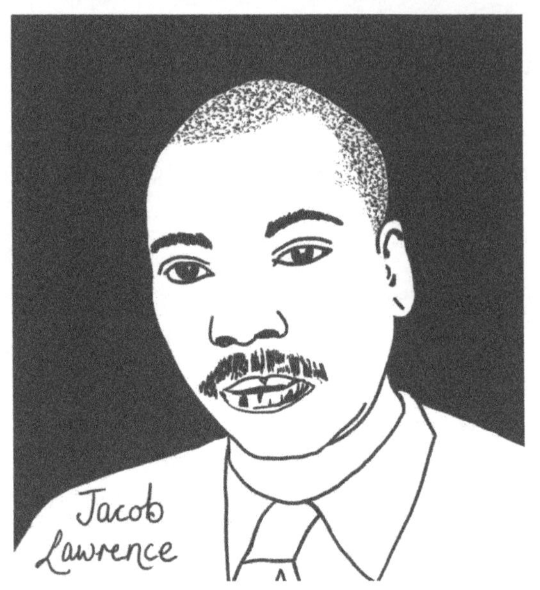

Jacob Lawrence

Born:	1917
Died:	2000
Birthplace:	Atlantic City, USA
Discipline:	Painting – expressive cubism

Jacob Lawrence was born in America at a time of extreme racial inequality and discrimination. When he was young his parents divorced and Jacob and his brother were put into foster care. When Jacob was 13, he moved to Harlem in New York where he was reunited with his mother. To keep Jacob occupied, his mother enrolled him in after-school art classes and that was where his long-term passion for art began.

In the beginning, Jacob would recreate the patterns on his mother's carpets with crayons, but as his confidence grew, he began to develop the signature style that he would maintain over the duration of his career. Jacob used his art to talk about the experiences of Black Americans, as did many artists of the Harlem Renaissance. Many of his paintings consisted of multiple panels that showed sequences of a story in bright, flat colours inspired by the vibrancy of Harlem. The simplified shapes of Jacob's work have many parallels with cubism.

In a time when Black Americans were denied their civil rights and much of public life was segregated, the significance of Jacob's work was still recognised. He was the first Black American to be represented in a New York gallery and he achieved national fame almost immediately.

Jacob has told the stories of many significant figures, including Harriet Tubman, who escaped slavery and devoted her life to rescuing other enslaved people, the abolition of slavery and women's rights. Jacob used his talent to shine a light on the struggles and triumphs of normal people.

Jacob's Migration series ensured that he is remembered as one of the most important painters of the twentieth century.

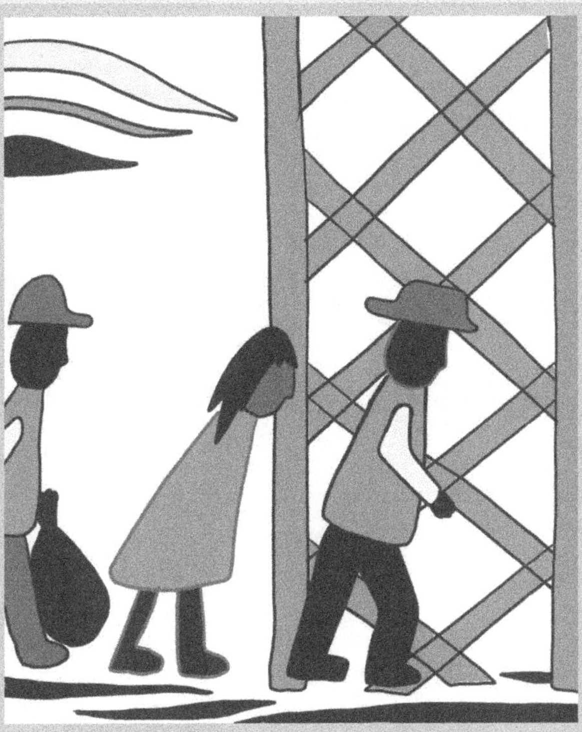

Find out more

Jacob Lawrence's portrayal of Harriet Tubman:

www.nga.gov/content/dam/ngaweb/Education/learning-resources/an-eye-for-art/AnEyeforArt-JacobLawrence.pdf

The full Migration series:

https://lawrencemigration.phillipscollection.org/the-migration-series

Images to inspire

Migration series panels: 1, 3, 12, 23 and 40

Other artist links

Charlotte Saloman: Charlotte also documented stories in multiple panels. Charlotte tells her own story as a Jewish girl living in World War 2.

Faith Ringgold: Faith tells stories, often with a social commentary, through her paintings and quilt making.

Caravaggio: A totally different style of painting, but children may recognise the Bible stories being told in these powerful paintings.

'When the subject is strong, simplicity is the only way to treat it.'

Jacob Lawrence (Arts WA, n.d.)

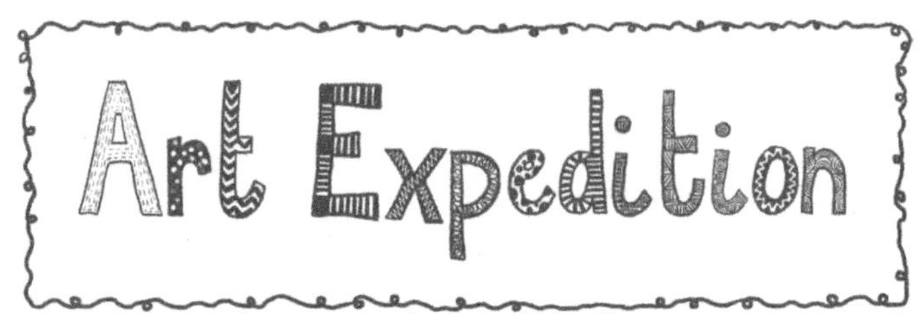

Jacob Lawrence • Lower Key Stage 2
Can art tell a story?

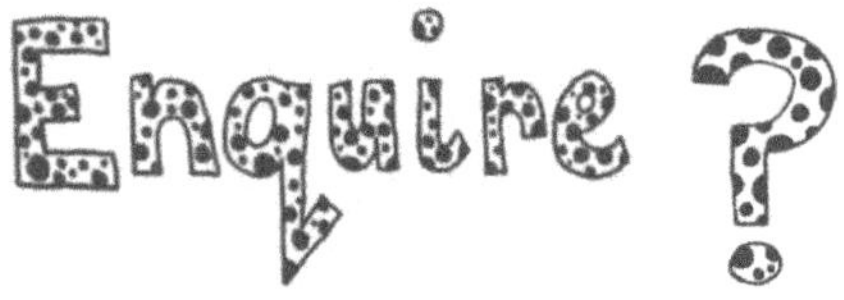

In what ways can art tell a story? Can children think of any stories they have seen where art is the prominent storyteller? Remember that illustration is a wonderful genre of art which will be very familiar to children!

Signpost: Through this project, we will be using paint to tell stories of our own.

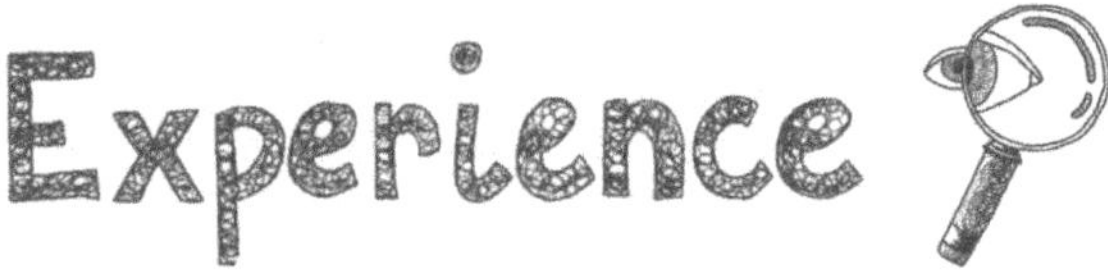

Turn famous paintings into stills from a bigger story. What happened before? What happens next?

Give children contrasting, narrative paintings to look at. What story do they think the artist was trying to tell? How do they know? What evidence supports their ideas?

You can use any paintings and artists that you feel your class will enjoy, but here are a few ideas that might provoke some interesting discussions:

- Guernica – Pablo Picasso
- Circe Turns a Companion of Odysseus into a Swine – Romare Bearden
- The Horse Fair – Rosa Bonheur
- The Scream – Edvard Munch
- In the Loge (At the Opera) – Mary Cassatt.

Give children small copies of your chosen paintings to stick in sketchbooks. Ask the children to treat the image as a picture from a storyboard. Can they draw what will happen next? Or what happened before? Encourage children to think outside the box and see the pictures as a moment from a bigger story, frozen in time.

Another way to encourage children to think beyond the literal is to give children speech and thought bubbles and ask them to imagine what the characters in the paintings might be about to say.

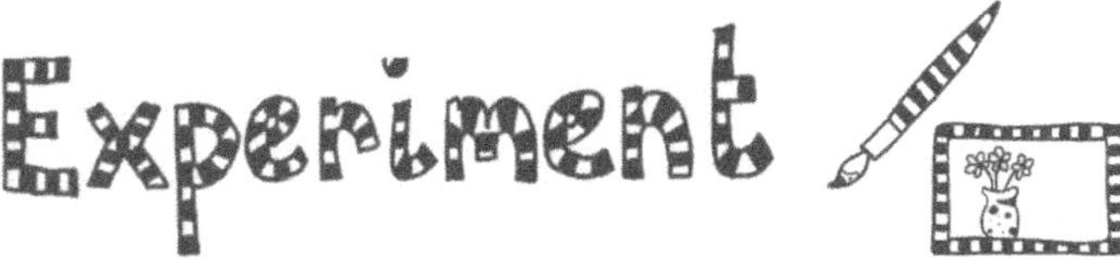

Look at Jacob Lawrence's paintings. Ask children to practise reducing images down to simple shapes and colours.

Look at Jacob Lawrence's work and think about the stories he told. Look at how he painted a series of paintings that told stories over many frames. How would we summarise his style of painting? Encourage children to identify the simplicity of the shapes and colours for the meaning of the painting to take centre stage. Show children how many of Jacob's paintings use triangles to represent perspective, where figures change size within an invisible triangle to give a sense of depth.

Ideally, this next section should be done from direct observation. Take children to places where they can observe people engaged in their daily lives. Maybe children could sit around the edge of the hall and observe their peers during assembly. Perhaps they could go to another class and watch the children busy with their work. Observing a PE lesson could be fun too!

Allow children to work directly into their sketchbooks to create quick drawings, reducing the people and their surroundings down to simple shapes and lines. Work in pencil and allow children a limited supply of coloured crayons to record the 'best fit' colours that they see. Encourage multiple drawings, where children make artistic choices about the information they record in order to recreate the 'essence' of what they are seeing, rather than a realistic rendering of the whole scene. Simplicity is key!

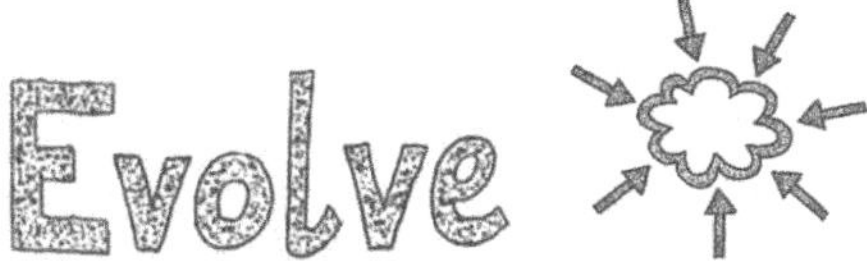

Divide up a story so that each child in the class has a part. Children design their part of the story.

Choose a story that the children can retell. It might be something as simple as the school day, or it might be a story that links to a topic or their English work. It could be something completely new! As a class, divide the story into parts where individuals or groups of children have their own element of the story to portray. This session is where the children will design the composition of their finished painting in isolation, but also how it will fit in with the paintings of the rest of the class to produce a consistent series that effectively tells the chosen story.

Jacob Lawrence used a consistent palette of colours to ensure that his individual paintings worked as a series of images. Children need to agree what their colour palette will be so that they have the colours they need for their individual paintings, but also so that the paintings work together as a group.

Ask children to paint several small compositions on a small scale so that they have a chance to decide which is most effective. This also gives children the opportunity to consider the best way to complete their painting, thinking about the order that the colours are applied to keep them pure and bold and avoid them mixing together. Make sure these designs are completed in paint and not pencil, so that children are learning how the paint will behave in their final piece.

Encourage the children to evaluate their designs as a class and make decisions about which compositions to choose to make the most effective whole-class piece.

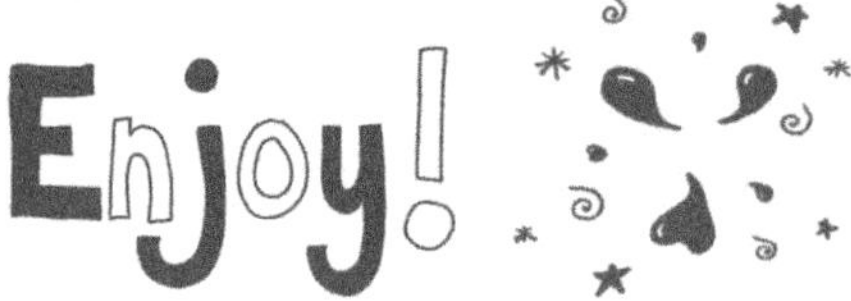

Paint the panel of the story and combine!

Children use their designs to recreate their part of the story, using the limited palette of colours agreed by the class in the previous session. Encourage children to think about the order in which they apply the colours to keep the shapes bold and geometric.

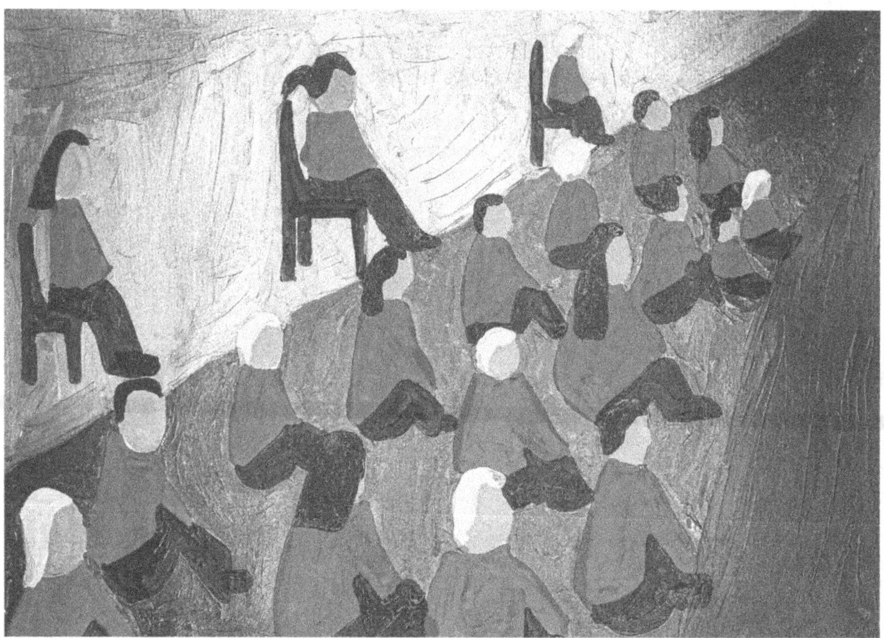

This panel has been painted as part of the story of the school day. This child has painted their peers sitting in assembly using Jacob Lawrence's signature use of flat colours and geometric shapes. They have also captured the use of perspective using a triangle to give a sense of depth and scale.

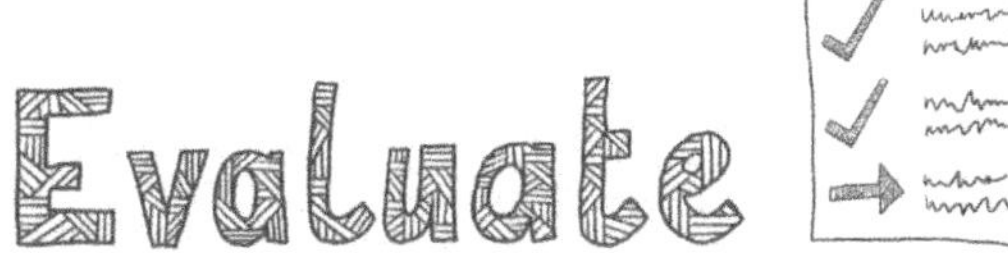

How did it go? Peer and self-assessment

Encourage children to evaluate their work as a class. Can they retell the story using the paintings the class have created? Use these suggested questions below to encourage your artists to think deeply about the effectiveness of what they have created.

Peer evaluation

- How effective is painting for story telling?
- Is there anything that could have made the story clearer?
- Can art tell a story?

Self-evaluation

- How did you find this style of painting?
- What part of your painting worked the best?
- If you had another go, what would you do differently?

Lesson plan Upper Key Stage 2: How is power depicted in art?

Artist biography

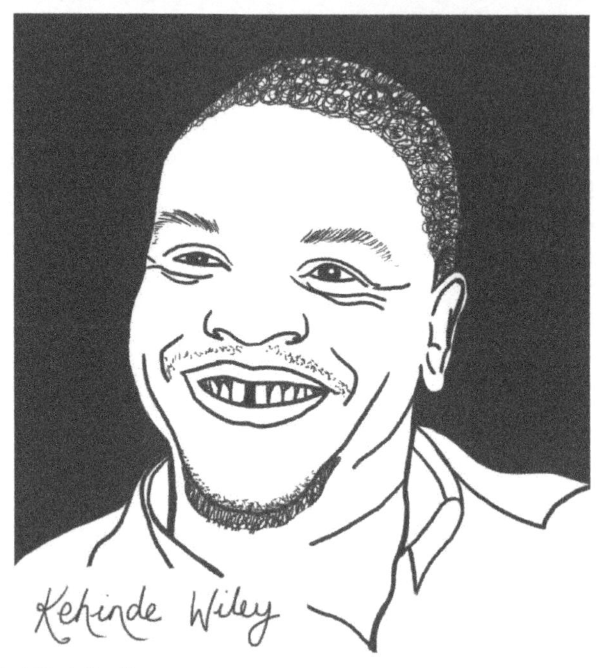

Kehinde Wiley

Born:	1977
Died:	–
Birthplace:	Los Angeles, USA
Discipline:	Painting – contemporary

Kehinde Wiley was born in Los Angeles and has a twin brother. From an early age, both boys became interested in art and enrolled in after school art classes where their talent was spotted when they were just 11 years old.

At age 11, Kehinde was given the opportunity to spend time at a Russian art school and this was when his passion for portraiture began. Kehinde was determined to be the very best artist that he could possibly be and he studied the work of the old masters such as Gainsborough and Constable. He was obsessed with his portraits becoming as realistic as possible.

Kehinde's studies of classical paintings inspired him to create a more modern style of portrait, which referenced the composition and positions of traditional art but featuring real people surrounded by the colours and patterns of their own cultures. Kehinde chose models from his hometown and encouraged them to pose in stances from classical paintings, elevating these everyday people into positions of grandeur.

One of Kehinde's most notable achievements was painting the official portrait of President Barack Obama. In the background of the painting, each flower represents an aspect of President Obama's life and heritage. The jasmine represents Hawaii, where Obama was born and raised, the chrysanthemums are the flower of Chicago where Obama met his wife, Michelle, and raised his family, and the blue lilies represent Kenya, which is where Obama's father was from.

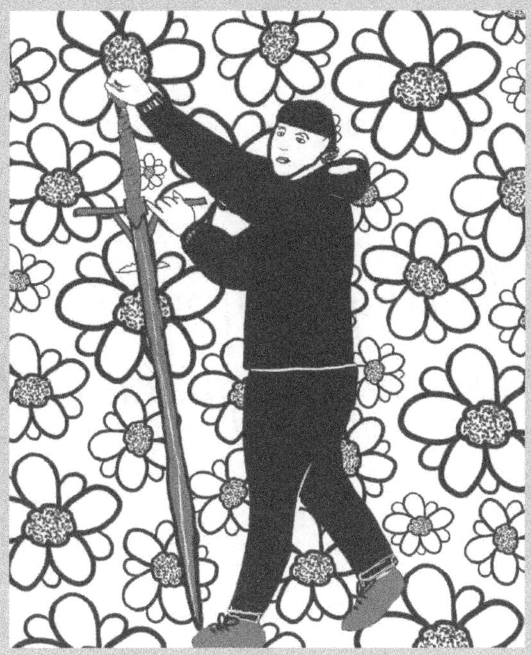

Find out more

Website:

https://kehindewiley.com

Instagram:

www.instagram.com/kehindewiley/

Images to inspire

President Barack Obama (2018)

Portrait of Jorge Wright (2017)

Anthony of Padua (2013)

Officer of the Hussars (2007)

Napoleon Leading the Army over the Alps (2005)

Ice T (2005)

Other artist links

Jacques-Louis David: Look at Jacques's version of Napoleon Leading the Army over the Alps. A great painting to draw direct comparisons between Kehinde's work and that of classical artists.

Artemisia Gentileschi: A good place to look for powerful women in classic art.

John Michael Wright: A brilliant source of inspiration for classical poses that can be found in portraiture.

'Art is about changing what we see in our everyday lives and representing it in such a way that it gives us hope.'

Kehinde Wiley (The Cut, 2016)

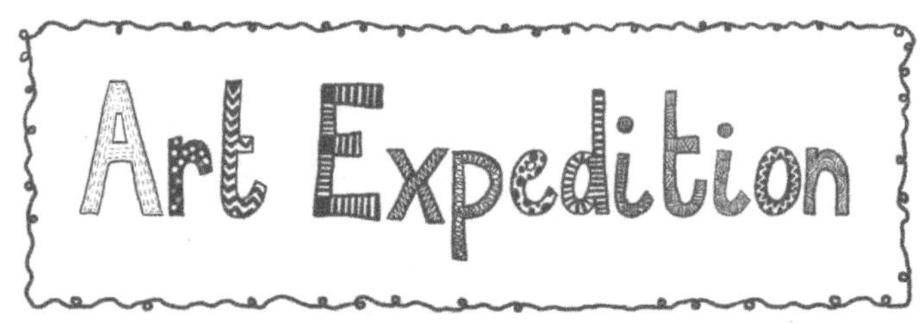

Kehinde Wiley • Upper Key Stage 2
How is power depicted in art?

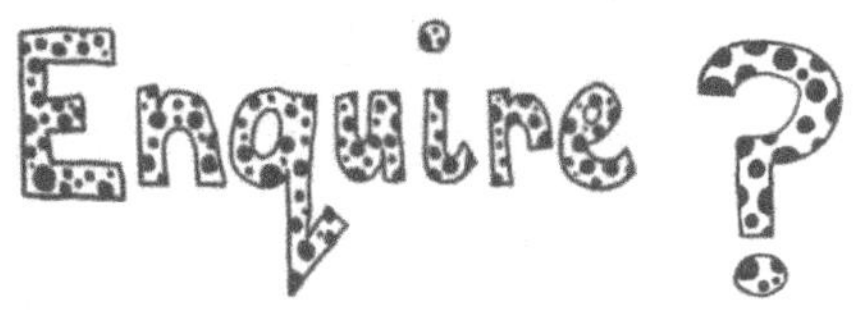

This question will be an interesting one to discuss. Who do the children consider to be 'powerful'?

Signpost: Through this project, we will be creating our own 'powerful' portraits using paint.

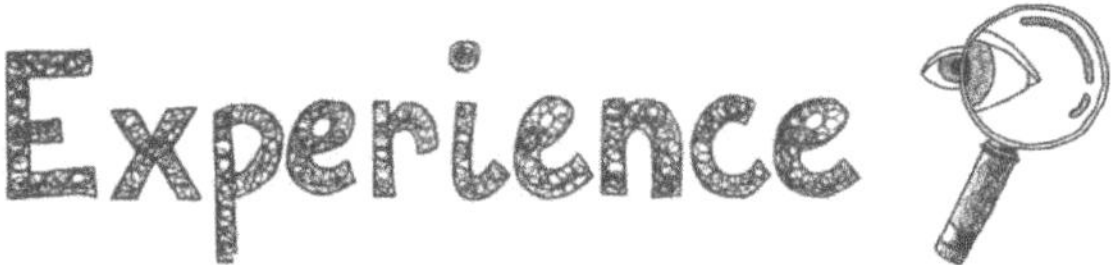

Look at classical portraits of significant figures from history. Children pose for quick paintings, experimenting with different stances that project power.

Give children several portraits from classical art to explore. How is the power of these figures conveyed? Stick some examples in sketchbooks and see if children can create a checklist of attributes from the paintings' compositions that signify the power and importance of their subjects.

You might want to encourage the children to research paintings for themselves, or you might want to provide a selection of images as a starting point. Here are some suggestions:

- Napoleon Leading the Army over the Alps – Jacques-Louis David
- Portrait of Queen Elizabeth I – Nicholas Hilliard
- King Charles II – Thomas Hawker
- The Ambassadors – Holbein
- Joan of Arc – Dante Gabriel Rossetti
- Philip II in Armour – Anthonis Mor.

Ask for volunteers to be models for the class. Provide some props (sticks and rulers will do just fine for swords and spears!). Models pose for a few minutes using the paintings they have seen to inspire their own 'power pose', whilst the class make quick, gestural sketches. Encourage children to focus on recording the shapes they can see rather than the detail. Fill a page with quick sketches that merge and overlap. The purpose of this session is to encourage observation and to practise capturing the 'essence' of the pose, rather than to create a life-like image. Don't rush this stage. The more chance children have to draw, the more control they will have over their final outcome.

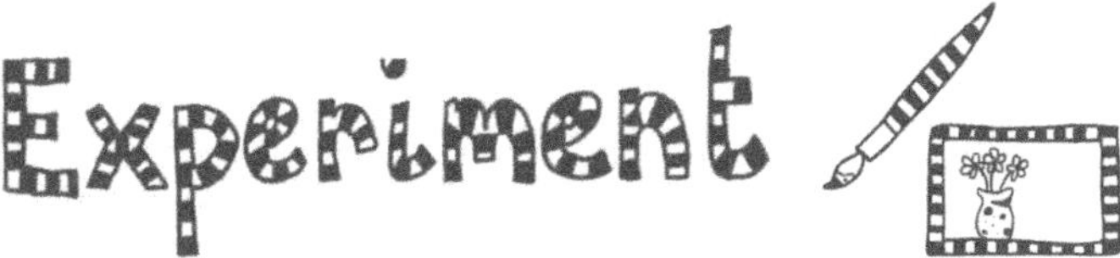

Discover Kehinde Wiley's work.

Show children images of Kehinde Wiley's work. This is a good opportunity to make the direct comparison between the two versions of 'Napoleon Leading the Army over the Alps'. Ask children to list the similarities and differences to see if they can unpick what Kehinde is trying to say in his artwork.

Show children the Barack Obama portrait. Explain the symbolism of the flowers in the background.

Ask children to think about patterns, flowers, trees or colours that might be significant to their own lives.

Using paint, encourage children to collect ideas in their sketchbooks, experimenting with different patterns, colours and textures to represent symbolism that might be important to them. Explore multiple ideas that can be narrowed down for the final piece.

Give children just the primary colours (red, blue and yellow) plus white and black so that they can rehearse their colour mixing skills as part of their experimentation.

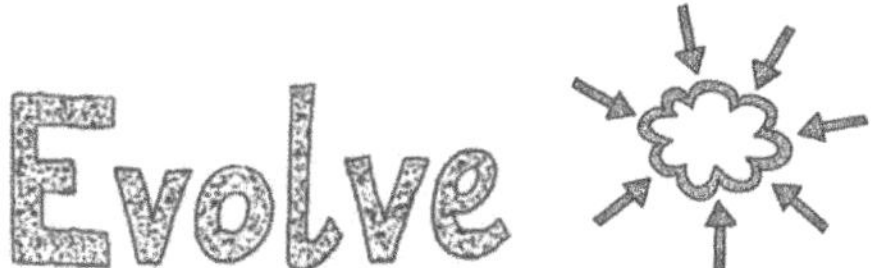

Consider the composition of the final piece.

The Evolve stage is where children begin to work on the composition for their final piece. Look back at the sketchbook ideas. Which power stance do they want to work with and which background do they think will best complement their portrait?

Encourage children to make sketches of their final piece and annotate with thoughts around colour and composition. Give the children the opportunity to take photos of each other in their chosen stance so that these can be added to the sketchbook as a supportive source ready for the next stage. Stress the importance of attempting several compositions and considering the colour choices of both the back and foreground and how they will work together.

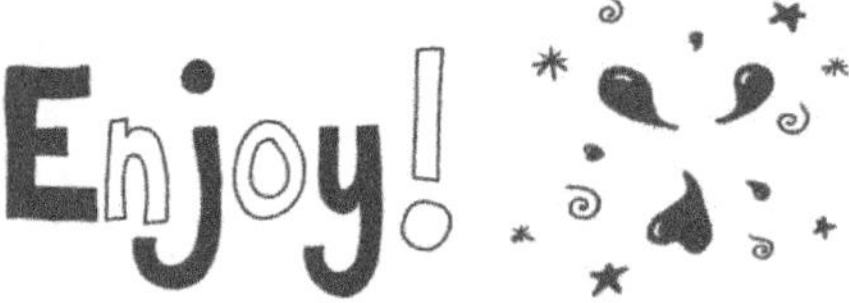

Create a portrait in the style of Kehinde Wiley.

This is the stage where the children produce their final portrait in the style of Kehinde Wiley: a painted, patterned background with a portrait of the child in a powerful pose in the foreground. This is a challenging project, so there are several adaptations that you could make to support children in creating something that is more manageable, but still effective.

- Paint the background and the portrait on separate pieces of paper. Then the portrait can be cut out to avoid one spoiling the other.
- Paint the background, but use a cut-out photo of each child in their 'power stance' as the portrait element.
- Use carbon paper. Put a photo of the child with the carbon paper between the photo and the background. Then trace over to create a carbon outline on the background that can then be painted. This could just be the outline of the figure or the spaces could be painted in too.
- Use a poly pocket. Put the photo of the child in the wallet and trace the portrait in paint; this could be just a black outline or a fully painted portrait. Then remove the photo and replace with the painted background. This will create a more abstract interpretation but will still look great!
- If you are brave and complete the project on one piece of paper, ensure that children have several sessions, with a chance for the paint to dry in between layers. Acrylic paint really is the best choice for this so that paint can be applied over the top of areas that might have been painted accidentally.

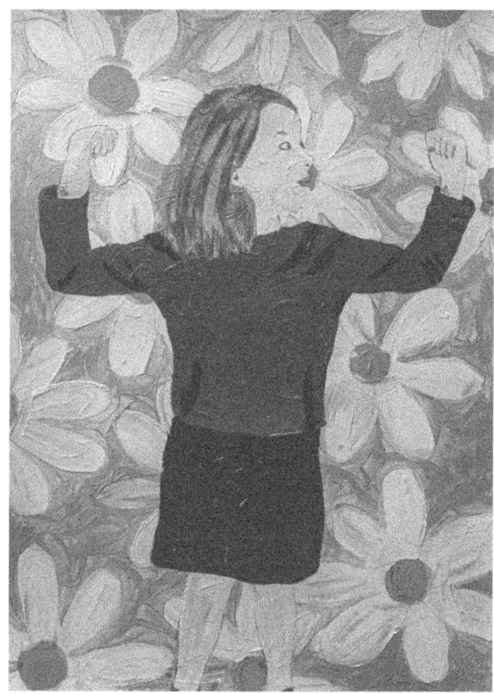

This child has used carbon paper to transfer the image of their 'power pose' to their background in order to create a realistic portrait in acrylic paint.

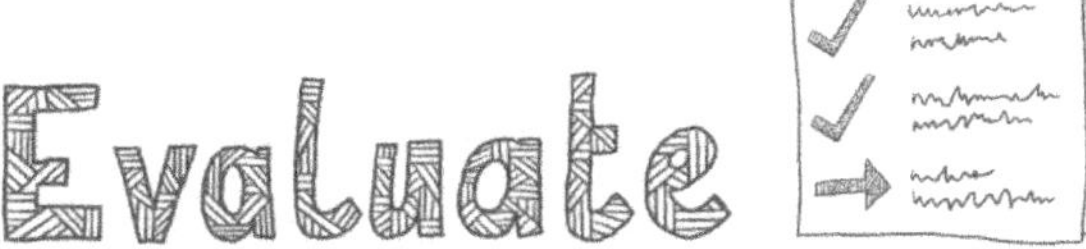

How did it go? Peer and self-assessment

Display all of the portraits around the room. Perhaps you could split your class in half so that some children stay with their work and the rest of the children move around sharing their thoughts about the portraits. They can then swap so that everyone has a chance to receive verbal feedback. Use these questions below to get your artists thinking carefully about what they have produced and the processes they have undertaken.

Peer evaluation

- How can you tell the subject of the portrait is important?
- Where has the artist shown perseverance?
- How could the painting be improved further?

Self-evaluation

- Explain the process you went through to develop this idea.
- How have you attempted to show yourself as 'powerful'?
- What would you like to work on to further develop your painting?

Chapter 4
Sculpture

Introduction to sculpture

Sculpture, or 'making', is without doubt one of the most engaging entry points for children as they embark on their artistic journeys. Yet despite this, three-dimensional work in school is often a rarity, which can potentially exclude many children from ever discovering their passion for art.

Working in 3D is often the moment when art suddenly 'makes sense' to some children. It is a totally different skill set to painting or drawing and you will often find that children will suddenly come alive when exposed to this totally unique way of working. The problem is that opportunities for sculpture are often limited, so this enthusiasm goes unharnessed. Restrictions on space, resources, confidence and time are just some of the reasons that sculpture tends to take a back seat. One way around this is to 'block' your art lessons into whole 'art days' when taking on a unit of work on sculpture, so that children can continue their work to completion without the need to store or tidy away in between sessions.

The other limitation with sculpture as a discipline is that often children do not have enough consistency in their use of a material to make tangible progress. There is a misconception that if a class has engaged in a project using clay lower down the school, that this means that they have 'done' clay. Sculpture, like all art forms, requires practice in order to develop mastery, so make sure that throughout your curriculum, children can rehearse their use of consistent, three-dimensional materials so that they can develop control and fluency.

Materials that can be used in sculpture

There are so many amazing materials that can be used to create three-dimensional artwork. This is by no means an exhaustive list but here are a few of my favourites.

Clay

This is normally the go-to three-dimensional material because it is so versatile and let's face it: cheap! But clay can be an extremely frustrating medium if projects are not carefully planned and pitched correctly. We need to ensure that children have the skills to mould, carve and attach pieces of clay before we expect them to complete projects that are dependent on this knowledge. Projects which explore form (Barbara Hepworth is perfect inspiration for this) need to be mastered before children can attempt the complicated process of building animals with limbs, heads and tails, which inevitably end up breaking into pieces once the clay has dried out.

Air-drying clay is incredibly difficult to join effectively, so encourage children to begin their sculpture experience by moulding from one piece of clay by stretching, smoothing and using tools. Try pinch pots lower down the school and then coil pots that can be shaped to create all kinds of exciting forms. Only then, once children have developed their confidence in this medium, should they learn to slip and score to join pieces of clay together to create more complex sculptures. Here is some further information about some of these key skills:

Pinch pots: Take a ball of clay and make a dent in the ball with your thumb. Then, using your fingers, pinch around the hole to create the walls of your pot. Young children can use cocktail sticks to make marks, holes and patterns as decoration on the surface of their pots.

Coil pots: Roll out a thin sausage of clay. Coil the sausage to make a shape similar to a snail shell. This is the base of your pot. Then, roll more sausages that can be layered on top of each other to create the walls of your pot. You can up-level this skill by using balls of clay in between the coils to make interesting patterns, or even curling the coils to make exciting shapes in the walls! These coils can then be blended together with fingers, just on the inside if you want the pattern to be visible, or on both sides for a smooth finish.

Slip and score: Leave a thumb-sized piece of clay in an inch of water overnight. In the morning, the clay will be soggy and can be mixed into the water to create 'slip'. This slip is like glue for clay. When children have perfected their clay skills and are ready for the next challenge, they can try adding separate pieces of clay by scoring both surfaces to be attached, painting on the slip and then pushing the surfaces together securely to create a strong bond.

Tin foil

I absolutely love using tin foil for sculptures. This material is so versatile! It can be bent and shaped in all manner of different ways and it can be reworked to encourage children to edit and improve. It is also light and holds its own weight which means that children can experiment with free-standing, balanced sculptures. Try using foil to create creatures with elongated limbs inspired by Louise Bourgeois, Elisabeth Frink or Alberto Giacometti. These could then be turned into stop-animation performance pieces, or children could explore and trace the shadows that these forms create. So many possibilities!

Paper

Using paper and card to create sculptures is highly underrated. With a bit of tape or a stapler, children can fold, twist, cut and tear paper to create amazing patterns. An interesting way to evolve paper sculptures is to encourage children to create 3D versions of 2D paintings. It is a very exciting way of getting children to engage with a piece of artwork and gives a unique insight into the child's sense of perspective.

Soap

See the Ai Weiwei-inspired art expedition later in this chapter. Soap is incredibly easy to carve using cocktail sticks, butter knives and clay tools. It is robust enough to hold its shape even when you are carving holes right through it, but soft enough to allow little fingers to carve patterns into the surface. If you want to use soap to practise carving, it is also easy enough to smooth down with a bit of water if you want to clear the surface for another go. Clean hands are just an added benefit of this process!

Ice

Creating ice moulds filled with interesting artefacts is a great way to show children how some artists create sculptures considering the way they will change over time. Have a look at Néle Azevedo's 'Minimum Monument' for inspiration. Give children a paper cup full of water and encourage them to choose interesting things to add before the cup is popped in the freezer overnight. On a sunny day, put the ice outside and use a tablet to create a timelapse of the ice melting; this project will definitely capture the children's imaginations and could provide an interesting talking point around climate change.

Wire

Wire is a wonderful way to empower children to produce 3D art. Children can develop their continuous line drawings into free-standing wire sculptures inspired by Alexander Calder or develop their understanding of geometric shape inspired by Gertrud Louise Goldschmidt. Both these artists have also perfected the art of 'kinetic sculptures', a perfect starting point for children to use wire to create hanging mobiles designed to move.

Sculpture and the design process

One of the most important things to remember when encouraging children to work in 3D is the differences that lie in the design process. In all the art expeditions I have created for this book, the Evolve stage is the point where children have an opportunity to practise the skills they will need to produce their final response. Although it is tempting for children to produce drawings to design what they would like to create, using a pencil does nothing to further a child's understanding of sculpture. In sculpture, the design process is in the 'macquette', a small model, made from the same materials as the final piece. This allows the artist to explore what it is like to use that material and discover whether their ideas will work using the properties of the medium they are working with.

A perfect example of this is clay. Imagine what a child would draw if they were designing a model of a giraffe. Would the child really understand the implications of using a malleable material to create such a long neck or such skinny legs? These discoveries would only be made if the design for their final model was done in clay. After this experience, in a low stakes environment, children will be able to make more effective choices in the making of their final responses.

Embrace sculpture

If you want to put 'making' at the centre of your primary art curriculum, consider 'Make First' (Crafts Council, 2022), a pioneering pedagogy that allows children to learn about materials through 'tweaking and tinkering'. This pedagogical approach throws children in at the deep end, where they solve problems and try new ideas right there in the making process. It acknowledges that the joy of working in 3D exists in the collaborative process of decision-making. Encourage your children to play, enjoy, work in groups and solve problems whilst responding to a question using three-dimensional materials. It takes a lot of bravery as a teacher to let the children lead the way, but the results are spectacular!

So, be brave and embrace sculpture! For some of your children it will be the light bulb moment that makes them believe they really can be artists.

Lesson plans

On the pages that follow are three art expeditions based on the work of Cecilia Vicuña, Ai Weiwei and Lubaina Himid. Each artist represents a very different style of sculpture. Although there are suggested materials within each lesson, you could use any of the processes above to make the expedition your own and develop your children's understanding of all that sculpture can be.

Lesson plan Key Stage 1: What is a sculpture?

Artist biography

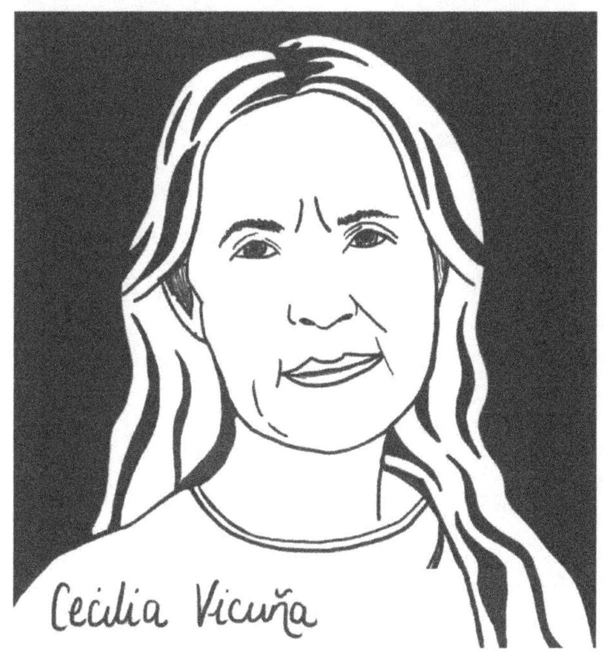

Cecilia Vicuña

Born:	1948
Died:	–
Birthplace:	Santiago, Chile
Discipline:	Visual art – installation

Cecilia Vicuña is an artist and a poet, born in Santiago, Chile. At 18 years old, her father built a studio for her to develop her artistic talents. From a young age, Cecilia wanted to make a difference and used art and poetry to talk about issues that she felt strongly about.

Cecilia found herself in exile in London following the military coup in Chile in the early 1970s, but this did not stop her from standing up for what she believed in. Cecilia continued to use her art to send a message supporting human rights and protecting the legacy of indigenous people.

In 1966, Cecilia began to construct sculptures called 'Basuritas', which is Spanish for 'garbage'. These sculptures were made of found objects, often washed up on the beach. Cecilia collected these objects and constructed them to make interesting forms that she would display in the environment in which they were found. Cecilia's 'Basuritas' are a form of land art and are a comment on climate change, an issue that Cecilia was ahead of her time in exploring.

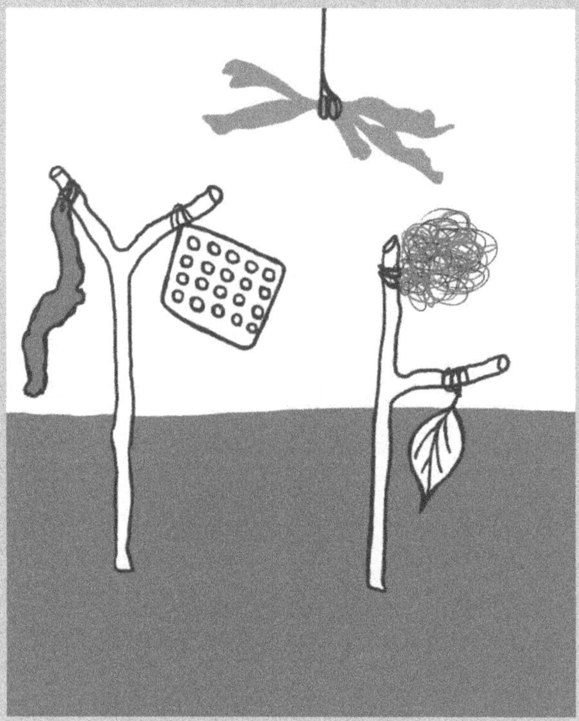

Find out more

Website:

www.ceciliavicuna.com/

Tate website:

www.tate.org.uk/art/artists/cecilia-vicuna-21412

Images to inspire

Precarious Improvisation (2009)

Pueblo de altares (1990)

Poncho Huiro (1990)

Paño e' sangre (1973)

Other artist links

Andy Goldsworthy: Andy is also a land artist, using materials found in the natural environment to create site-specific art.

Tim Noble and Sue Webster: These artists use rubbish to create incredibly life-like shadows of figures.

Michelle Stitzlein: Michelle creates incredible murals from recycled objects, turning rubbish into flowers and foliage.

'My best works are the ones I don't make.'

Cecilia Vicuña (Schorske, 2022)

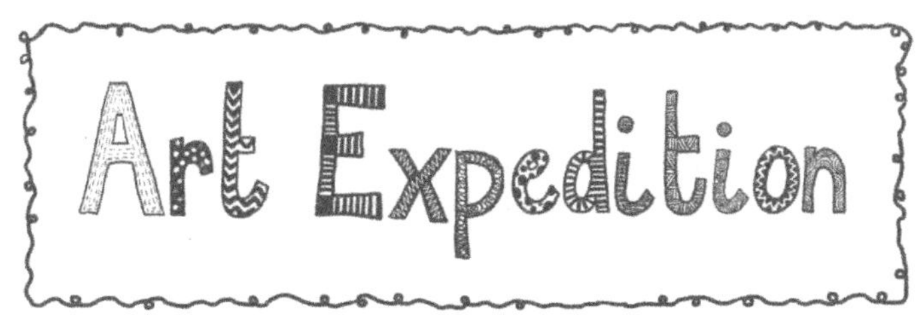

Cecilia Vicuña • Key Stage 1
What is a sculpture?

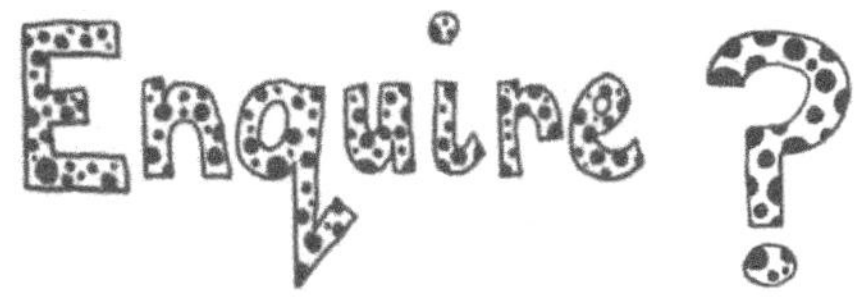

Ask children the question and see if they have any knowledge of art in 3D. How would they define what a sculpture is?

Signpost: Through this project, we will be making sculptures using 'found objects' from our own environment.

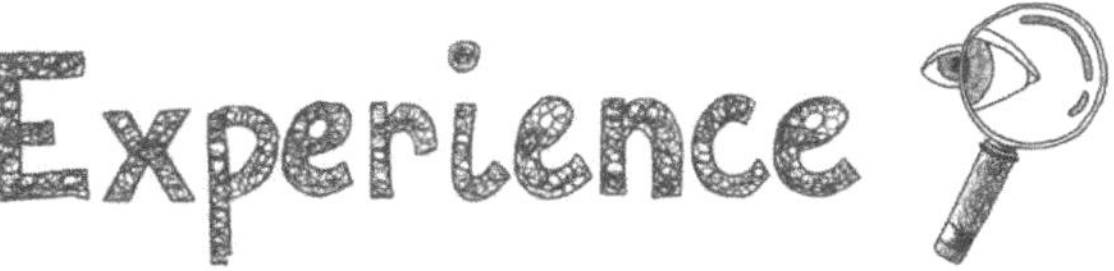

Show children a selection of different sculptures. Ask them to recreate clay maquettes (small models) from each inspiration and discuss the similarities and differences.

Show children a wide variety of sculptures as inspiration. Encourage discussion to further children's understanding of the materials used, the shapes represented and the sites in which the sculptures exist. The aim is to challenge children's preconceptions of what sculpture can be and extend their thinking beyond the statues they might have seen in towns and city centres. You can use photos of any sculptures you like (direct observation would be even better if you are lucky enough to be situated near any real-life sculptures!).

Give children five different images of sculptures on their tables. You can use any images you like, but here are some interesting sculptures that might produce a nice variety of results:

- Cloud Gate – Anish Kapoor
- Repetition Nineteen III – Eva Hesse
- Field – Antony Gormley

- Balloon Dog – Jeff Koons
- Eat Me Now – Chila Kumari Singh Burman.

Encourage the children to respond to what they see using a piece of clay or plasticine. Ask children to discuss how their different maquettes feel, the different ways in which they were constructed and how each model they make differs from the last. Take photos of all the mini sculptures for sketchbooks!

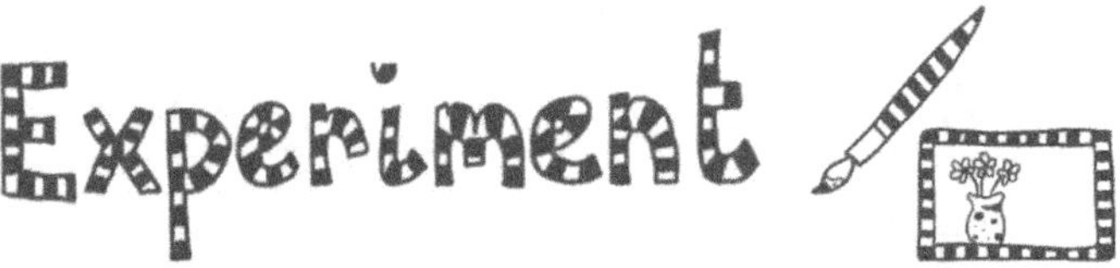

Introduce Cecilia Vicuña's 'Basuritas' and 'Precarious'. You can find these on Cecilia's Instagram: www.instagram.com/ceciliavicuna/

What can we use to make 'form'?

Show children Cecilia Vicuña's work with 'found objects'. What materials does she use to create her sculptures? Explain to children that the element of art we use to describe three-dimensional work is 'form'. Anything with form can be a sculpture.

Give the children access to a selection of materials to explore and turn into sculptures. Here are a few ideas that might work well:

- lolly sticks and sticky tack
- plasticine
- wire
- pipe cleaners
- foil
- paper (plus tape and staplers)
- LEGO®
- art straws.

Encourage children to play with the materials and see what they can make. A carousel might work well here to encourage multiple explorations rather than becoming embedded in one idea. Remember to facilitate new ideas too! If a child suggests something else from the classroom that could be used for making, this is a sign of them exercising their creativity!

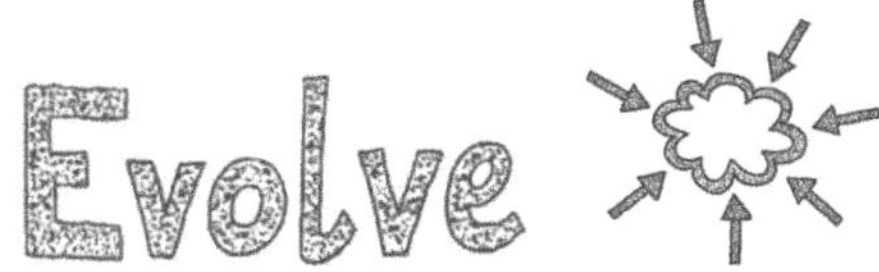

Introduce the idea of site-specific art. Work in different locations (outside / classroom / cloakroom / dinner hall).

Talk about how Cecilia Vicuña uses 'found objects' and creates sculptures within the environment where the materials were found. Go on a walk around the school and its grounds. What materials can you see that could be turned into sculptures? It could be natural materials from outside, recycling, packaging from lunchtime... whatever you would like the focus to be.

Remember, Cecilia has a passion for environmental issues, so a sculpture that comments on litter or the natural world would be particularly appropriate. Collect your chosen materials and give children a chance to practise joining and assembling. Remember, this design process needs to happen using the actual materials so that the children know what will work and what tools they will need when they come to make their final sculpture.

Give children photos of the environment they are in so that they can draw their sculpture design directly onto the photo once they have evolved their ideas.

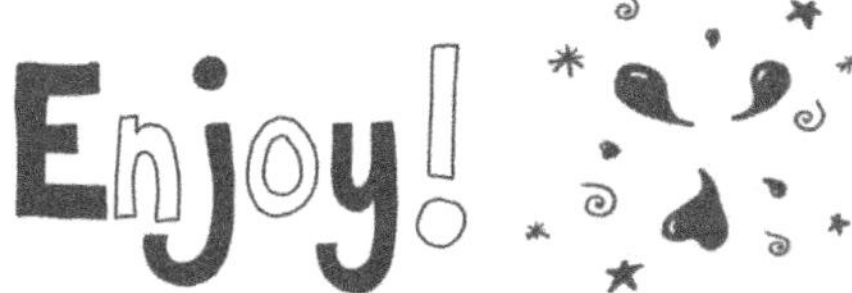

Make and photograph!

Children can revise their ideas and then set to work! Go into the environment that the children have chosen and create sculptures using the materials they have found there. Take photographs of the final pieces for sketchbooks.

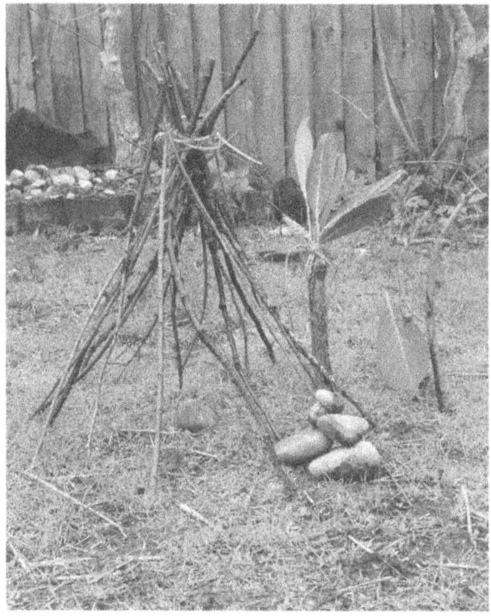

These children have combined leaves, pebbles and sticks with string to create this interesting free-standing sculpture using the objects they found in this specific environment.

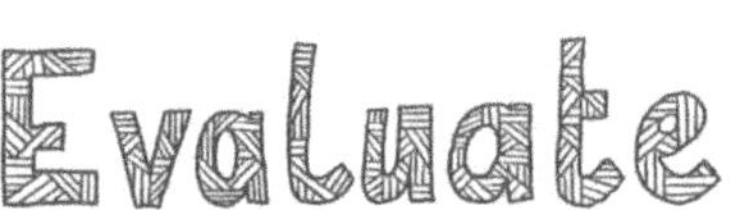

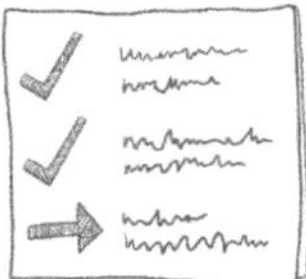

How did it go? Peer and self-assessment

Share the children's photos on the whiteboard.

Peer evaluation

This can be done as a class. Share the images of the found object sculptures and encourage children to think about the questions below:

- What materials have been used?
- Does the sculpture fit with the environment?
- What else could be added?

Self-evaluation

Ask children to annotate around their photo in their sketchbook.

- Give your piece a title.
- What was your favourite part of this art expedition?
- Can you explain what a sculpture is?

Lesson plan Lower Key Stage 2: What does it mean to be individual?

Artist biography

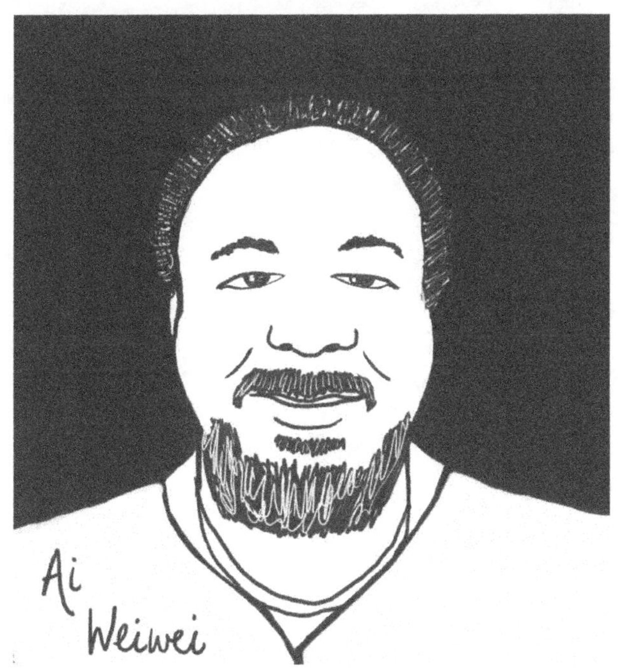

Ai Weiwei

Born:	1957
Died:	–
Birthplace:	Beijing, China
Discipline:	Sculpture and photography

Ai Weiwei was born in China where he lived in poverty with his family. His father was a poet who opposed the Chinese government and as a result, he and his family were sent to a labour camp when Ai Weiwei was just one year old. Three years later, the family were exiled for a further 16 years. After returning to Beijing, Ai Weiwei continued to stand up for what he believed in and was later arrested on spurious 'economic charges' resulting in him spending 81 days in a Chinese jail.

Ai Weiwei's early experiences have led him to become a fierce critic of the Chinese regime and he has used his art to shine a light on political and social issues. One of Ai Weiwei's most famous sculptures is 'Straight', an installation of 150 hand-straightened steel rods retrieved from poorly built Chinese schools that collapsed in an earthquake, resulting in the deaths of 5,000 children.

Another controversial artwork is 'Dropping a Han Dynasty Urn', which consists of three black and white images of Ai Weiwei smashing a valuable antique vase. This work was designed to demonstrate Ai Weiwei's political beliefs about China's past but many historians felt this was senseless destruction of an irreplaceable historical artefact.

Ai Weiwei's installation 'Sunflower Seeds', which saw him place millions of tiny, handcrafted porcelain seeds on the floor of the Turbine Hall at the Tate Modern, made a statement on mass production versus individuality.

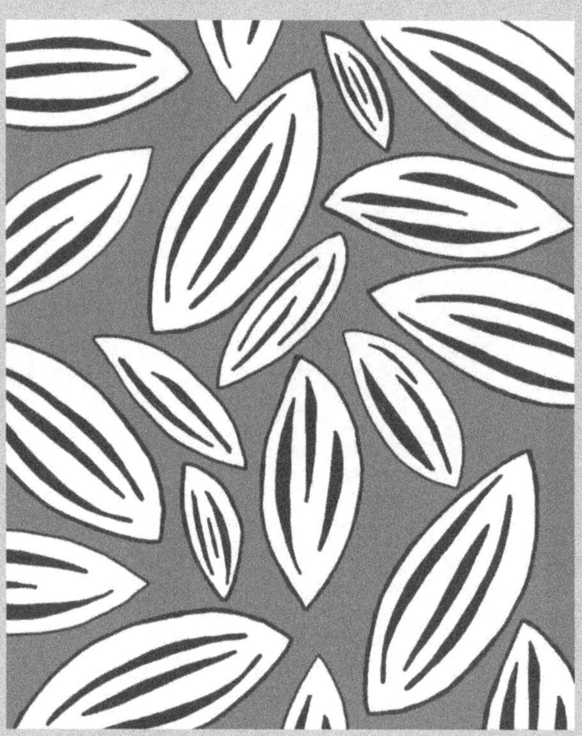

Find out more

Instagram:

www.instagram.com/aiww

Tate website:

www.tate.org.uk/art/artists/ai-weiwei-8208

Images to inspire

He Xie (2010)

Straight (2008-2012)

Sunflower Seeds (2008)

Dropping a Han Dynasty Urn (1995)

Other artist links

Yayoi Kusama: Similarly to 'Sunflower Seeds', Yayoi immerses the viewer in an obliteration of identical images, in this case polka dots.

Antony Gormley: 'Field' is another example of multiple, similar objects (figures in this case) arranged on the floor.

Félix González-Torres: In 'Untitled (Portrait of Ross in L.A)', the floor is littered with sweets that the audience are encouraged to pick up and eat!

'Creativity is the power to act.'

Ai Weiwei (Weiwei, 2011)

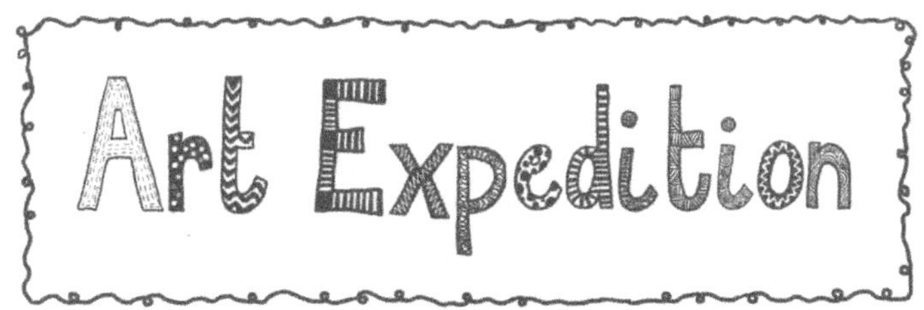

Ai Weiwei • Lower Key Stage 2
What does it mean to be individual?

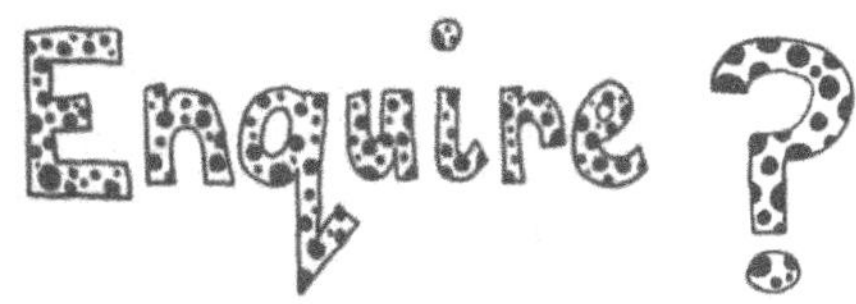

Ask children what it is that makes them 'them'. Spend time celebrating the uniqueness of the class and the ways in which the children's differences make them special.

Signpost: Through this project, we will be creating a sculpture that represents us as individuals using soap or clay.

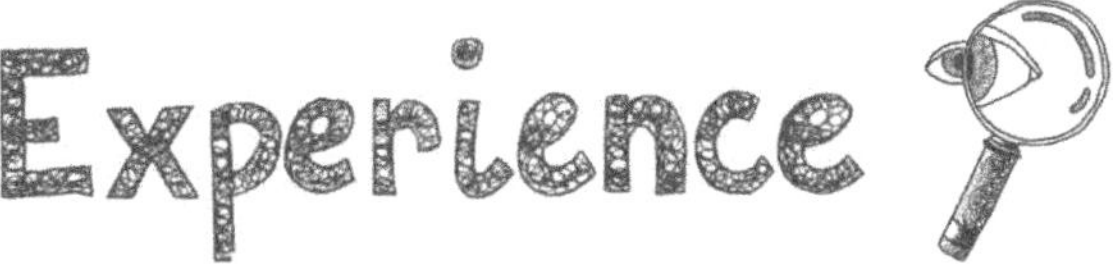

Ask children to fill a sketchbook page, exploring the things that make them unique.

Ask children to think about how they can represent themselves artistically. Give them a selection of art materials to use to create their sketchbook page. Encourage children to consider ideas beyond the way that they look. They could represent:

- favourite colours
- clubs they are part of
- hobbies
- family
- foods they enjoy
- places they have been
- people that are important in their lives
- their favourite music, films or TV.

Once children have completed their pages, encourage them to move around the room and share their sketchbooks with the class. What similarities and differences do the children find amongst their peers?

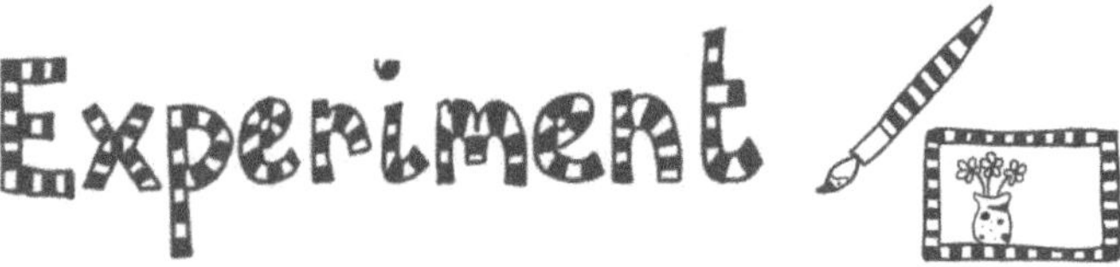

Introduce Ai Weiwei's 'Sunflower Seeds'. Children practise reducing their images from the Experience stage to simple shapes and patterns that can be carved.

Talk about Ai Weiwei and how he uses his art to stand up for what he believes in. Show children images of Ai Weiwei's 'Sunflower Seeds' at Tate Modern. Ask children to discuss what they can see. The likelihood is that children will talk about the similarities – millions of tiny seeds scattered all over the floor. Share with the class that every single seed is handcrafted and is completely unique. What does this artwork say about us as people? Ai Weiwei made this piece to talk about the power of conformity. As an individual, it is easy to get lost in the masses, but each of us is beautiful and unique. Individuals also have their own thoughts and feelings and we can make a difference if we work together to make our voices heard.

Encourage children to look back at the images they collected in the Experience stage. Which are they happiest with? This is the stage where children need to decide which of their images they will reduce to simple shapes and patterns for their final piece.

As this is an art expedition exploring carving, encourage children to paint sunflower seed shapes in thick paint and 'carve' into the wet paint with cocktail sticks. This will give children a better understanding of the level of detail that will work well on their final piece than just drawing could do. The beauty of this method is that the wet paint can be smoothed over to make changes, although children should be encouraged to leave the designs they like least as evidence that their thinking is progressing.

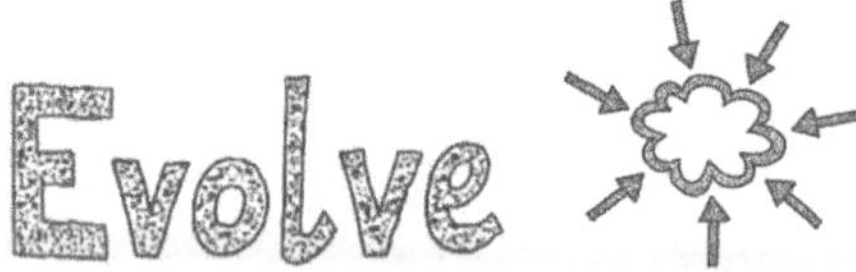

As children rehearse soap carving, their sunflower seed ideas evolve into a unique three-dimensional design to represent their own identity.

N.B. You can do this project with clay if you prefer; just ensure that the design process and the final piece are made in the same medium, so children get the opportunity to rehearse their skills.

Give children a tiny piece of soap (you can buy hundreds of little hotel-sized soaps very inexpensively). This is where the children can practise for their final piece. Using cocktail sticks, butter knives or clay tools, encourage children to practise their carving skills to give them a better idea as to which of their ideas from the Experiment session will transfer well onto their 3D form. The beauty of soap and clay is that the carved surface can easily be scratched or smoothed away for further attempts. It is important that this stage is not rushed so that children gain better control of the medium they are working with.

Once the children have a good understanding of the medium, they can sketch a finished design that represents their chosen ideas to be carved in the next stage.

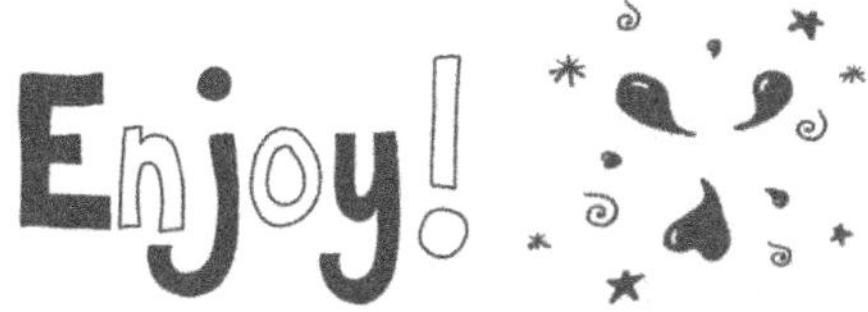

Carve a full-sized piece of soap (or clay!) with intricate designs.

Give children their full-sized soap (or piece of clay). Emphasise that all the soaps are identical but that the class are going to make them unique with the different designs they carve. From a distance the soap carvings will look the same, but up close, each will represent an individual from the class. Adding a thin layer of grey acrylic paint to the surface of the soap will bring out the carvings (white paint will do this if you are working with clay). Photograph the carvings as a class set, spread out over the floor but also individually for sketchbooks.

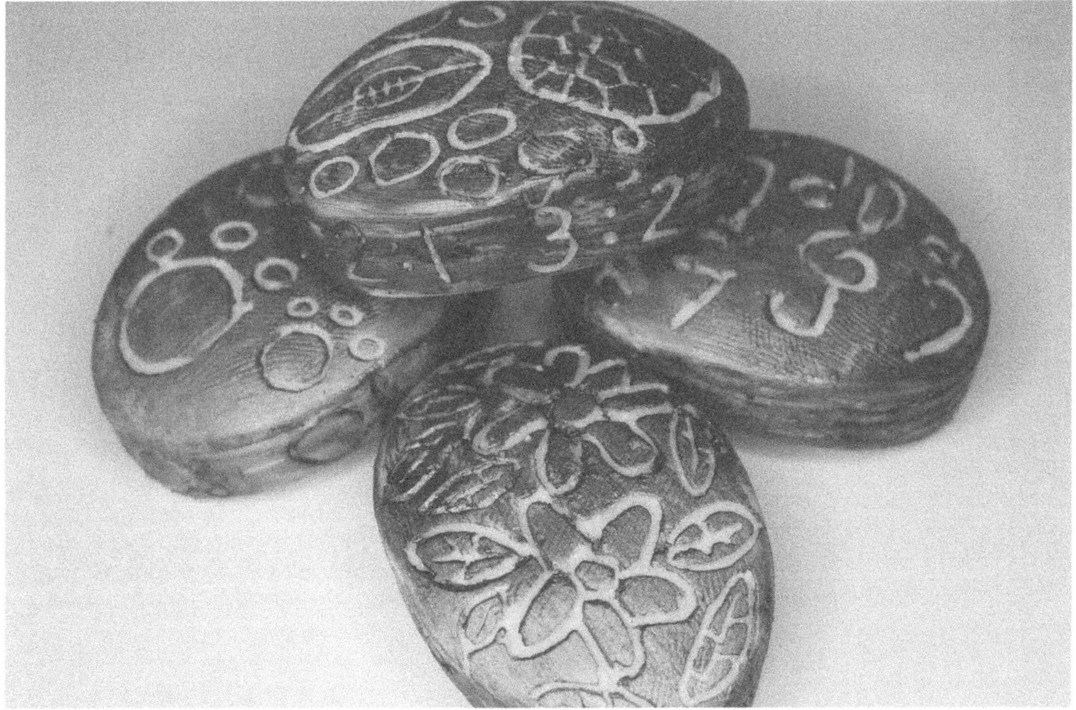

These children have decorated their soaps with imagery that represents a love of animals, sport, music and the outdoors. We painted a layer of grey acrylic over the designs to accentuate the carvings and to make our soaps look more like Ai Weiwei's sunflower seeds.

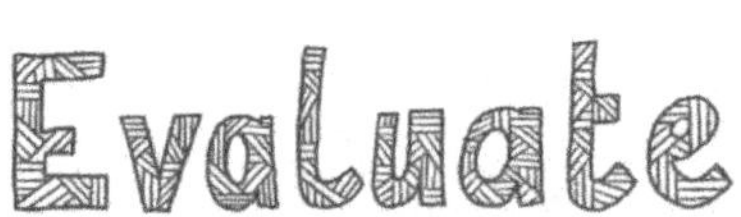

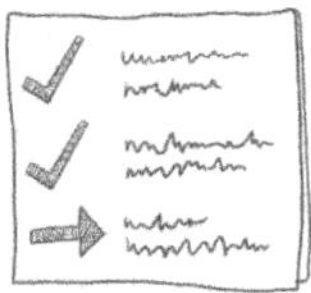

How did it go? Peer and self-assessment

Peer evaluation

Encourage children to pick up the carvings and comment on them individually.

- What is unique about this carving?
- What do you think this carving represents?
- How does seeing the finished piece make you feel?

Self-evaluation

Ask children to annotate around their photo.

- Why did you choose the designs you did?
- How did you find carving soap?
- How have you shown individuality?

Lesson plan Upper Key Stage 2: What do we remember?

Artist biography

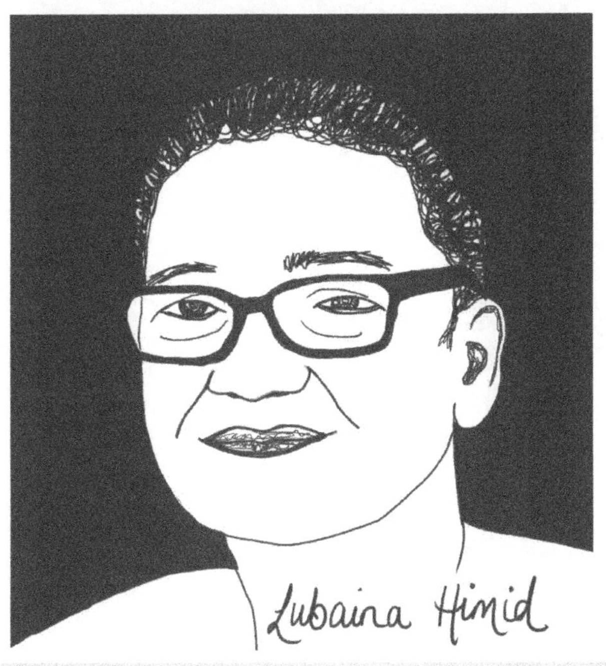

Lubaina Himid

Born:	1954
Died:	–
Birthplace:	Zanzibar Sultanate (modern day Tanzania)
Discipline:	Visual art – painting, installation and drawing

Lubaina Himid is a British artist who has spent her life studying and creating artwork that explores ideas around belonging and self.

At the beginning of her career, Lubaina studied theatre design and many of the skills she learned during these early years are still apparent in her work today. Her large, colourful cut-outs of people are arranged in stage-like settings and this helps tell the story of each individual character. Much of Lubaina's work explores the way that immigrants to the UK were forced to give up their identities and often also their names, and aims to reconnect people to their cultural heritage.

Lubaina was a member of the British Black Arts movement, which aimed to gain recognition for the pioneering work of Black artists in the UK. She remembers being told 'Black people don't make art' and being determined to prove them wrong.

Lubaina has been awarded many accolades for her artwork, including being the first Black woman to win the prestigious Turner Prize. She was also recognised by Queen Elizabeth II, receiving a CBE for 'services to art'.

'Jelly Mould Pavilions' is a sculpture that Lubaina hopes will celebrate the significant contribution of people of African descent to the history and culture of Liverpool.

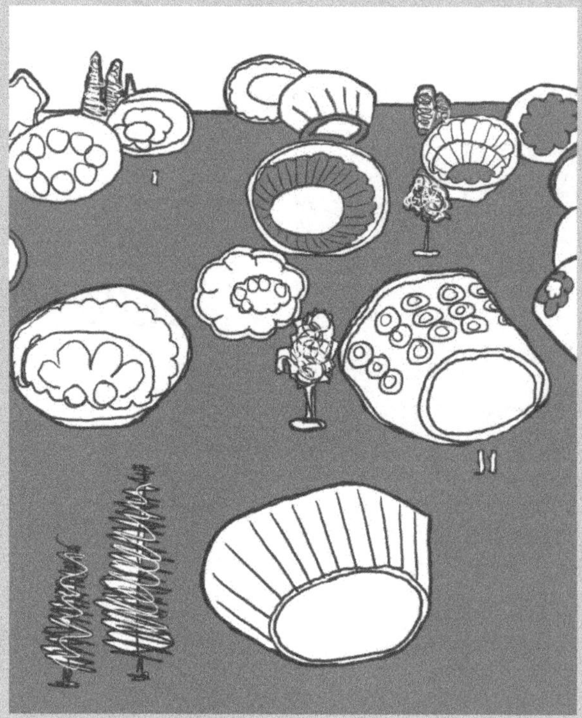

Find out more

Tate Kids:

www.tate.org.uk/kids/explore/who-is/who-lubaina-himid

Jelly Mould Pavilions:

https://blogs.kent.ac.uk/artistry/2022/06/13/lubaina-himids-jelly-mould-pavilions-for-liverpool-by-gillian-brooke-turner/

Images to inspire	**Other artist links**
Jelly Mould Pavilions (2010)	**Jacob Lawrence:** Jacob explores representations of Black American life in his larger-than-life paintings (see Chapter 3).
Naming the Money (2004)	**Grayson Perry:** Grayson explores identity and personal histories through his ceramics.
A Fashionable Marriage (1986)	**Yinka Ilori:** Yinka explores the patterns and colours of different cultures in order to design chairs that specifically consider a person's history or identity.

'You bring your baggage, your opinion, your life and I'll bring mine – and let's try to talk about it.'

Lubaina Himid (Higgins, 2017)

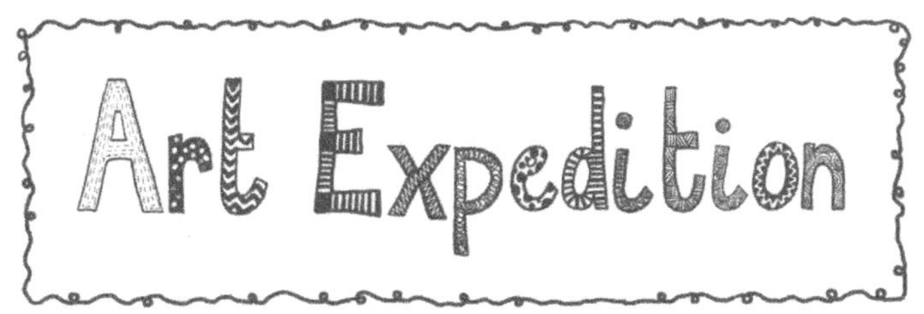

Lubaina Himid • Upper Key Stage 2
What do we remember?

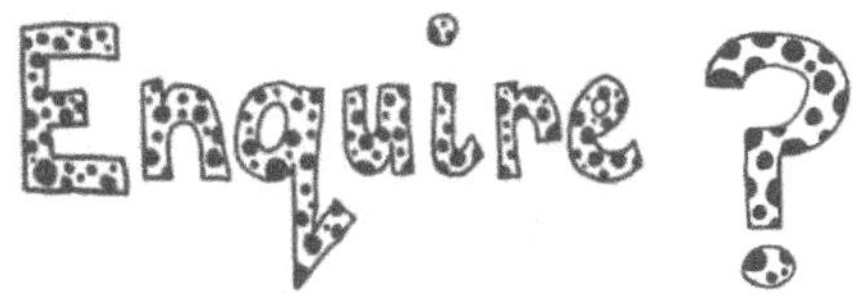

Ask children to list what events and people from history they are aware of. Why do we commemorate some events over others? What makes an event from history more significant than another? It would be interesting to look at the list children generate in terms of the people they have included. Are there an equal number of women? People of colour?

Signpost: Through this project, we will be choosing a special person or event to commemorate through our own sculpture.

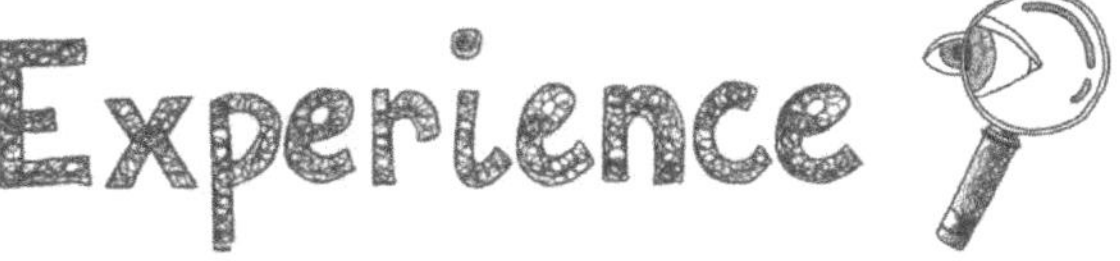

Collect artistic evidence that represents local history. This could be from buildings, war memorials, gravestones, plaques or internet searches to reveal more about the history of the children's locality.

You could take children for a walk to find historical evidence that can be recorded in sketchbooks. This could be lists of names from war memorials, rubbings of signs of interesting road names, sketches of old buildings or anything else that is local to your school that gives a glimpse of the past. It might be more appropriate to do this from the classroom and use the internet. What has happened in the history of the local area?

Children could research famous people with links to their home, or famous events that have happened in local history. A useful source of information for this session would be leaflets from your local tourist information centre that the children can cut out, stick in and sketch from. You could also provide photos of local historical sites or encourage children to bring in their own.

Children should collate this evidence on one sketchbook page as they begin to build a picture of the history of the school's locality.

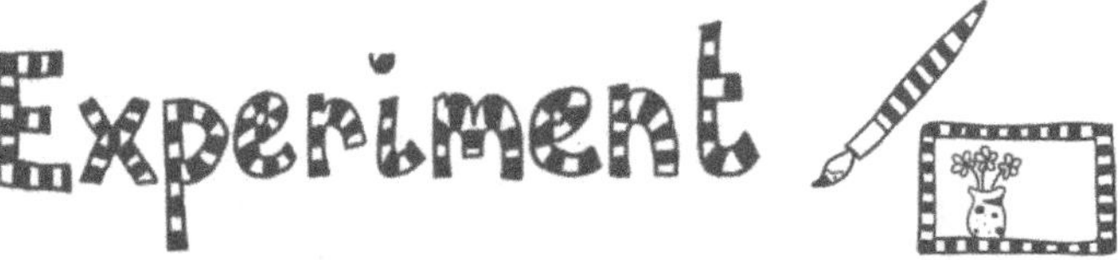

Introduce Lubaina Himid's 'Jelly Mould Pavilions'. Ask children to think about whose contributions have shaped the history of their local area.

Show children Lubaina Himid's 'Jelly Mould Pavilions'. Explain that Lubaina created this work to celebrate the 'hidden histories' of Liverpool and to shine a light on the contributions of Black communities that have been overlooked. It is worth holding an interesting discussion at this point about who decides what we commemorate historically and why some stories are remembered and others aren't.

Who has contributed to the history of the children's local area? This is a wonderful opportunity for children to seek out people from history that have contributed to a town or city but who may have been overlooked. It could be people living or working in the community now. You may need more research time at this point or children may be able to develop an idea from the Experience stage.

Once children have decided on an area that piques their interest, ask them to represent their person or place using paint on a paper cup, to create a prototype of the class's own 'Jelly Mould Pavilions'.

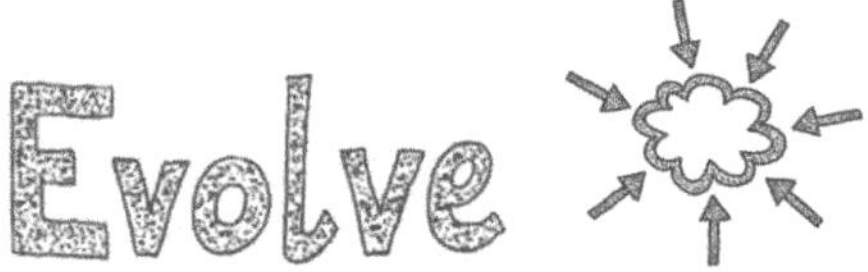

Children use papier-mâché to create their own mould.

Children will need to choose a shape for their mould. Provide different options and encourage children to consider their subject when making their choice. The base for the mould could be anything: bowls, actual jelly moulds, balloons, pencil pots; anything that has an interesting shape. Just cover the mould in clingfilm and then apply papier-mâché to create the shape.

Encourage children to complete four layers of papier-mâché, alternating newspaper and white paper so it is easy to keep track of the layers. Watered down PVA glue makes great paste and can be painted over the surface to ensure a nice, smooth, shiny finish. When it is thoroughly dry (leave it a good week to be sure!) you can peel the clingfilm off and you should have a rigid shape ready to paint.

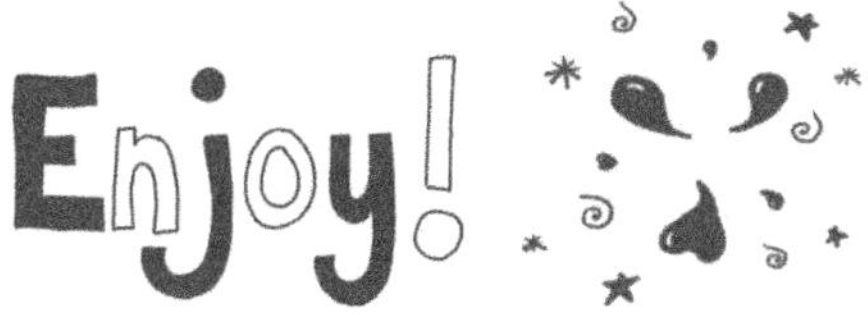

Make and photograph!

Once the children have their own completed mould they can paint the papier-mâché to represent the person or place from their local history that they feel should be remembered. Look back at the sketchbooks and the paper cup designs for inspiration. Use acrylic paint that will ensure coverage of the newspaper and will produce a shiny finish.

Once the moulds have been painted and have been left to dry, push the tables together and cover with backing paper. Display the class's finished Jelly Mould Pavilions by spreading the moulds around the tables. Pop down to Reception and borrow some of the small-world toys to add trees, figures and other details. Take photos for sketchbooks.

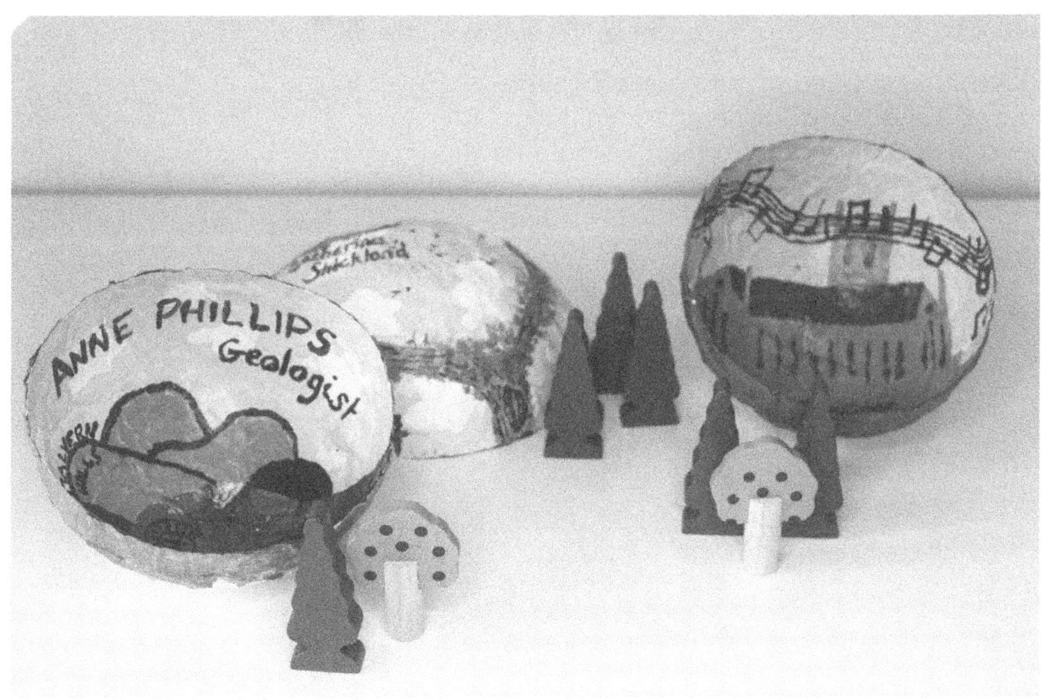

These children have used papier-mâché casts of balloons painted with acrylic paint to create bowls that celebrate some of the hidden histories of Worcester: Anne Phillips, Catherine Strickland and Samuel Coleridge-Taylor.

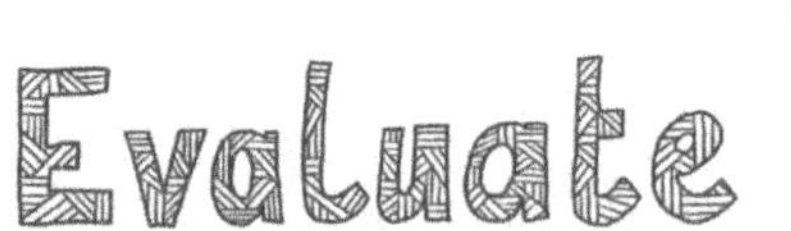

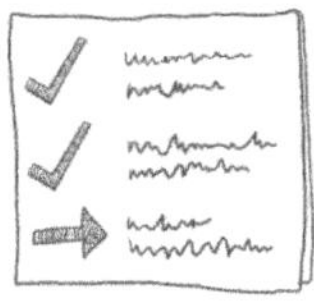

How did it go? Peer and self-assessment

Peer evaluation

Ask children to write comments directly onto the backing paper beneath their Jelly Mould Pavilion.

- What does this 'building' represent?
- Why is it important that this is remembered?
- How could the design be refined to make the meaning clearer?

Self-evaluation

Ask children to annotate around a photo in their sketchbook.

- What should your building / person be called?
- Why did you choose this aspect of local history?
- What else could you add to the Jelly Mould Pavilion to better represent your history?

Chapter 5

Collage

Introduction to collage

Collage is one of the most versatile and satisfying art disciplines to teach in primary schools. The fact that children are manipulating pre-existing images and materials means that they can step away from any art anxiety they may have and experiment creatively in a way that feels less intimidating. Having photos or images to start from is hugely supportive, especially for those who find it hard to separate the enjoyment of artistic process from the quest for realism.

There is also something special about the flexibility and semi-permanence of collage. Throughout the entire process, children are able to add, remove, manipulate and change elements of their composition, without having to commit until the very last moment. And even then, this is assuming that you want your collages to be stuck down. Mobile collage, where the children enjoy moving loose materials around on the desk or the floor, enjoying the process of trial and error but with no finished outcome, is just as valuable and encourages the same learning as a finished, stuck-down collage in a sketchbook.

How can you use collage effectively at school?

Going beyond traditional paper-based materials, there are many other ways that collage can be effectively employed in school.

Natural collage

Children can use a whole range of different natural materials to create incredible collages, whether it be leaves, flowers, bark, grasses or any other objects that can be found outdoors. The beauty of collages like these, sourced from the natural environment, is that they will look different depending on the time of year. So it's well worth repeating this activity in different seasons to further engage your children artistically with their surroundings.

Fabric collage

Children can make the most amazing, brightly coloured and textured collages using scraps of material or old clothes. These can be fixed with glue; just make sure that your class has decent scissors!

Or, to create a more textiles-focused unit of work, you could ask children to pin their designs and then one at a time, free-machine embroider over the top of their work to fix it in place. If you are lucky enough to have access to a sewing machine, free machine embroidery works really well with even small children. Just guide the fabric in a haphazard fashion across the design and the stitches will not only fix the layers of fabric, but they will also add interesting patterns and marks to the finished work.

3D collage

3D collage (assemblage) can be made from pretty much anything. Children could create an assemblage design from the contents of their pencil cases or from items in the classroom. They could use papercrafts to give a 2D collage a third dimension by adding folded springs, holes, flaps, zig zags or pop-ups. You could even make an assemblage out of PE equipment! These kinds of collages made from found materials are an excellent way to get children's creative juices flowing as a quick starter activity, as well as a more formal project.

Text collage

You can use letters and words from newspapers and magazines to create some really interesting responses to a theme. Sometimes being restricted by the words that can be found from a particular source forces children to think outside the box in their word choice. Using a 'ransom note' style (words or letters cut out and reassembled from an existing text e.g. a newspaper) or adding printed words to existing pictures can be a great way to tell a story or respond to an issue.

Mosaics

Making paper mosaics from small pieces of coloured card is a lovely activity, but nothing beats the real thing if you have the resources. You would be surprised at how many parents have old tiles knocking around in their garages and local tile companies (for a nod in the newsletter) can be incredibly generous with their end-of-line stock. Then all you need is tile adhesive, grout and of course a hammer! If you pop the tiles in a sturdy plastic bag to protect children from the sharp edges, under supervision, children will *love* being able to hammer the tiles to break them into pieces.

Decoupage

Pretty much anything can be given an artistic overhaul with a bit of decoupage! Choose any object (perfect opportunity to explore surrealism) and cover with layers of small pieces of coloured paper. You can buy beautiful, purpose-made decoupage paper but it is often prohibitively expensive. The same effects can be created with tissue or, my preference, old used wrapping paper. Wrapping paper tends to hold its shape better than tissue once covered in PVA glue and comes in beautiful patterns and designs, and can often be sourced for free if parents are given a heads up!

Transfers

Adding transfers to collage is an exciting way to create layers that are often translucent, allowing the design below to shine through. Two ways to do this really effectively are sticky tape and acetone transfers.

Cover a picture printed from your school photocopier with sticky tape and soak in water for 10 minutes. Then, the paper can be rubbed from the back using a cloth, leaving a translucent image on the sticky tape. This can then be placed over the top of an existing collage to add an extra layer.

Similarly, paint the back of the image with nail varnish remover (one with acetone), and place it face down on the collage. When you rub the back of the damp picture with a hard object like a pencil, the image will transfer onto the surface below. You can experiment with different marks and scribbles to reveal parts of the picture you want to transfer, or scribble over the entire image to create an impression of the whole thing.

You will be surprised at the quality of the transfer that is produced in both these examples!

Digital collage

There are many amazing ways that digital collage can be used in the classroom. This has never been more accessible than it is now, with many free apps that allow you to easily combine pictures and graphics.

Apps like Canva are free for educators and it is simple to remove the backgrounds from images and to use the stock art to create really amazing digital collage. Canva also allows you to set up a virtual classroom so that children can 'hand in' their work to be stored as evidence or printed for sketchbooks.

Lesson plans

The three artists explored in the following lesson plans use a variety of different collage techniques. You could start your collage unit exploring some of the techniques listed above and allow children to choose which style produces the best outcome for each particular project. This would encourage children to make their own choices about tools and techniques and give them the opportunity to produce something truly individual.

Lesson plan Key Stage 1: How are we different? How are we the same?

Artist biography

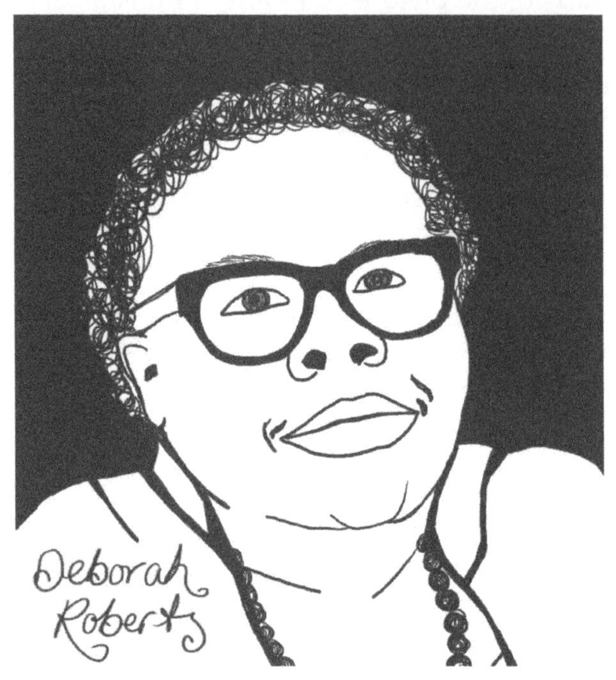

Deborah Roberts

Born:	1962
Died:	–
Birthplace:	Austin, USA
Discipline:	Visual art – collage

Deborah Roberts is an American collage artist who uses art to explore ideas of beauty and self-image. Deborah noticed that both the media and traditional art portrayed beauty in particular ways, making it both unrealistic and unobtainable for many young women.

As a little girl growing up in America, Deborah was aware that she did not see herself, or other Black Americans, represented in art or media. She noticed that fashion magazines always focused on White, Western women meaning that traditional beauty ideals were not relevant to her or to many people in her community.

Deborah uses her art to portray a more diverse idea of what 'beautiful' can be by exploring the different roles and identities of girls in a more realistic way. She creates beautiful images of children, often on white backgrounds, that put the figure as the sole focal point of her work. Deborah often incorporates imagery of fists, boxing gloves and flexed biceps that show the strength yet innocence of her subjects.

Deborah's collage work takes facial features from different people and combines them to create new images that incorporate a wider view of identity, beauty and self-image. She sources images from the internet to cut up and reassemble to create her iconic collages.

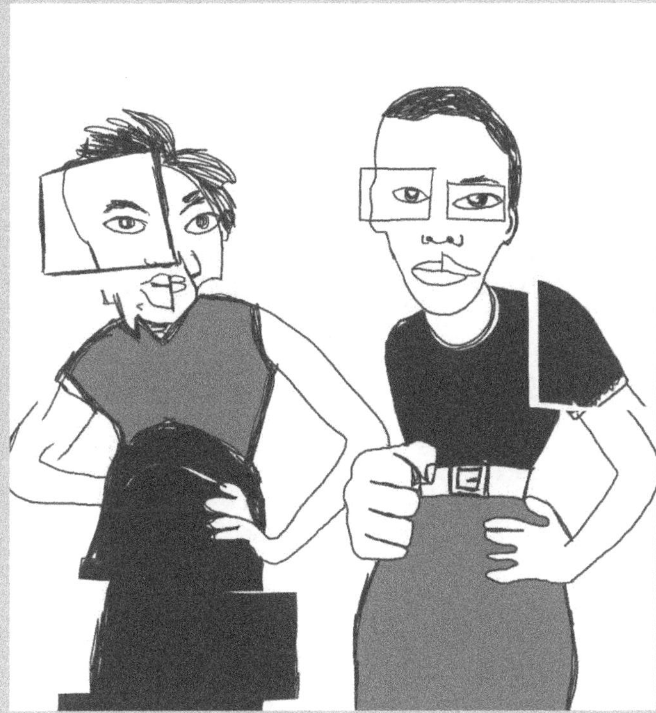

Find out more

Gallery website: www.stephenfriedman.com/artists/51-deborah-roberts/

Website: www.deborahrobertsart.com/

Images to inspire

Delilah (2021)

Laying my Burdens Down (2021)

True Believer (2020)

The Duty of Disobedience (2020)

Hip bone (2019)

This Ain't no Fairytale (2018)

Other artist links

Hannah Hoch: Hannah uses photographs from newspapers which she cuts up and reassembles to create strange new worlds and interesting portraits of composite images.

Tschabalala Self: Tschabalala uses a mixture of different materials and paint to assemble brightly coloured figures from collage.

Peter Blake: Peter uses collage to portray ideas around identity. His most famous work is the album cover for The Beatle's 'Sgt Pepper's Lonely Hearts Club Band'.

'I want everyone to be successful in the art world.'

Deborah Roberts (Ryzin, 2022)

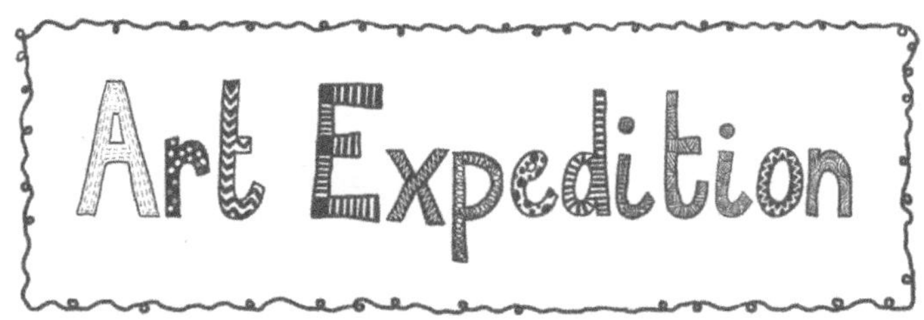

Deborah Roberts • Key Stage 1 • How are we different? How are we the same?

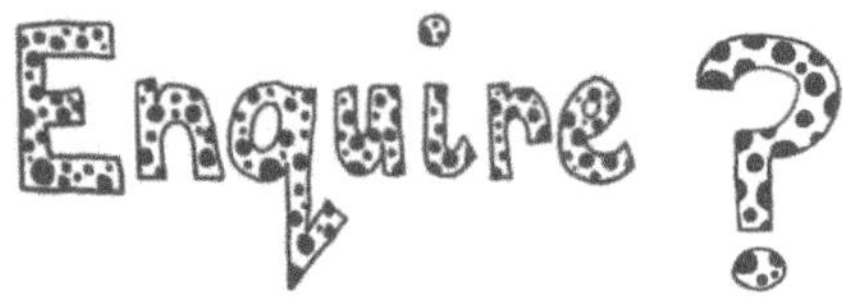

Ask the children to look around the class and explore this question. Encourage them to think beyond the way we look.

Signpost: Through this project, we will be creating photo collages using the class as models!

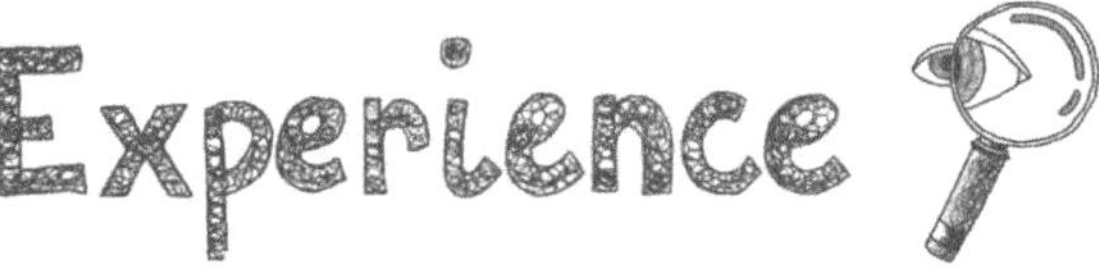

On two separate sketchbook pages, ask children to artistically record their similarities and differences.

Give children access to a range of drawing materials that they can choose from. Encourage the children to move around the class and choose different friends to work with. Ask children to chat with their partner until they find a way that they are both the same. Once they have chosen a similarity, get them to record it in their sketchbook using a self-selected drawing tool. It could be something to do with their physical appearance, e.g. eye colour, hair length, shoe size, glasses. Or it could be something that cannot be seen, like a shared hobby, a pet at home or a favourite colour. Once they have drawn something on their page, encourage the children to move on and find a new partner. Continue until the sketchbook is full, then do the same activity but for differences.

For older children, you might want to narrow the focus of this session to include more observational drawing. You could ask children to focus just on eyes and move around the class sketching each other's eyes and thinking about the way that even one feature can have a multitude of similarities and differences.

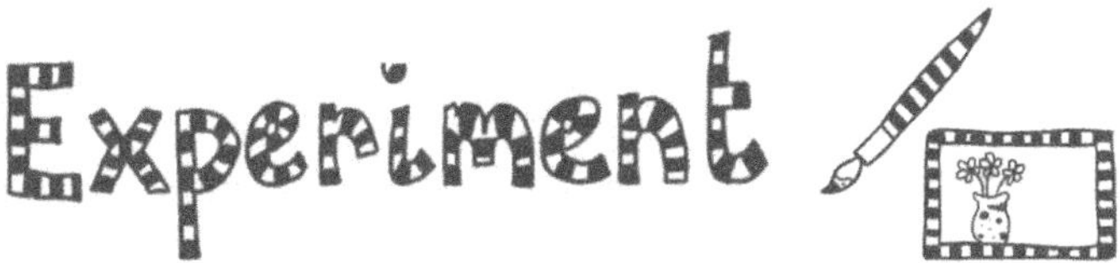

Look at the work of Deborah Roberts and experiment with collage.

Introduce children to the work of Deborah Roberts. What do they notice about the figures in her artwork? In what ways are they the same? How are they different?

See if children can unpick how Deborah has created her images. It is important for them to notice that Deborah does not just use photographs in her work; some of the components are joined together with painted sections or pieces cut out of coloured paper.

Give children access to lots of different newspapers, magazines, and different kinds and colours of paper. See what they can create in their sketchbooks. Maybe they will choose to create people or maybe they will experiment with different images. At this stage what they create is unimportant; all we want is for children to experiment with cutting, sticking and reassembling images. Encourage children to respond creatively to the task and they are likely to create all kinds of exciting images!

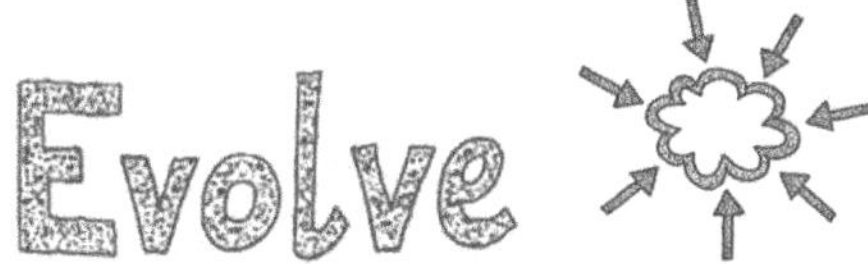

Start to design a collage using different features from children in the class.

Ask children to start to design their own unique portrait of a person using features from the class. Included in their design should be annotations to explain why they are choosing to use specific parts, e.g. Jill's eye, Mo's hair, Hussain's nose.

The design should be drawn at this stage so there is another opportunity for some observational drawing. The children can move around the room to look carefully at the owner of the feature they are using. It would be useful to create several different designs so that children can make choices about which they think will be most effective.

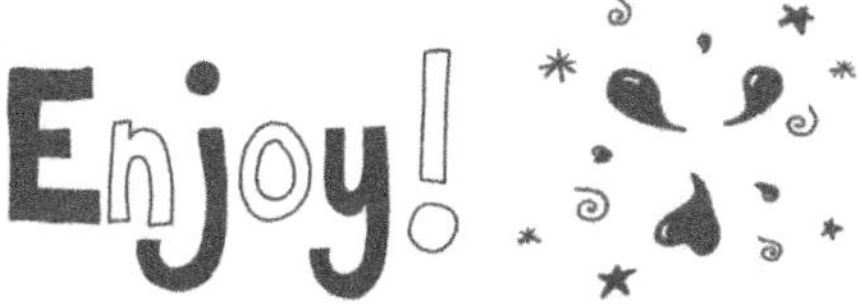

Create a final piece – a collage made up of class body parts!

Take a photo of each member of the class (or even better, get the children to do it!). Encourage children to cut out and reassemble the photos to make a composite image of a person from the pieces they planned in the last session. We want children to embrace the fact that the pieces might be different sizes, shapes or from different perspectives and encourage the use of coloured paper to add details or to help fit pieces together.

This activity will work best if the photos are printed onto A3 and provided in a mixture of colour and black and white.

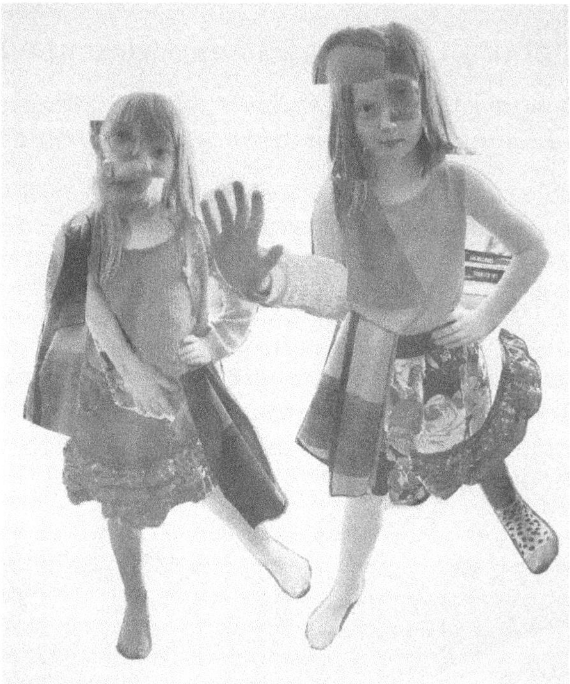

This final piece is a composite image of three different children created from printed photos cut up and rearranged.

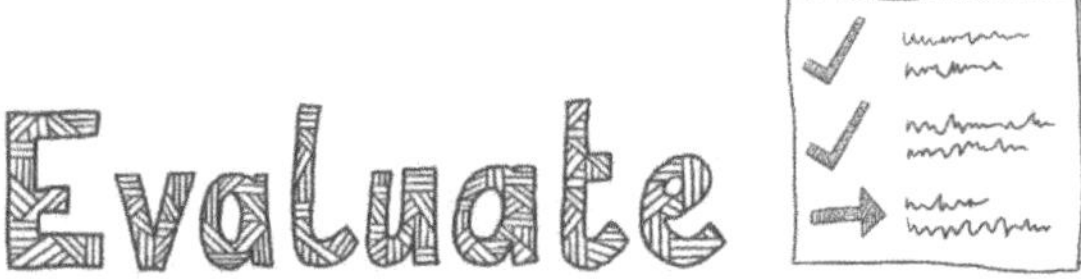

How did it go? Class and self-assessment

Class evaluation: Share the images as a class and use these questions as a starter for class discussion.

- How are our portraits the same?
- How are our portraits different?
- Who can you see in these portraits?

Self-evaluation: Ask children to think about the questions below. They could discuss with a partner, an adult or record their thoughts in their sketchbook.

- Which part of your collage worked best?
- Which part of your collage would you change and how?
- How are you the same as this portrait? How are you different?

Lesson plan Lower Key Stage 2: Can shadows be art?

Artist biography

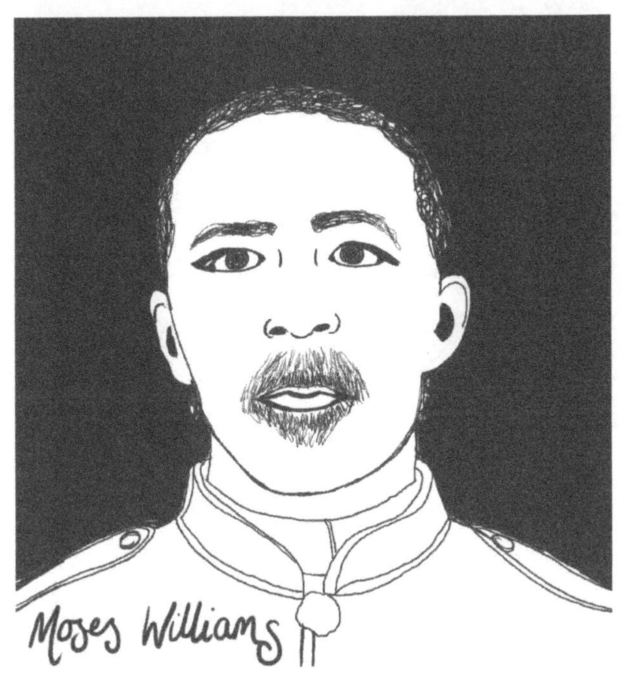

Moses Williams

Born:	1777
Died:	1825
Birthplace:	Philadelphia, USA
Discipline:	Silhouette making

Moses Williams was born in America in 1777 into slavery, when it was still legal. His parents, Lucy and Scarborough Peale, were enslaved people owned by the famous artist Charles Willson Peale. Moses' parents were freed in 1786, but the law at the time meant that Moses was forced to stay working for the Peales until his 27th birthday. Once Lucy and Scarborough were freed, they changed their last name to Williams and passed this name on to their son.

As Charles Peale was an artist, Moses grew up surrounded by art. Charles had many children, many of whom enjoyed art from an early age, so the house where Moses worked was filled with artistic inspiration. Moses was never taught to paint, as this would have been considered 'inappropriate' for an enslaved person, but he was taught other skills to support him with his work at Charles Peale's museum.

One of the skills that Moses learned was to use a physionotrace to create silhouettes of people's portraits. Silhouettes (or profiles as they were then called) were a very fashionable and inexpensive way of having your portrait recreated on paper and could be mounted or framed. Moses was paid 6–8 cents for each profile, so when he was released from enslavement, he was able to marry and buy his own house.

It was not until 100 years later that collage and paper cutting became recognised as a serious art form. But now, Moses' silhouettes have been displayed alongside the work of great artists in institutions such as the Philadelphia Museum of Art and the Smithsonian.

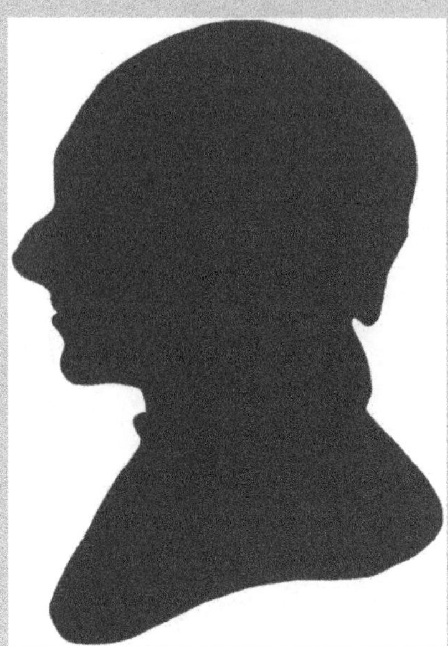

Find out more

Artsy:

www.artsy.net/article/artsy-editorial-slave-american-painter-moses-williams-forged-artistic-career

Article:

www.silhouettesbyhand.com/news/2015/1/19/black-silhouette-artist-and-entrepreneur-in-early-america

Teacher guide:

https://cdn.sanity.io/files/f23a1pgq/pma_production/643148501ad269ee079be566dfd29d878f7379c3.pdf

Images to inspire

There is a good range of images to show children here:

https://philamuseum.org/search/collections?q=Moses%20Williams

Kara Walker

www.pinterest.co.uk/pin/391602130069357983/

Kumi Yamashita

https://kumiyamashita.com/light-shadow

Tim Noble and Sue Webster

www.artworksforchange.org/portfolio/tim-noble-and-sue-webster/

William Kentridge

www.artbasel.com/catalog/artwork/32666/William-Kentridge-Small-Silhouette-Sewing-Machine

Other artist links

Kara Walker: Kara uses silhouettes to tell stories from Black history and also to shine a light on the racial injustice. Be aware that some of these images portray scenes that would be inappropriate for young children.

Kumi Yamashita: Kumi uses physical objects to create amazing shadows from very small forms.

Tim Noble and Sue Webster: This pair of artists use rubbish to create interesting silhouettes.

William Kentridge: William works with paper cut-out silhouettes in a similar style to Moses Williams.

'As he cut into the paper, Williams wrote his own story.'

Gwendolyn DuBois Shaw (DuBois Shaw, 2005)

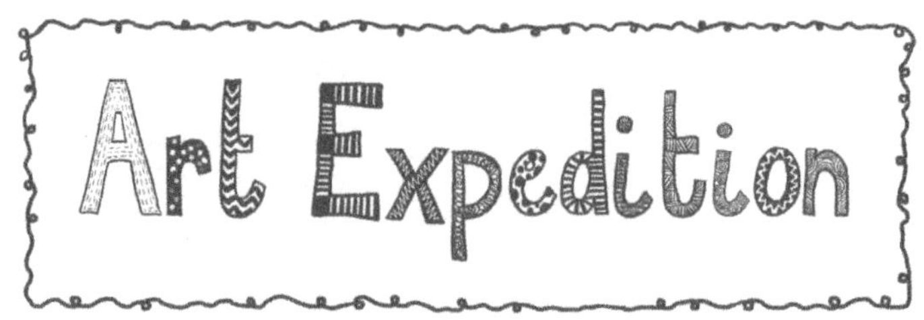

Moses Williams • Lower Key Stage 2
Can shadows be art?

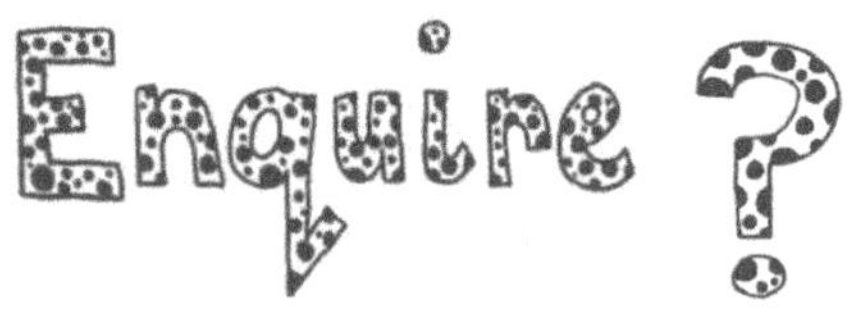

Ask children if they can define what a shadow is and how shadows change. This art expedition works well in Year 3 when children might be studying the science unit of light.

Signpost: Through this project, we will be creating our own silhouettes out of paper.

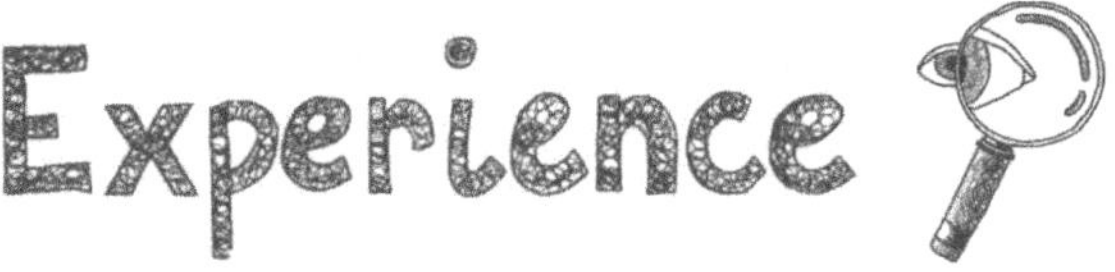

Give children a chance to experience shadows and play with the way that they are made.

Give children torches and do your best to darken the room. Allow time for experimentation and play as children find out what shadows can do. Pose questions that might further children's understanding of shadow:

- How do you make a shadow?
- How do you make the shadow bigger? Smaller?
- Can you make the shadow move?
- How can you improve the details you can see in a shadow?
- Can you make a coloured shadow?
- Can you combine shadows to make new shapes?
- Can you predict what a shadow will look like?

Once the children have a good understanding of how to manipulate shadows, get the sketchbooks out! Keeping the lights down low, see if children can place objects onto their pages and then sketch the shadows they create. Make sure they are tracing exactly what is there rather than trying to make the shadow look like the original object. Do this on just one page so that the different shadows overlap and merge together. Don't worry if the shadows spill off the page, just trace what is there! Give children different colours or drawing materials with which to do this, so that once the lights go back on, they will have a sketchbook page full of interesting lines, shapes and patterns.

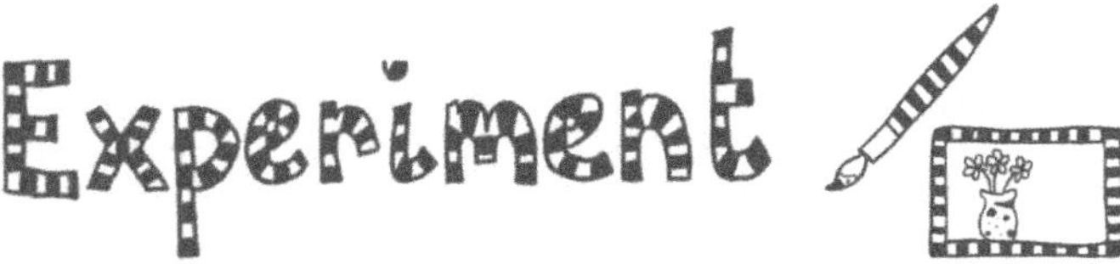

Introduce children to Moses Williams and practise paper cutting.

Show children the work of Moses Williams, Kara Walker, Tim Noble and Sue Webster, Kumi Yamashita and William Kentridge. What do the children think? Can they unpick how the later examples have been made? Encourage them to talk about the differences between a silhouette and a shadow.

Discuss the difference between 'solid cut' (cutting a solid shape out of paper) and 'hollow cut' (removing the shape to leave an outline) so that children are able to experiment with both types of silhouette cut.

Give children different types, textures and colours of paper and let them have a go at creating their own silhouettes by 'drawing with scissors'. Encourage children to stick their attempts into their sketchbooks, keeping both the solid and hollow cut images. They may want to do each other's profiles, or they may prefer to do objects around the classroom. Either way, try to encourage them to cut straight into the paper without drawing first and to work from direct observation if possible.

As this is the Experiment stage, ensure that children choose simple manageable objects initially and attempt to capture the essence of the subject rather than a realistic outcome. You could also use carbon paper to allow children to transfer shapes from photos that they have found in magazines or taken for themselves.

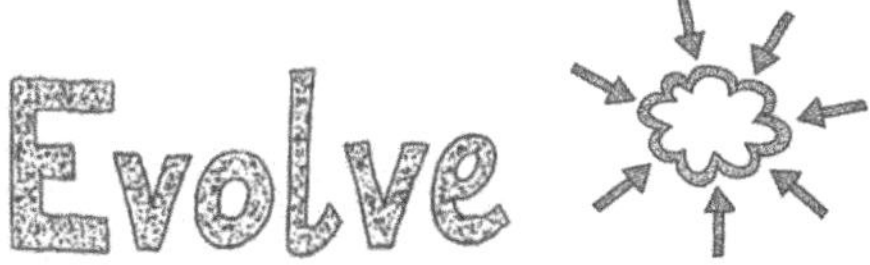

Design a collage using silhouettes and paper cutting.

You could give children free rein to choose a subject that they are interested in, or you could link this to a topic or class theme. The idea is to create a collage bursting with interesting shapes, cut from different colours and textures of paper. Try to encourage children to use a mixture of solid and hollow cut images that overlap and spill from the page to add interest and variety.

Here are some examples of potential themes.

- Cut out the child's own profile and collage with silhouettes of things that they believe form part of their identity.
- Same as above but for a famous person from history.
- Cut out a silhouette of a country and collage with images of landmarks or other features of that place.
- Cut a silhouette of a character from a story and surround it with other elements that relate to their character journey.
- Cut out shapes of different animals / birds or flowers from the local area or from a contrasting habitat.

Children design their final outcome, labelling their picture with the materials they plan to use. Suggested materials for cutting might be:

- sandpaper
- newspaper
- magazines
- tissues
- foil
- envelopes
- newsletters
- anything from the recycle bin!

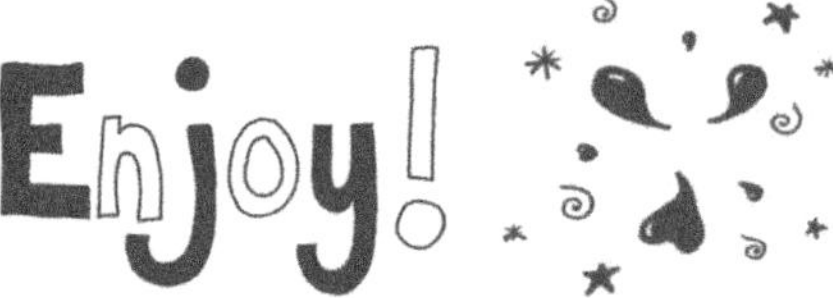

Create a final piece – collage!

Give children time to complete their collages. The beauty of paper cutting is that the composition can be moved and rearranged before it is glued, which allows the option for elements to be reworked if necessary.

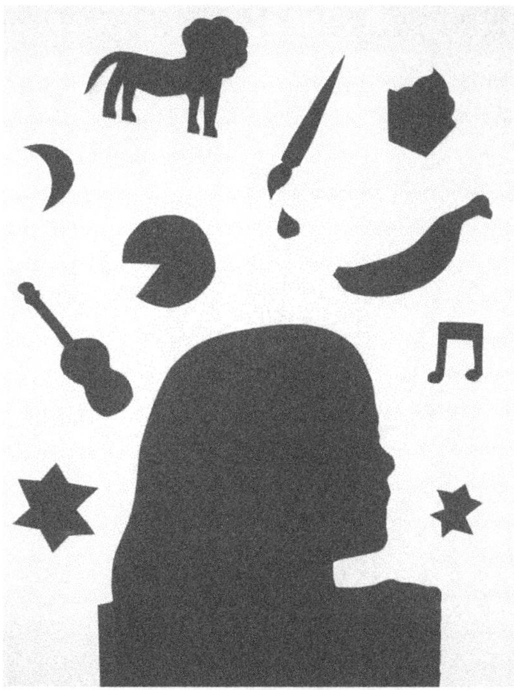

We used carbon paper to transfer a realistic silhouette from a photo. The other shapes represent things that this child feels are part of their identity and are cut freehand out of black paper. The lovely thing about collage is that you can make multiple attempts at cutting out a shape and then choose the most effective for your final piece!

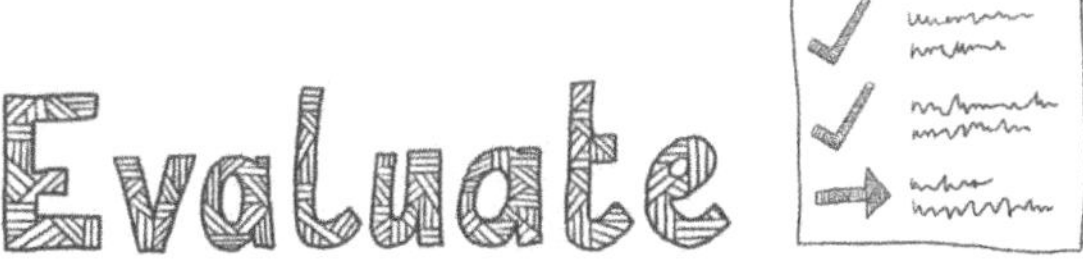

How did it go? Peer and self-assessment

Peer evaluation

Ask children to move around the room looking at the final pieces. Use these questions to stimulate interesting discussion.

- What do you see when you look at the collage?
- What is your favourite shape and why?
- Which part looks most challenging?

Self-evaluation

Children could record their ideas in their sketchbooks or use these questions to share their ideas verbally.

- Why did you choose the shapes you did?
- How did you decide which paper to use?
- Is there anything else you would have liked to add?

Lesson plan Upper Key Stage 2: How does food connect us?

Artist biography

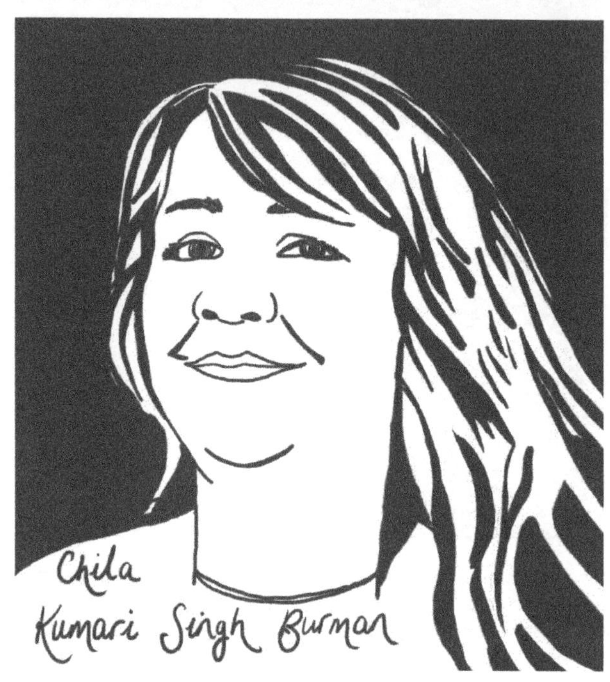

Chila Kumari Singh Burman

Born:	1957
Died:	–
Birthplace:	Liverpool, UK
Discipline:	Collage, etching, sculpture, printmaking

Chila Kumari Singh Burman is a Punjabi Liverpudlian who uses her pop art style to combine influences from her Indian heritage with modern art.

When Chila's father came to England in the 1950s, he was unable to find work as a tailor which had been his profession in India. So he bought an ice cream van, called it 'Burman's' and put a big tiger on the top. These motifs from Chila's childhood are prominent features of her work. Regular family trips to see the Blackpool illuminations have also influenced her art, particularly her neon installations, one of which was displayed on the external wall of the Tate Britain.

As a child, Chila discovered a love of art at school and her teachers encouraged her to continue her studies at university. Chila became a prominent figure in the British Black Arts movement, which sought to raise the profile of the work of Black artists to gain recognition from art institutions. Much of Chila's work explores issues that she feels strongly about, such as women's rights, politics and the abolishment of nuclear weapons.

She does not allow her art to be classified as one thing. She is a sculptor, painter, collage and mixed media artist, exploring and experimenting with different materials. Her work is always heavily embellished with sequins, beads, fluorescent paint, glitter and found treasures that are repurposed to create her signature, flamboyant style.

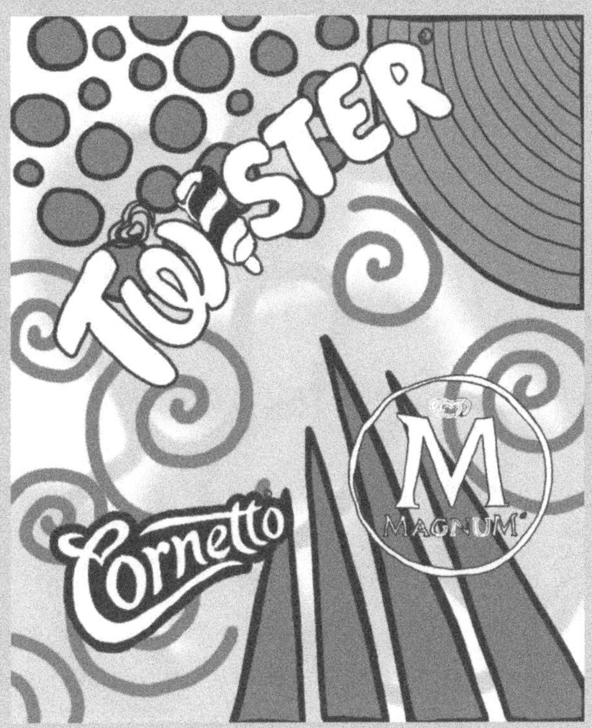

Find out more

Tate Kids:

www.tate.org.uk/kids/explore/who-is/who-chila-kumari-singh-burman

Website:

www.chila-kumari-burman.co.uk/

Images to inspire

Love Hearts (2006)

Mint (2006)

Self Portrait in Sugar (1979)

Other artist links:

Claes Oldenburg: Claes also uses food as a theme to his work. His oversized sculptures of ice creams have many similarities to the work of Chila Kumari Singh Burman.

Andy Warhol: Andy's print making often used labels of food or drink as inspiration.

Richard Hamilton: Richard creates collages out of cuttings from newspaper and pieces of packaging.

'I just want to create and do things ... that's why I love being an artist!'

Chila Kumari Singh Burman (Tate Kids, n.d.)

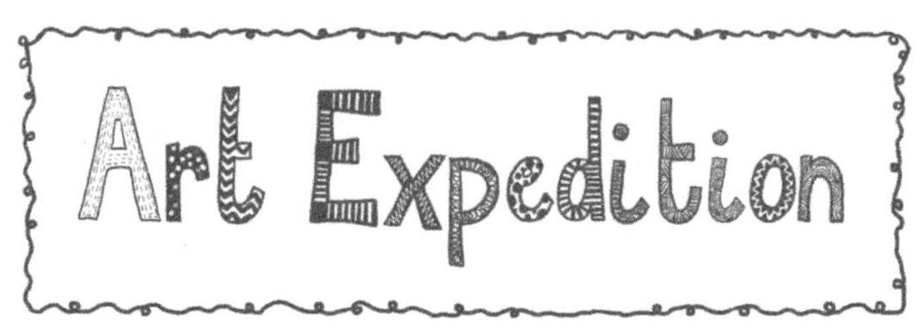

Chila Kumari Singh Burman
Upper Key Stage 2 • How does food connect us?

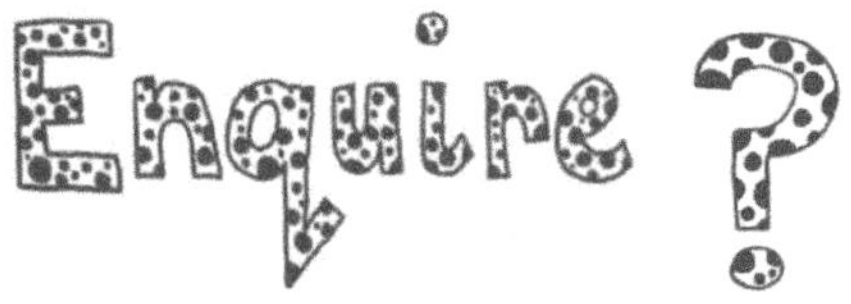

Ask children to think about the question of food as a connection to others. Who do they eat with? What memories do they have of meals or treats with family and friends? Are there people in their lives they associate with a particular type of food?

Signpost: Through this project, we will be creating a colourful, exciting collage celebrating foods that hold a special significance to us.

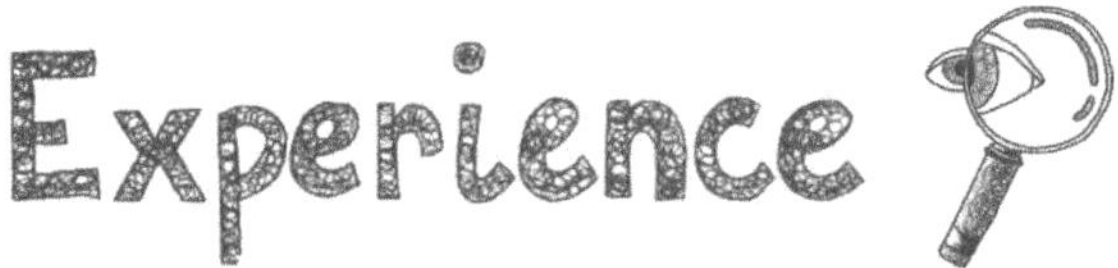

Create a sketchbook page of different foods that have a personal significance.

Ask children to share memories that can be evoked by a specific food. It might be a certain type of cake they always have at Granny's house, the snack they have after swimming, a favourite food from a party they have attended or the consistent item that they always like to have in their lunchbox.

Ask children to draw their ideas in their sketchbooks, with annotations and illustrations that explain the significance of each food.

Giving children the opportunity to draw from direct observation is best here, but you might decide to give access to secondary sources such as photos or the internet to diversify the options the children have. Maybe children could bring in packaging in the days leading up to this session, which they could draw from or use as collage. Or they could draw directly from items in their lunchboxes! Anything that gets the children sketching and mark making. Encourage the children to look at each item from different perspectives or to draw a magnified detail to further enhance their understanding of the subject.

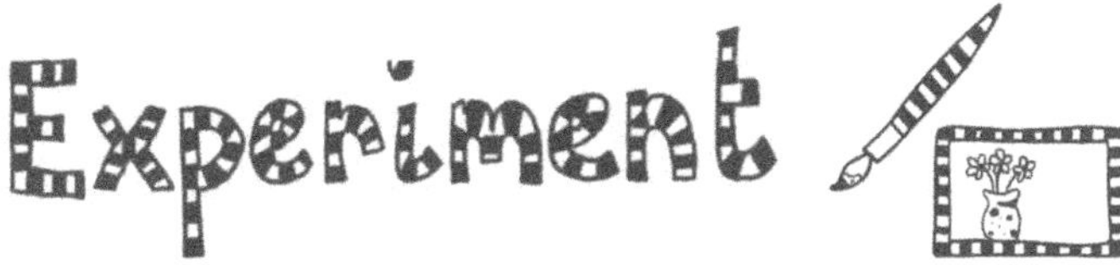

Experiment with mixed media to create different collage papers that can be used for a final piece.

Look at Chila Kumari Singh Burman's work. Give children time to enjoy the artwork and see if they can spot any recurring themes, e.g. tigers and ice creams, and ask them to make observations around the colour palette used in Chila's work. Explain that the colours and symbolism used are a reference to Chila's family, in particular to her dad who used to own an ice cream van with a giant tiger on the top.

Focus in especially on Chila's 'Self Portrait in Sugar' exhibition and individual ice cream themed work such as 'Mint', and encourage children to look closely at the background to start to gain some inspiration for patterns, colours and designs.

Give children a selection of coloured papers to choose from, as well as access to a wide range of art supplies. Encourage the class to create different patterns on the paper that will be used to collage an exciting background for their final piece. They could use ideas from the backgrounds of Chila's own work, or create their own. Encourage printing, painting, scribbling, frottage (rubbings)... whatever they like. The more different papers the children create, the more options they will have for their finished piece. They could even collect wrappers to be used within their collages.

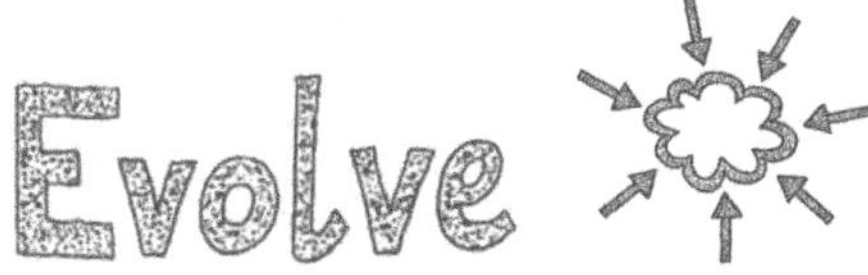

Choose the motifs and create them on individual pieces of paper.

The beauty of collage is that decisions can be made and reversed in action, so a formal design process is not as important. In the Enjoy section, pupils will be able to choose what they add and remove as an iterative process; all they need is to have enough materials to give them artistic options.

In this session, we want children to hone in on the specific food they want to explore, and to create components that represent why that particular food has been chosen. It might be that the food is a birthday cake and the other chosen images might be a party hat, some streamers and pictures of the people who were present at the celebration.

Children should create these images in any medium they like, on separate pieces of paper. These can then be cut out and added to the collage in the final stage.

It is always worth over creating for collage, so encourage children to create multiple images that can be selected from in the final stage.

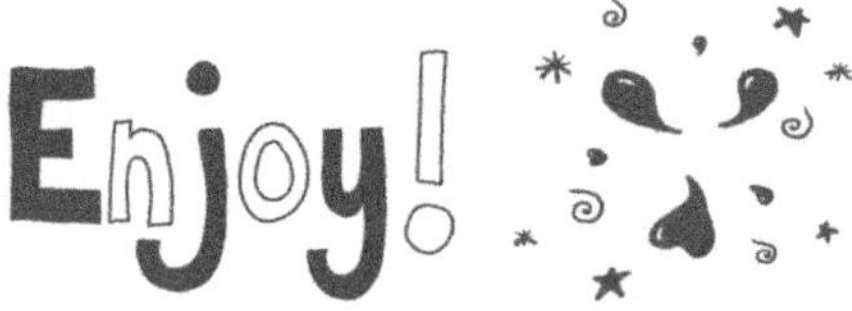

Create a final piece – a colourful montage that celebrates a food and how it connects us!

Children collect their collage pieces: the imagery that represents the food they have chosen and the collage papers created during the Experiment stage.

Do not use glue to start with. Remember, collage is an iterative process, so the children need to experiment with different combinations of their materials to find a composition that works best.

Once the colourful background layers and foreground images have been placed, children can glue them down and add embellishments like Chila Kumari Singh Burman. Put out options of sequins, glitter, metallic paint, beads, and let the children decorate and enhance their images. More is more in Chila's world, so encourage children to go for it!

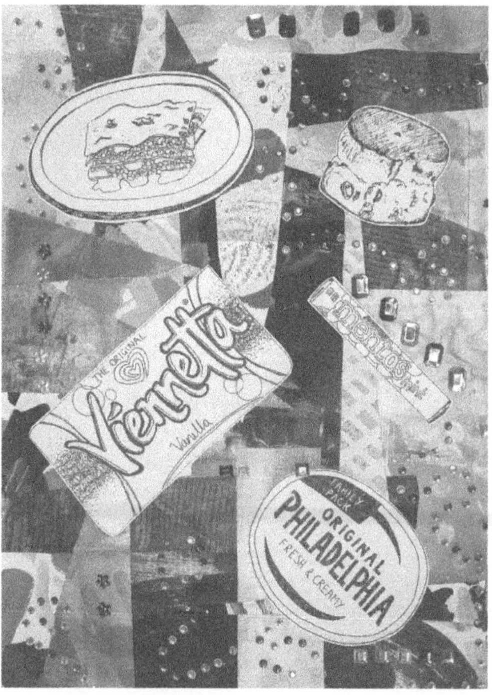

This piece, entitled 'Nanny's House', is a celebration of the foods this child enjoys on a visit to their grandparents' house. The colourful printed background is embellished with a range of sticky gems and glitter for the full Chila effect!

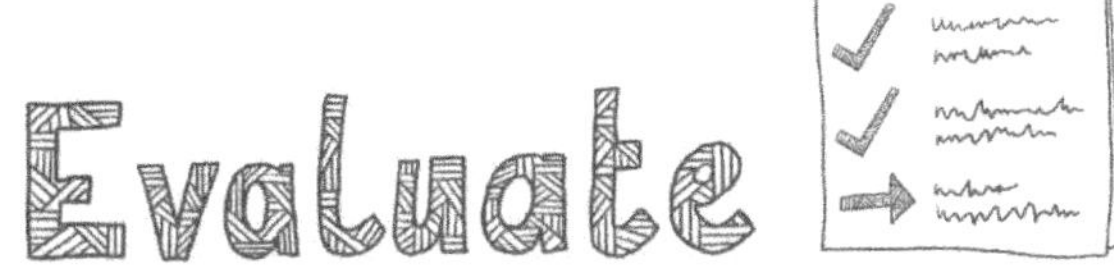

How did it go? Peer and self-assessment

Children in Upper Key Stage 2 should be given the opportunity to respond to these questions in their own way through their annotations. Peer assessment can be verbal or on a sticky note, so that children are not writing in each other's sketchbooks.

Self-evaluation

- Why did you choose this imagery?
- What could you have added to improve the piece further?
- Which collage element is the most effective?

Peer evaluation

- What can you learn about how food connects us from the imagery used?
- What could make the connection clearer?
- What ideas from this could you use to develop your own work?

Chapter 6

Photography

Introduction to photography

Photography has never been as accessible in the classroom as it is now. With tablets firmly embedded in most schools as a learning tool, children not only have easy access to cameras, but there are also incredible options for photo editing at the touch of a button.

Children also enter primary schools from a more advanced starting point. Even Reception children will generally be confident taking a photo on a device and there are very few primary children who have never taken a selfie or two!

But despite some experience of the technology, teaching photography is still an exciting and challenging thing to do in primary art. Teaching children the power and meaning behind some of the world's most famous photos is something that will never get old. Photography is also not an 'easy option' compared to drawing and painting. There are some topics that only a photo can do justice; the impact of having something so real presented to the viewer can be what connects us and makes us care about the subject.

The introduction to any unit of work based on photography would be greatly enhanced by a lesson discussing the impact that photography has had on the world. Children could be encouraged to consider everything we wouldn't know about, if not for photos. How many children have actually seen a tiger in real life? Or visited the Eiffel Tower? Or been diving under the sea? And yet, because of the power of photography, most of us are very familiar with these images. Photos also help us connect to our past. My children talk about 'remembering' family events that they are only aware of because they have seen themselves there in photographs.

Ways to develop children's understanding of photography

There are many ways that you can progress children's understanding of photography beyond just taking pictures using a tablet. Here are a few ideas.

Shadows

Instead of focusing on capturing an image directly, ask children to search for interesting shadows. These could be naturally occurring shadows or children could manipulate objects to create interesting shadows. Artists such as Tim Noble and Sue Webster create human-shaped shadows out of rubbish and Kumi Yamashita also creates interesting silhouettes in different ways.

Perspective

There is lots of fun to be had playing with perspective in photography. Encourage children to move objects and people into the foreground and background to create distorted realities. Can the children take pictures where a child close to the camera appears to pick up another child who is standing in the background of the photo? What other ways can children manipulate this technique to play with our perceptions? These effects are great team projects that will get the children working together to produce a shared outcome.

Close up

Many objects take on new and interesting shapes when photographed close up. This also gives children an opportunity to experiment with the focus of the camera they are using. Taking close-up photos of everyday objects and then adjusting the colourisation can produce some incredible surrealist images that are often unique and interesting. Challenge children to create and edit a close-up image that the rest of the class are unable to identify!

Cubism

Cubist photos are lots of fun! Have a look at David Hockney's 'Joiner' photos for inspiration. Encourage children to take multiple photos of a person or object from different angles, distances and perspectives. Once these photos are printed, challenge children to reassemble them, by cutting, overlapping and rotating to create their own image that captures the essence of the original subject, but moves away from the realism of a standard photo.

Mirrors

Using mirrors as a subject is a great way to extend the idea of photography. Ask children to set up mirrors in different ways to create interesting, abstract images. Instead of relying on mirrors alone, perhaps children could experiment with different reflective surfaces? You could challenge children to create a series of 'selfies', with their reflection captured in a different way each time.

Homemade filters

Children will undoubtedly be familiar with the idea of using different filters to create effects on photos. Try taking this idea further by using different materials to create your own. Materials that might create interesting results include cellophane, sticky tape, paper with holes cut out or teased cotton wool. Experiment with these filters at different distances from the lens; obscure and partially obscure or even place objects in front of the camera in a way that deliberately blocks parts of the image in translucent or opaque ways. This is a great way to encourage artistic trial and error in the low stakes environment of digital photography, where unlimited images can be taken and then the most successful chosen to be retained.

Photofolding

Photofolding can produce some really effective outcomes. One way to interpret this would be for children to take photos and then fold them into standalone sculptures using origami, nets or random folding. Aldo Tolino's geometrical designs are a good starting point for work on photofolding. Multiple identical photos could also be printed out, folded and then stuck back over the original image to create a new image that is very similar, but slightly distorted.

Cyanotypes

Cyanotypes (or sun paper as it is sometimes called) is a great way to introduce primary age children to the way that photos are developed without the need for a dark room. The paper can be bought ready-made and reacts to sunlight, so children will need to pre-plan their composition as the paper develops quickly. Take the paper outside and lay toys or natural materials such as flowers or leaves on top. The areas of the paper that are left uncovered will develop into bright vibrant blue, leaving the covered areas white. Have a look at Gohar Dashti's cyanotypes for inspiration!

Photo challenges

If you want to raise the profile of photography as an art form in your school, a photo challenge can be a really exciting project! Decide on some weekly prompts that could be shared with the school and encourage children to email their contributions each week to be shared in assembly. If time is tight, the pictures could simply be put on slideshow mode whilst children walk into assembly, celebrating the photos from the week before. Keep the prompts simple and everyday, e.g. my walk to school, my family, the view from my window, dinner time, etc., so all children can relate to them. Most children will have access to a mobile phone via their parents, so there should be few barriers to participation for those who want to enjoy sharing their photos.

Anything that gets children engaging in art both at home and at school is a wonderful thing!

Lesson plans

All three of the artists on the pages that follow use photography in fun and imaginative ways. The subject matters are easily accessible so that you can adapt each art expedition to work for you and your class. Hopefully the different techniques will also inspire you to create some exciting journeys of your own!

Lesson plan Key Stage 1: What do toys do when we aren't there?

Artist biography

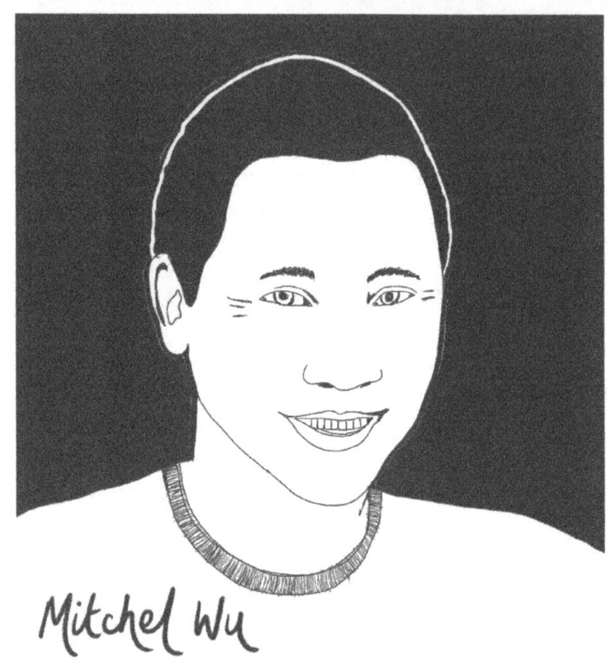

Mitchel Wu

Born:	unknown
Died:	–
Birthplace:	Los Angeles, USA
Discipline:	Photography – advertising and marketing

Mitchel Wu is a photographer who has the enviable job of photographing toys for high-profile companies such as Marvel, Hasbro and Disney.

With a background in art and illustration, Mitchel has always been a creative. He worked in product design for many years and then spent time as a wedding photographer until he began to struggle with working every weekend and being away from his family.

Photographing toys was something Mitchel had seen on social media and never imagined it could be something someone did as a full-time job. It just seemed like too much fun! But in 2016, Mitchel's images had gained so much attention that he was able to devote all his time to this exciting profession.

Mitchel's photographs bring well-known characters to life by putting them into positions that give them movement. He also plays with the unexpected, making us challenge our preconceived notions about the personalities of some of our best-loved toys.

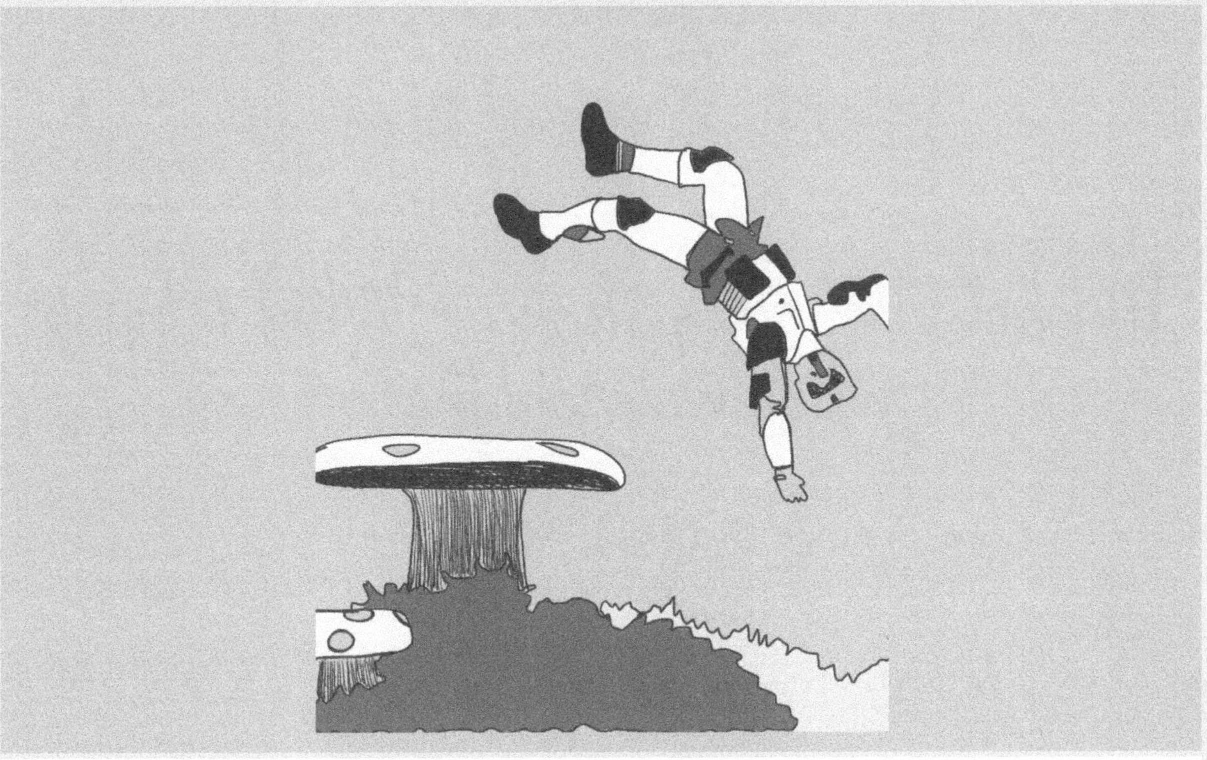

Find out more

This is a good place to see lots of Michel Wu's amazing images:

https://museemagazine.com/features/2018/5/13/toy-photographer-mitchel-wu-you-need-to-create-the-emotion-and-motion

Website:

www.mitchelwutoyphotography.com

Images to inspire

Mitchel Wu's images are untitled, but let the class loose to search on the Internet. Most of their favourite characters will be there and all the images are suitable for young children.

Other artist links

David Gilliver: David creates incredible scenes in miniature, combining tiny toy figures and unexpected items, e.g. dolls hiking up mountainous strawberries!

Renate Müller: Renate used to make stuffed animals to support children in hospitals, but now these brightly coloured animals exist as sculptures in their own right.

'The beauty of toy photography is that one is able to make so much out of so little.'

Mitchel Wu (Wu, 2018)

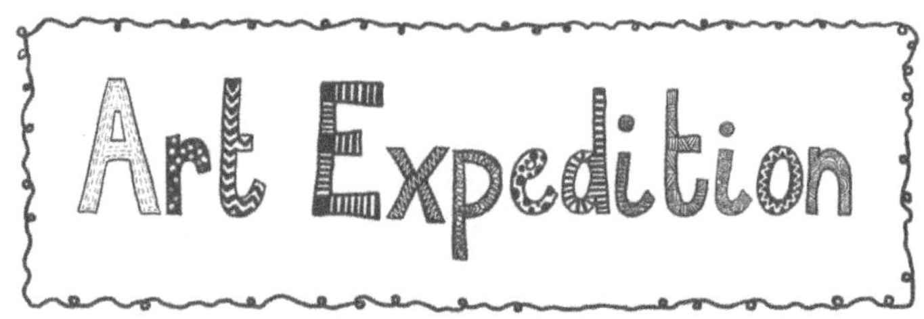

Mitchel Wu • Key Stage 1 • What do toys do when we aren't there?

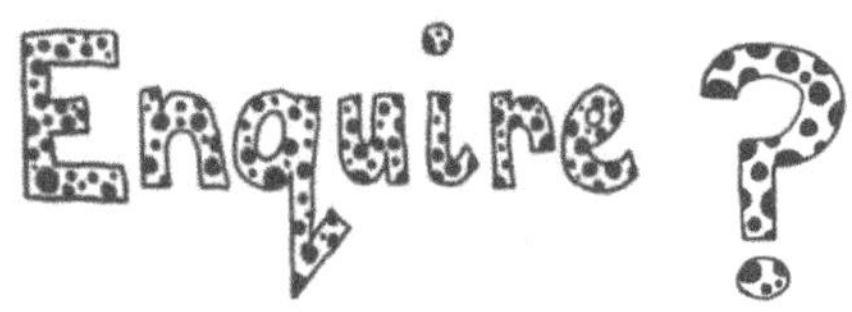

Ask children to list their favourite toys. What might they get up to when no one is at home? Ask children to share stories!

Signpost: Through this project, we will be using photography to capture the adventures of our favourite toys.

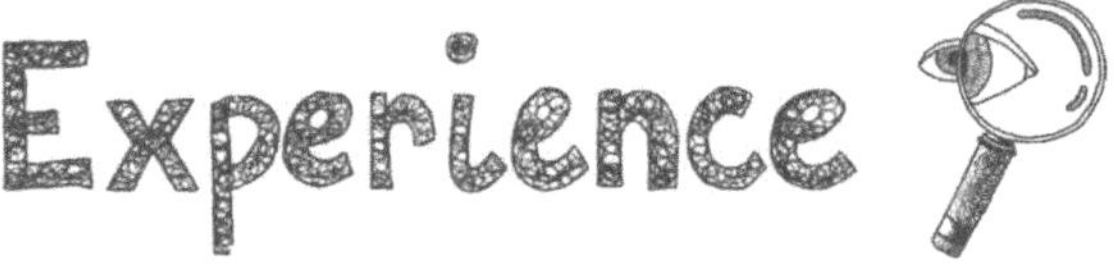

Ask children to bring in toys to inspire their art!

Let children know in advance that this session is going to happen if you would like them to bring in their own toys for inspiration. If not, then collect toys from around the school for children to choose from – character toys work best for this art expedition, but some other toys to use as props might be useful too!

Ask children to fill a sketchbook page with responses collected from direct observation of a range of different toys. Allow children to use a range of media so that they can enjoy creating. Try to encourage them to look closely and draw parts of the toys in detail, as well as looking at them as a whole. Put the toys in different positions so that children can fill a page with sketches and images that overlap in an exciting and colourful way.

You may want to give five minutes per toy/position or work in a carousel so that children get braver at making quick marks to represent lots of characters rather than getting burdened with the intricate details of just one.

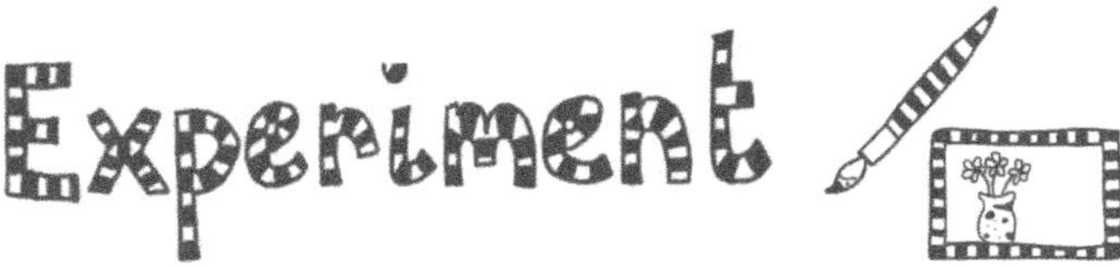

Introduce Mitchel Wu's amazing toy photography.

Give children plenty of time to really enjoy Mitchel Wu's work. The characters will be very familiar to the children! Give out printed photos for the children to have a look at and see if, in groups, they can verbally tell the story of what is happening in each image. Ask children to compare ideas. Did each group come up with the same story?

Look closely at Mitchel's photos. Introduce the words 'foreground' and 'background'. Can the children see how Mitchel has made the foreground stand out by blurring the background?

Teach children how to blur the background of a photo. If you have newer iPads, this feature already exists in portrait mode. If not, the free app Snapseed does this brilliantly. Just upload a photo, select 'Lens Blur' and children will be able to choose an area of focus leaving the background blurred. You may want to let the children experiment with some of the other editing features too!

Give children a selection of toys to photograph, experimenting with the blurring tool until they can do it independently.

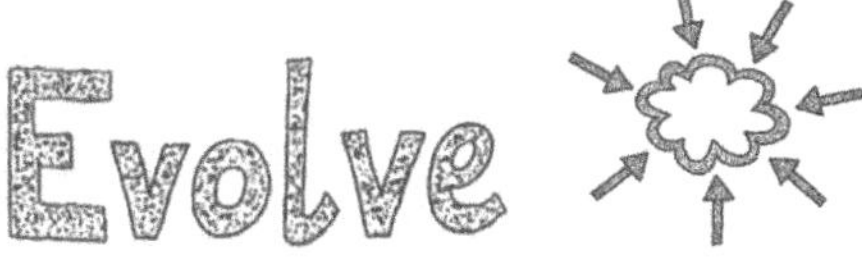

Design the composition for a final piece.

Let children choose a character to be the star of their photo. This could be a toy from home or a selection from school. Encourage partner talk, where the children imagine what this toy gets up to when no one is looking. Ask children to draw a quick sketch and write a short sentence about what this might be. How could we recreate this in a photograph? What would we need? This is the opportunity for children to test anything that might need hanging, attaching or balancing to ensure that their composition is achievable. They will also need to think about the background. Where will the photo be taken?

Once a final composition has been decided, children will need to make a list of props ready for next week.

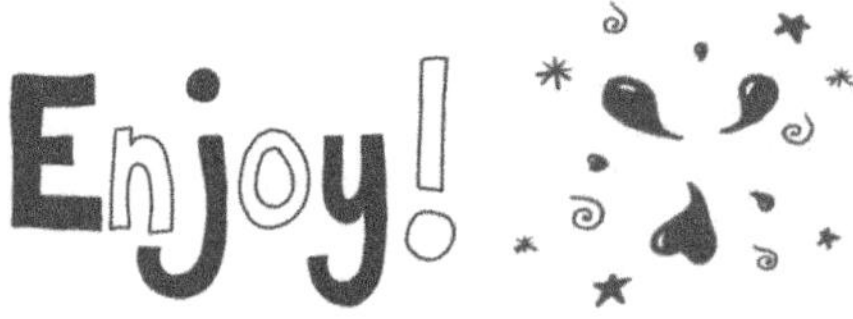

Make and photograph!

Create the scenes and take a photo! Children might need to work in groups to create each picture if there are constraints on tablets or props. It might also be useful to have an extra pair of hands to hold up backgrounds and hold items that are suspended.

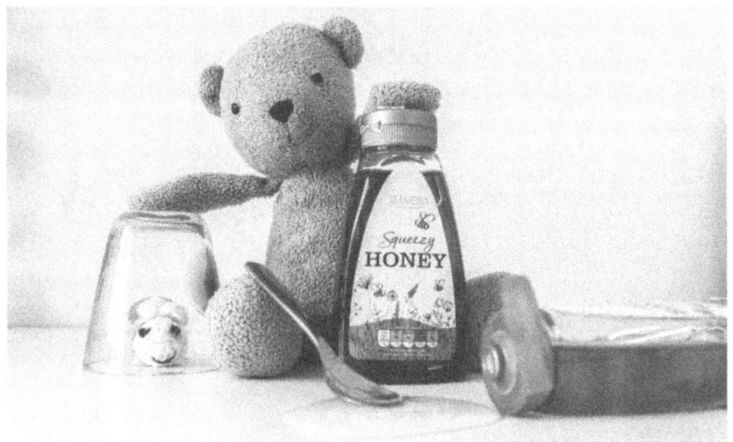

Everyone knows that bears love honey! This naughty teddy has been raiding the pantry. He has even trapped an unsuspecting bee to ensure he is never short of his favourite treat again!

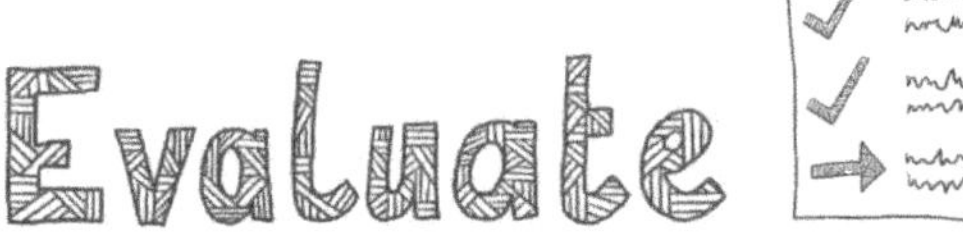

How did it go? Peer and self-assessment

Share the children's photos on the whiteboard.

Peer evaluation (this can be done as a class)

- What is going on in this picture?
- How has the artist made the story clear?
- What do you think happens next in the story?

Self-evaluation

Ask children to annotate around their photo:

- What is your toy doing?
- What challenges did you have to overcome to create your scene?
- What new skill have you learned to help you edit photos?

Lesson plan Lower Key Stage 2: Who do I want to be?

Artist biography

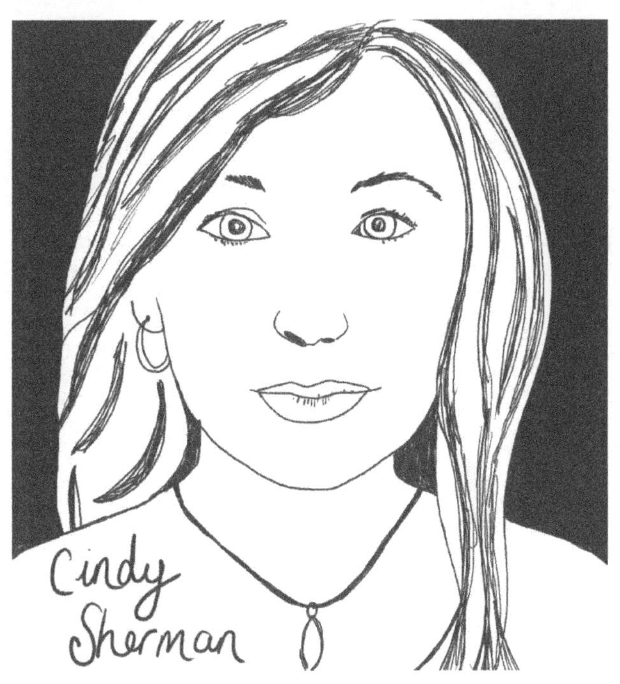

Cindy Sherman

Born:	1954
Died:	–
Birthplace:	New Jersey, USA
Discipline:	Photography – postmodern

Cindy Sherman began her artistic career as a painter but soon became frustrated with what she considered to be the limitations of this artistic discipline. She felt that her time could be better spent creating new ideas which could be photographed quickly, rather than the laborious process of using paint to 'copy' an image.

Cindy has always explored ideas around identity, her most famous work being 'Untitled Film Stills', a collection of black and white images, portraying herself as different female film characters. Cindy aimed to capture 'every woman' within her photos, exploring the way that people perceive women by the way that they look.

When Cindy creates her photographs, she works alone. She is in charge of the make-up, wardrobe, set design and character creation, using herself as the model. Through the many different costumes that Cindy wears for her photos, she explores the idea of the many 'parts' we play in our lives.

Cindy is particularly interested in considering the role of women and how they are portrayed in media and film. She challenges the viewer to reconsider the stereotypes that we are exposed to every day.

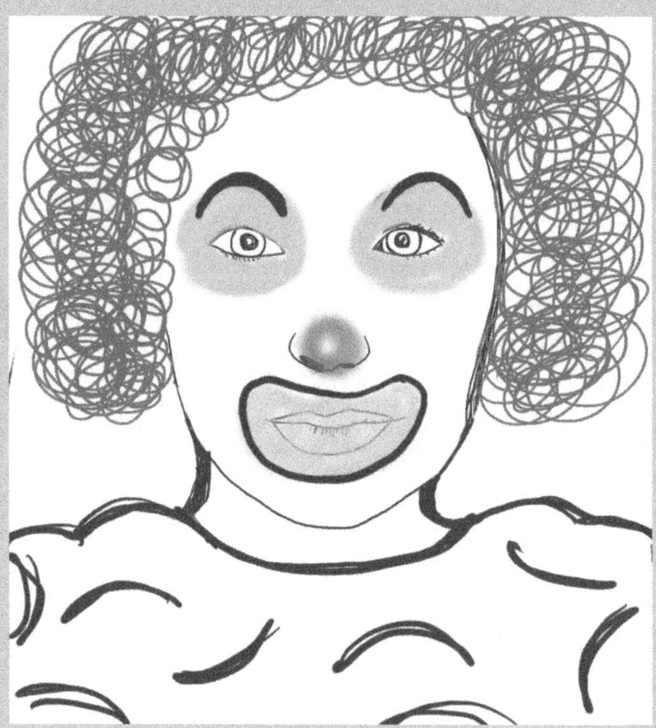

Find out more

The Art Story:

www.theartstory.org/artist/sherman-cindy/

The Museum of Modern Art:

www.moma.org/artists/5392

Images to inspire	**Other artist links**
Untitled Film Stills Untitled 414 (Clown) Mrs. Claus Untitled 477 Untitled 474 Untitled 602	**Juno Calypso:** Juno becomes her alter ego 'Joyce' in her work, using different costumes and settings to create alternative characters. **Silin Liu:** Silin superimposes herself into photos with famous people, assuming a character to make herself seem part of the original image. **Andy Warhol:** Andy's self-portraits often depict himself playing with his identity.

'The still must tease with the promise of a story the viewer of it itches to be told.'

Cindy Sherman (MOMA, n.d.)

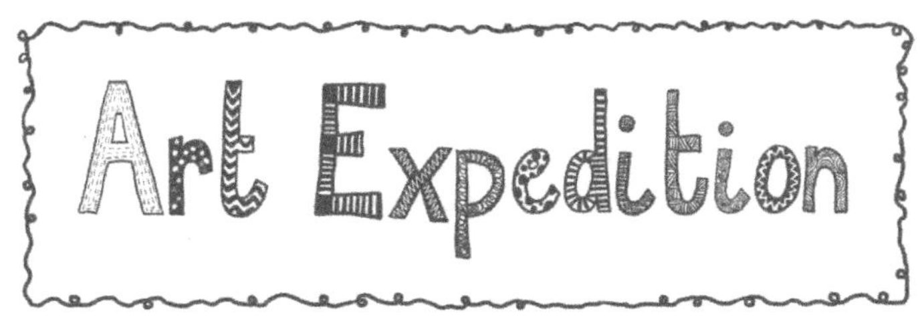

Cindy Sherman • Lower Key Stage 2
Who do I want to be?

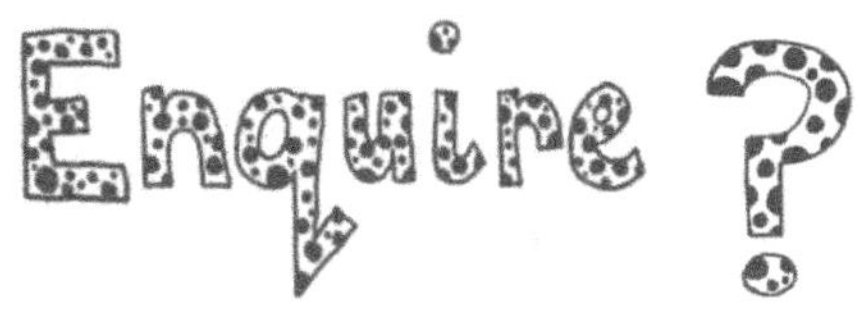

Ask children what they want to be when they are older. Who are they now? Try to unpick the children's ideas beyond just a future occupation. What kind of person would they want people to think they are?

Signpost: Through this project, we will be exploring our own identities to create self-portraits using photography.

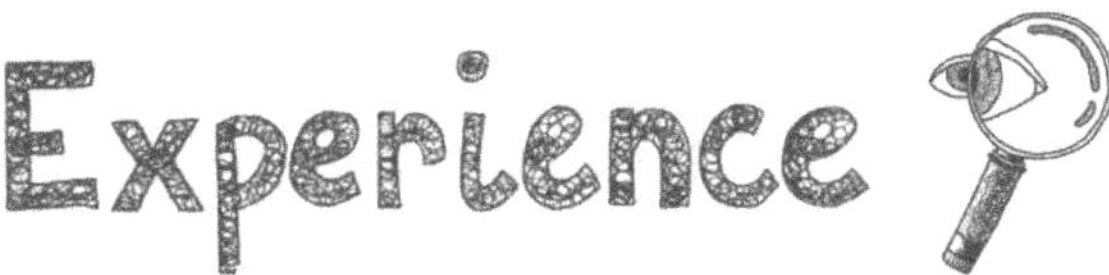

Ask children to create a sketchbook page imagining their lives when they are older.

Ask children to imagine the future and represent their ideas on a sketchbook page using a range of art materials. It would be worth having access to newspapers and magazines so children can find images and words that might inspire them. Here are a few key questions you might want to use as prompts:

- What will you look like?
- What might your family be like?
- Where will you live?
- What will be your job?
- What could your hobbies be?
- What clothes will you wear?
- Who will your friends be?
- Will you have any pets?

- How will people describe you?
- What will your personality be like?

Encourage children to find words as well as pictures. These could be written but they could also be collaged. Think about the kind of person children would like to be as well as the more tangible attributes.

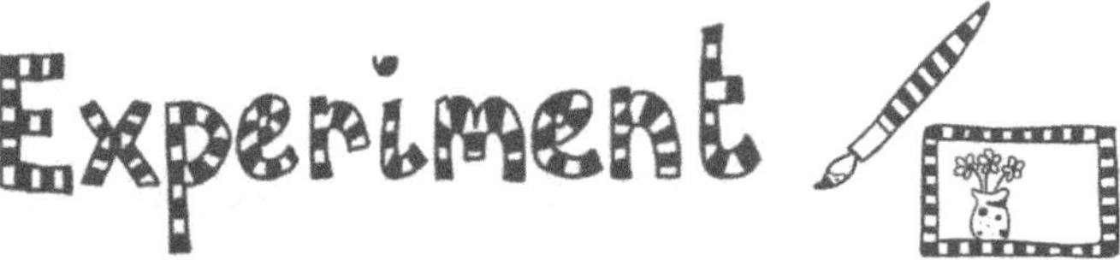

Introduce Cindy Sherman's 'Untitled Film Stills'.

Show children Cindy Sherman's 'Untitled Film Stills' (there are lots of them, so pick a selection that you feel are appropriate for your class). What do the photos have in common? What is different about them? See if children recognise that it is the same person. Also show some of Cindy's more modern work where she might be portrayed as a man, clown or cowgirl. Look at how Cindy's series of images are often related, e.g. heavily colourised or black and white.

Give children time to familiarise themselves with the photo editing software that is used by your school. Children will need to work in pairs so that they can take images of each other in different poses. Children can then choose different images of themselves to edit. Using free software like Canva, teach the children how to remove the background from their images so that they can add their portrait to different backgrounds to create the illusion that they are somewhere else. They could even add props to their images by downloading stock photos and combining them with their original image. Encourage lots of experimentation, chopping images and recombining them to create a brand-new portrait.

Print examples for sketchbooks so the children have a record of what combinations and techniques worked well.

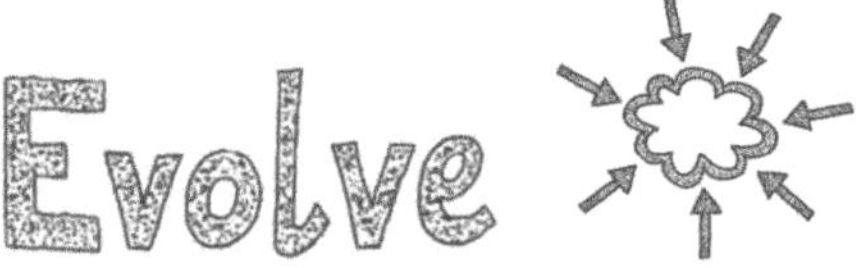

Begin to design the final piece where children plan four photos that represent an element of how they imagine they will be when they are older.

Ask children to start to sketch ideas for photos that will represent the way they imagine they will be when they are older. Give children small rectangles of paper on which they can start to design the way their photos will look. There will be four images in the final piece but encourage children to design more than this, so they have options for the final design.

Be as ambitious as possible! Do the Evolve stage at least a week before the final piece so there is time to try and source the props that might be needed to recreate the different aspects of the child's future persona. Encourage children to think about the use of face paint, clothes, hats, settings, etc. to bring the different images to life and make the meaning clear. Children can bring in props from home, borrow them from other classes, or be really creative and make things that represent any props they are unable to source. Children can also consider how they may use stock photos from the internet to add props or costumes that they can't access.

By the end of this session, children should have decided on their four images and written a list of the things they will need to recreate them – all recorded in their sketchbook.

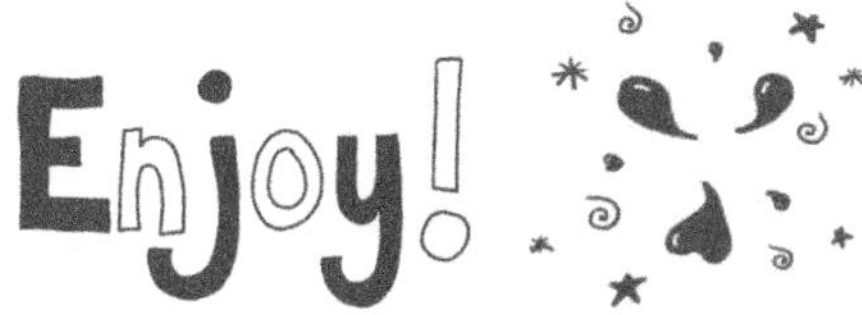

Take the photos and edit them to create a consistent series.

Creating the final piece may take some time! Get children to dress up and take the four photos of each other for the final piece. Ask whoever is taking the photos to take multiple images so that the child whose photo has been taken can select the ones they want to include.

Once four images have been selected, use the photo editor to enhance each photo to further develop the theme of the picture. Arrange the photos either in a line or as a square, then print!

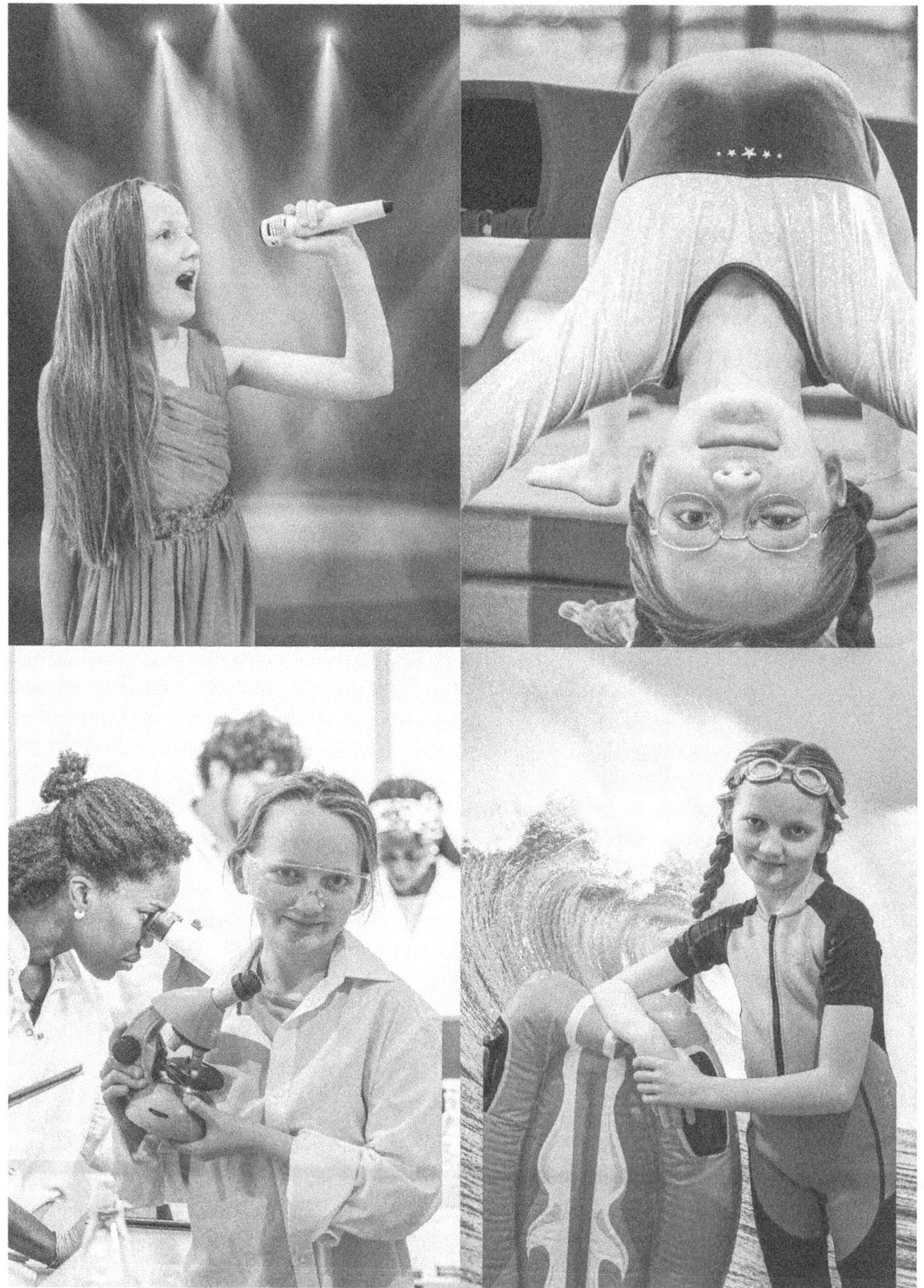

These four images were created using Canva. We removed the original backgrounds of each photo and replaced them with stock photos that enhanced the theme of each picture.

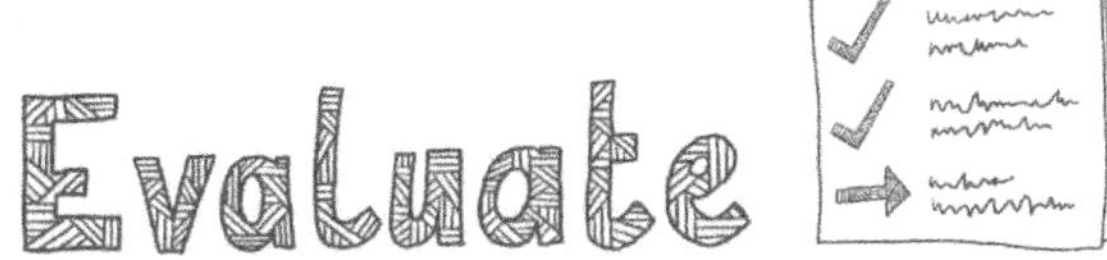

How did it go? Peer and self-assessment

Peer evaluation

- Look at the images. What can you learn about what your friend would like to be?
- Choose three words to describe what the person in the photos is like.
- What differences are there between the person you know and their future self?

Self-evaluation

Ask children to annotate around their own photo series.

- Which photo do you think was most successful and why?
- Do the photos look like you expected?
- What would you have done differently?

Lesson plan Upper Key Stage 2: Why is water important?

Artist biography

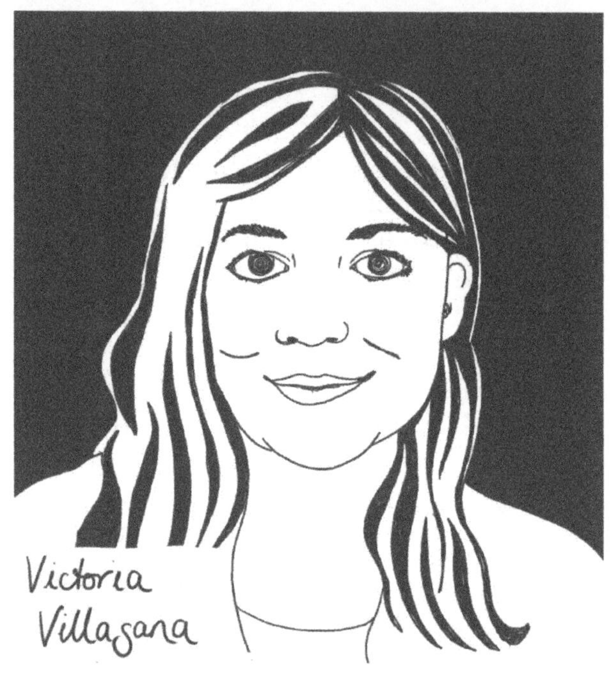

Victoria Villasana

Born:	1982
Died:	–
Birthplace:	Guadalajara, Mexico
Discipline:	Textiles, installation and street art – contemporary

Victoria Villasana was born in Mexico where she studied design. Her love of textiles began as a child when she used to make clothes for her dolls.

Victoria spent a decade living in London, spending her time studying different artistic processes from floristry to fashion. During her time in the city, Victoria arguably reinvented street art, creating vibrant designs using her signature combination of photos and colourful threads. She was inspired seeing a street artist at work one day pasting one of their images to a wall. Victoria decided that instead of keeping her work to herself, this was the perfect way to share it with the world.

In her work, Victoria chooses images of famous artists, politicians and musicians, picking important figures from different cultures to celebrate. Her use of yarn is a nod to her Mexican heritage where textiles are very important, but this is also a way of repurposing wool as something modern and relevant, and bringing it beyond its historical place of being traditionally 'female'.

Many of Victoria's pieces leave the wool uncut, spilling out from beneath the picture. These raw edges give her work a dynamic feel, as if the images are a work in progress, waiting to be finished.

Victoria's work with WaterAid was a collaboration designed to demonstrate the life-changing impact that access to clean drinking water can have on a community.

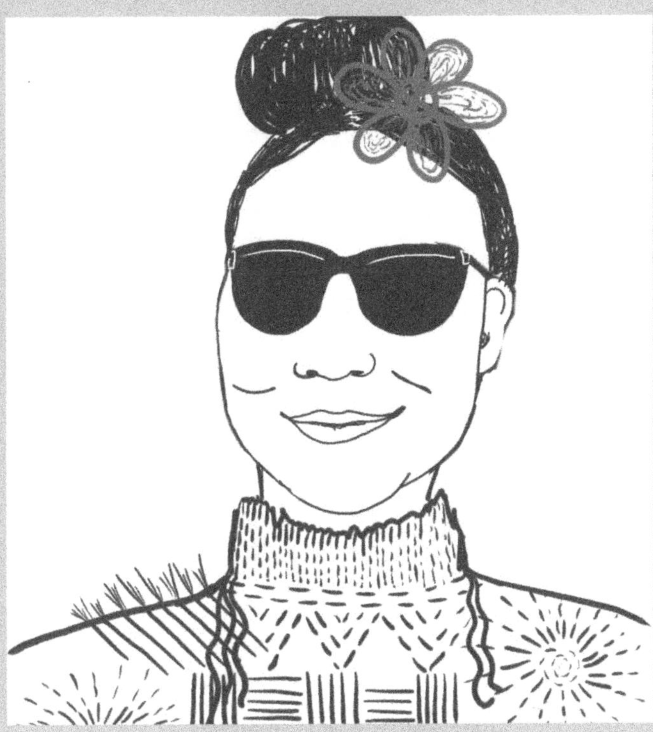

Find out more

YouTube: 'Fashion Revolutionaries: Victoria Villasana' https://www.youtube.com/watch?v=cjCawawrV1s

Website: https://victoriavillasana.com/

Images to inspire

Victoria Villasana's images are untitled but they can easily be found by the famous person they depict.

For this project, look up the images Victoria created to support WaterAid.

Other artist links

Joana Choumali: Joana takes photographs of her local area and enhances them with embroidery.

Melissa Zexter: Melissa uses thread to stitch intricate patterns and designs into photographs to create a magical quality.

Maurizio Anzeri: Maurizio uses straight lines to create curves using stitching. His patterns use 'parabolas' (curves) to create interesting shapes and designs.

'I think we need to stop labelling and putting people in boxes.'

Victoria Villasana (Robinson, 2018)

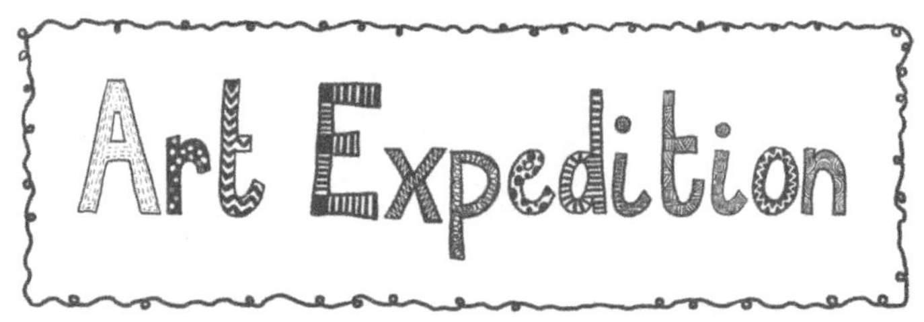

Victoria Villasana • Upper Key Stage 2
Why is water important?

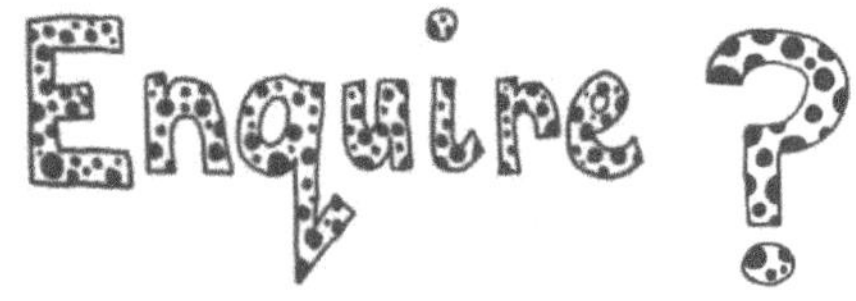

Ask children to think about why we need water. Can they imagine what life is like for those who do not have access to clean water? Or have to walk miles to obtain it? Make sure children realise that access to clean water is not just an issue in developing countries. There are many reasons why people might not have unrestricted access to water.

Signpost: Through this project, we will be combining photography and textiles to celebrate the ways that water is important to us.

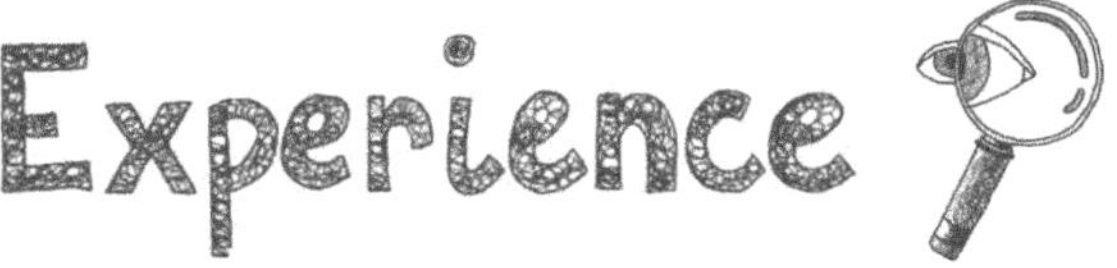

Children create a sketchbook page on the theme of water. Make sure children have access to sources for observation.

Ask children to fill a sketchbook page on the subject of water. Encourage them to collect water in different pots that they can sketch. Also ensure that children have access to secondary sources so that they can make sketches about water sources that they cannot directly observe.

Encourage children to think beyond the literal. As well as drawing water, can children draw with water? Can they create different effects using water combined with other artistic materials? Can they make marks that represent the movement of water? Can they use onomatopoeia (words that sound like the noise they refer to such as 'buzz' or 'hiss') to collect words to do with water that could be presented artistically? For example, children could draw the flow of water, a whirlpool or a wave using 'water-related' words.

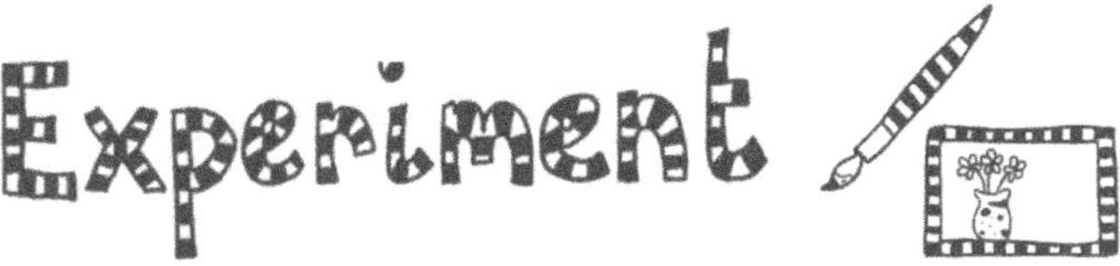

Introduce the work of Victoria Villasana. Look at the way that thread is used to enhance her photographs.

Show children the five images taken by Victoria Villasana for WaterAid, which you can find online.

This series of pictures is a celebration of life with access to clean water. Ask children to move around the school with tablets and see if they can photograph evidence of ways in which their lives are enhanced by water. It could be plants in the school garden, the dinner hall, children taking part in PE, water bottles, hand washing, etc. Try not to give too much guidance and see what the children can come up with. These should be quick photographs from which to make choices later.

Return to the classroom. Show children how to crop their photos and change them to black and white using your tablet's editing software. Also demonstrate how to change the contrast and shadows so that children can experiment with different effects.

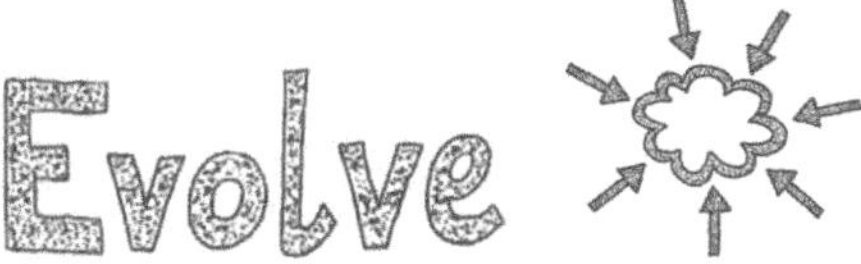

Children choose an area of focus and create a design for a final photograph, practising stitching into paper.

In their sketchbooks, children can make choices about the theme of their final photo. Look at the trial images from the Experiment stage and make notes about how the image could be enhanced when the final shot is taken, e.g. more light, better focus, a change in composition.

Then, the children will need to make choices about the enhancements they will add using stitching. Stick some small photos of Victoria Villasana's work in sketchbooks and ask the children to use these as inspiration by stitching directly into the page. Experiment with different stitch designs. You may just want children to perfect running stitch or you may want to offer tutorials in more elaborate stitching patterns. It is definitely worth getting a cheap pack of needle threaders for this session!

By the end of this stage, children should be able to sketch their photographic composition and plan their stitch design ready for the next session.

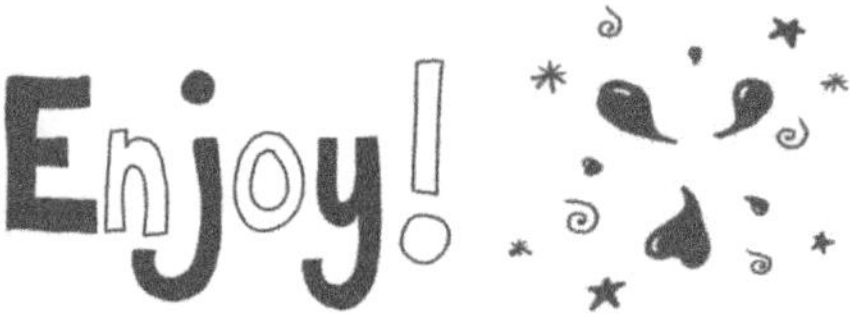

Take the finished photograph, print and embroider!

Children should take their final image to represent a celebration of water. Use the editing skills learned during the Experiment stage to crop the image and make it black and white.

Print the images onto card and then add the embellishments planned during the Evolve phase.

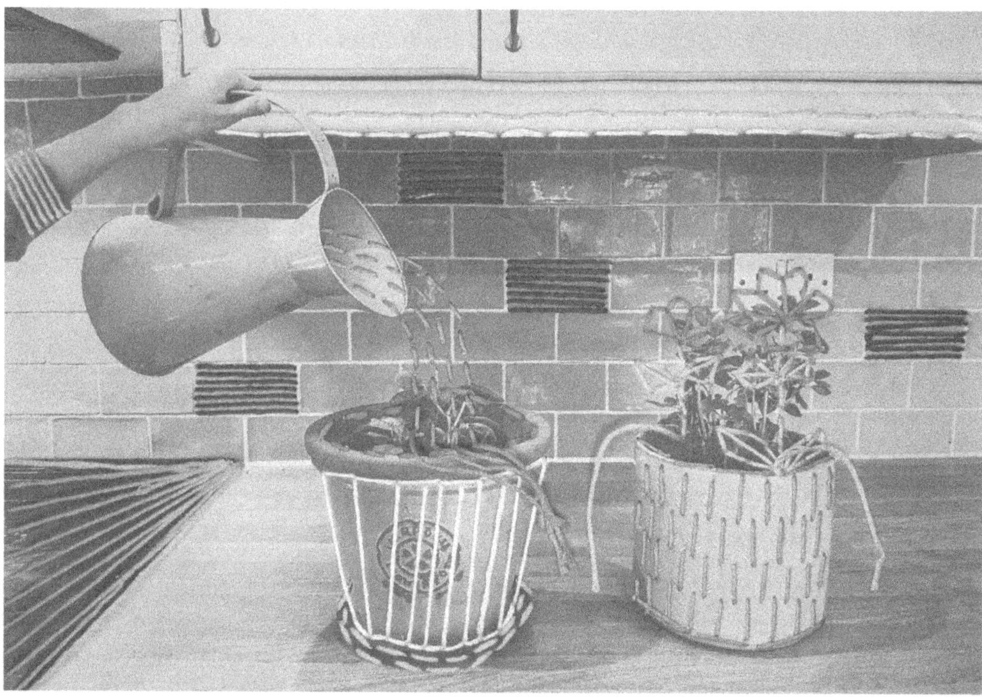

This photo has been enhanced using a range of different stitches using embroidery thread. There are even some hanging threads left unfinished true to Victoria's style.

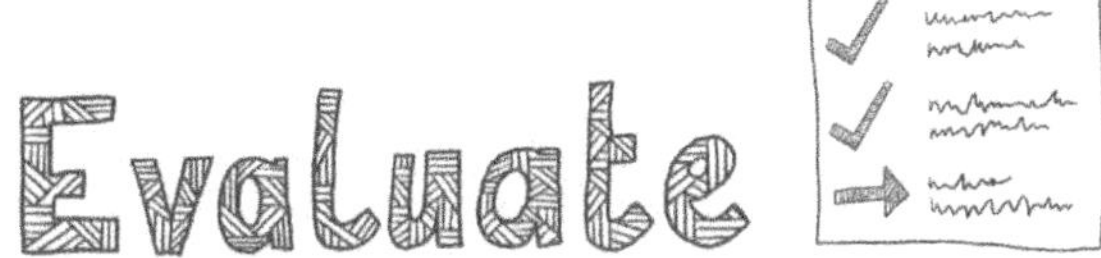

How did it go? Peer and self-assessment

Peer evaluation

Ask children to write comments onto sticky notes as they move around the room celebrating the final pieces. These sticky notes can be added to the child's sketchbook as a record of the feedback that they have received from a peer. These questions could be used as prompts to support this:

- How does this image celebrate water?
- What is the most effective part of the image?
- Victoria Villasana is a street artist – where could this image be displayed?

Self-evaluation

Ask children to annotate around their photo in their sketchbook.

- What worked well in your final piece?
- What changes could you make to enhance your image further?
- How could you use this art style to raise awareness of another important issue?

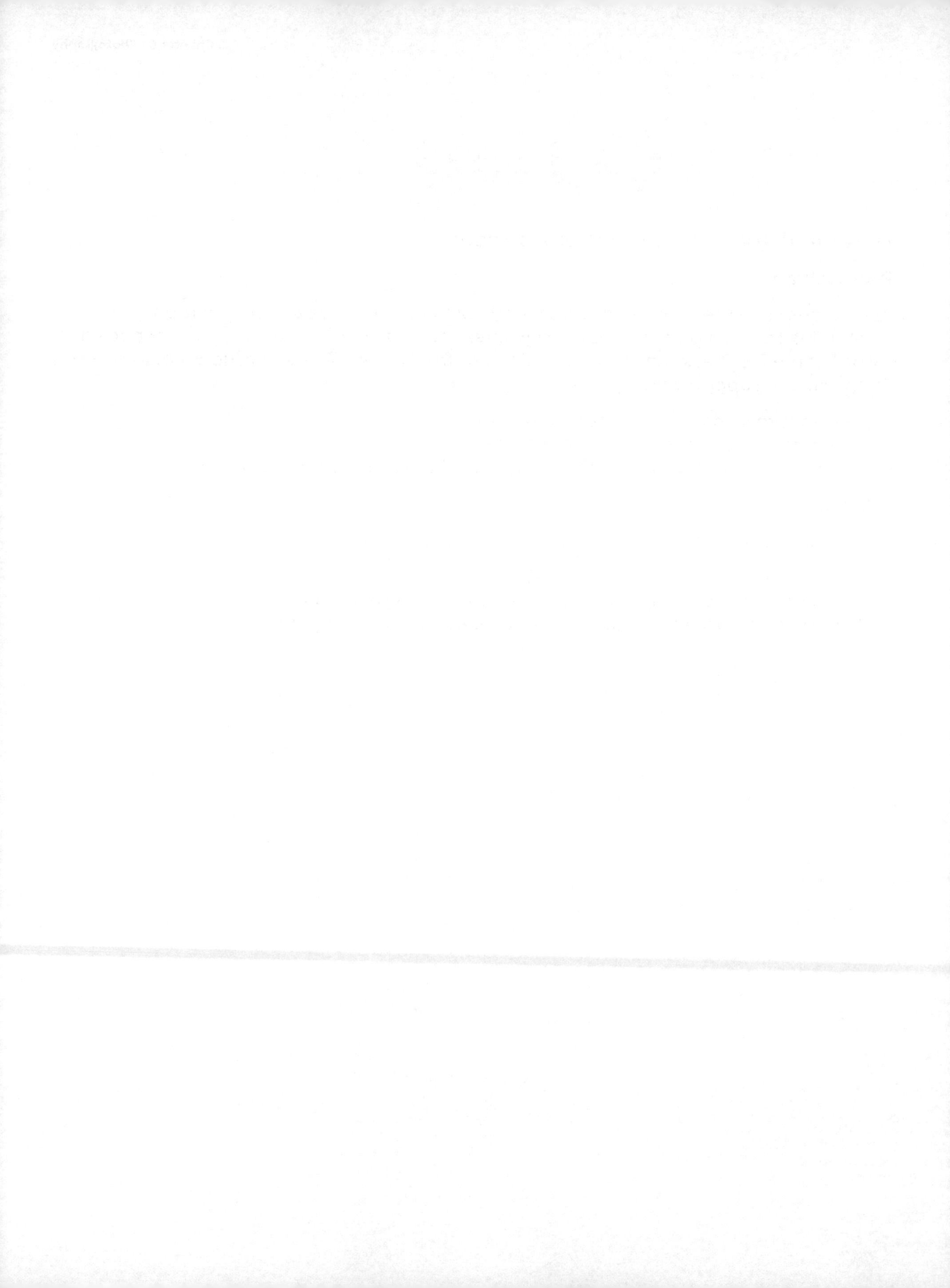

Chapter 7
Printing

Introduction to printing

There is something very dynamic and exciting about printing with children. The ability to be able to create multiple pieces of work from the same matrix empowers children to make changes, improve and evolve their print designs and manipulate different variables such as paint-load and pressure. Printing incorporates a wealth of other artistic skills such as cutting, painting, mark making, colour mixing and carving. The outcomes are often bold, powerful and full of contrast. Creating multiple prints also provides you and your class with a fantastic bank of collage materials that can be used to great effect in other projects.

Printing ideas to try

Here are a few printing ideas that you could try in school.

Monoprinting

Monoprinting is where an image is transferred from one surface to another in a way that can only be achieved once. Using carbon paper is a great example of this. Children can draw on the back of the paper, pushing the carbon onto a surface beneath. Although this is a wonderful opportunity for children to make marks of their own, you can also give children photocopied images or select images from newspapers and magazines that they can place on top of the carbon paper to trace over. This is a wonderful way to build confidence and show children the potential of a medium without the anxiety often associated with drawing. It is also a brilliant way to transfer pre-prepared designs to another surface.

There are lots of other surfaces that you can use in this way. Try scribbling on paper with oil pastel or applying a thin layer of printing ink with a roller onto a piece of laminated paper. Both will transfer marks onto the paper below as children put pressure on the reverse.

Polystyrene foam

Polystyrene foam is a surface that children can carve into with a pencil or other sharp tool, to create an amazing matrix from which to print. This is a go-to printing medium in schools because it is relatively cheap, easy to work with and can even be rinsed so that children can print multiple designs in different colours. It is worth the investment in proper printing ink as this gives a really crisp image with intense colours. A little goes a long way though, so encourage your children to be sparing and really roll the ink onto the polystyrene foam to give a thin layer of colour.

Lino printing

There are many reasons why primary teachers recoil at the idea of lino printing, but this technique is such an effective way to create prints and can be done safely, particularly in Key Stage 2. Lino (or linoleum) is a rubbery surface that can be carved into using V-shaped or U-shaped tools. You can now buy soft lino which is much easier to carve, and as long as children are taught the correct technique (place your supporting hand nearest to you, then cut away from the body) you should not have any accidents! Lino also gives the opportunity to produce reduction prints, where you cut a basic design, print, then make further cuts and print again in a different colour. This process can be repeated to build layers of ink that add detail to the finished image.

Gelli printing

I absolutely love gelli printing! A class set of gelatine printing plates can be hundreds of pounds but a similar effect can be created using a piece of laminated card as a surface. This kind of printing creates monoprints, but layers can be built up using different colours and designs. Add a layer of ink or acrylic paint on laminated card, then draw or make marks into the surface, then press a sheet of paper on top of the laminated card to transfer the print. You can leave interesting marks on the laminated sheet before you remove the print by pressing feathers, bubble wrap or other textures into the paint. You can even use stencils as a barrier between the paper and laminated card when you print, so that interesting designs can be retained as further printed layers are added. For a more detailed step-by-step guide, see the art expedition under Favianna Rodriguez later in this chapter. There are also loads of great ideas at this link if you would like to explore this process further: www.gelliarts.com/.

There are more ambitious options to consider, such as distressed ink and image transfer. Search online for gelli printing. You will be hooked!

Collagraph printing

Use a piece of corrugated card as your matrix and stick on pieces of craft foam, bubble wrap, string or other interesting surfaces. This can then be printed from to create exciting patterns and interesting textures. PVA glue works well if you leave the collagraphs to dry overnight, but a glue gun is an even better option because the collagraphs will be ready to print from immediately!

Screen printing

Screen printing is where ink or paint is pushed through a fabric 'screen' and a barrier prevents the colour from reaching the printing surface. Although traditional screen printing is done with light-reactive chemicals, there are still highly effective options that can be done safely in primary school. You can use paper stencils which go between the screen and the printing surface as a barrier, or paint directly onto the underside of the screen, using masking fluid to prevent the colour reaching the paper.

You can buy screen printing frames and squeegees (tools that drag the paint across the screen) from most educational suppliers, but they are very expensive and bulky to store. They are definitely worth the investment if your school can justify it, but there are other ways to achieve similar results on a budget. Screen printing mesh can be bought cheaply and you can create your own homemade press by stapling a section of mesh to a piece of laminated card along the top edge. Fold the mesh out of the way, put your printing surface on top of the laminated card, place your stencil on top of that and then replace the mesh. Use a piece of corrugated card as a squeegee to drag the paint or ink from the stapled edge to the bottom. The paint will transfer to the printing surface everywhere except the stencil which can then be peeled away to reveal your own version of a screen print. Give it a go, it is lots of fun!

Lesson plans

The following three artists employ very different methods of printing which will give your children a good understanding of the different ways that printing can be achieved. You could incorporate other printing methods into each expedition to give your children the opportunity to explore a wider range of techniques. Favianna Rodriguez's work would also lend itself to an exciting expedition into collage if you fancy moving into a mixed media project!

Lesson plan Key Stage 1: What can we learn about trees?

Artist biography

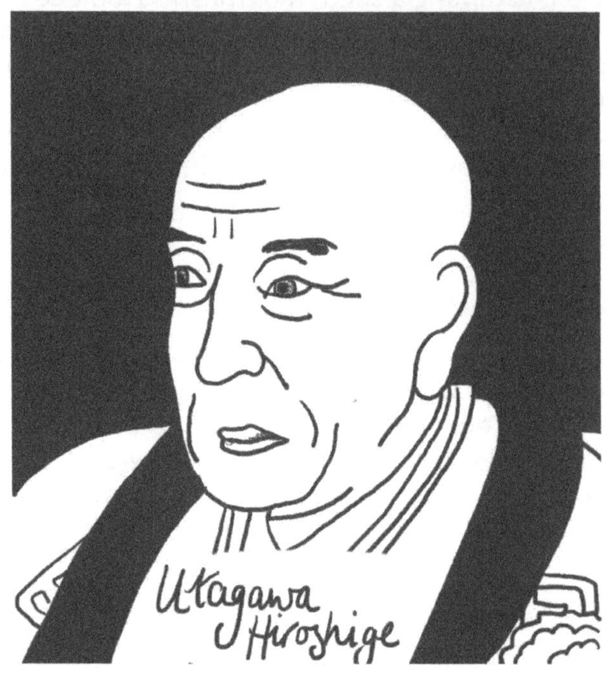

Utagawa Hiroshige

Born:	1797
Died:	1858
Birthplace:	Edo, Japan
Discipline:	Painting and printmaking – ukiyo-e woodblock

Utagawa Hiroshige was born in Edo, which is now called Tokyo. His ancestors were Samurai and his great grandfather was a powerful member of the Tsugaru clan.

Hiroshige initially began by following his father's career, as was traditional, so at 12 years old he became a fire watchman. Both his mother and father died when Hiroshige was just a child and it was not until then that he began to paint. He attended art school and learned from other Japanese masters such as Toyohiro. It was here that he embraced the art of ukiyo-e. Ukiyo-e translates as 'pictures of the floating world'.

Hiroshige created many of his paintings to document his travels. The trend at the time was to paint beautiful women and movie stars, but Hiroshige was more interested in landscapes and nature. His most famous work 'Fifty-three Stations on the Tōkaidō Road' is the culmination of the sketches Hiroshige produced whilst travelling along the Tōkaidō road.

Throughout his life, Hiroshige changed his name many times, often to symbolise a change in his artistic style. This was customary for Japanese artists at the time. Utagawa is actually the name of Hiroshige's school!

Hiroshige even caught the eye of Vincent van Gogh, who was deeply influenced by Japanese art and displayed many examples in his studio. He even copied Hiroshige's 'Plum Park in Kameido' in an effort to learn more about Japanese art.

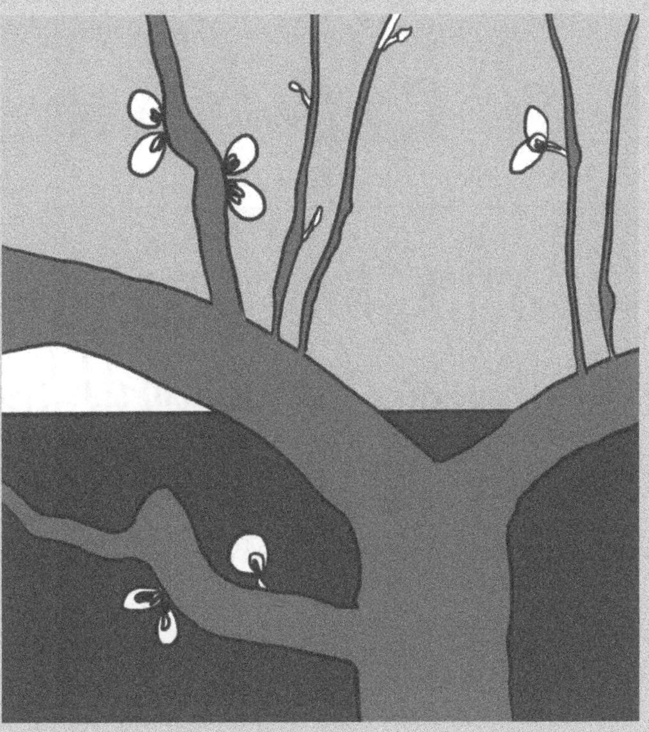

Find out more

The Art Story: www.theartstory.org/artist/hiroshige-utagawa

Art Institute, Chicago: www.artic.edu/artists/34946/utagawa-hiroshige

Images to inspire

Macaw on a Pine Branch

A Red Plum Branch Against the Summer Moon

Sparrows and Camellia in Snow

Plum Garden at Kameido

Red Blossom Plum

Cherry Blossoms and Shrike

Other artist links

Vincent van Gogh: Show children the two versions of 'Plum Park in Kameido'. Hiroshige's is a print and van Gogh's is a painting. See if the children can spot similarities and differences.

Peter Doig: Peter is a contemporary artist that also makes prints of trees.

Wang Chao: Wang uses traditional Japanese printing methods such as wood block, to create beautiful, large-scale prints on fabric.

'I leave my brush in the East and set forth on my journey. I shall see the famous places in the Western Land.'

Utagawa Hiroshige (Jay, 2018)

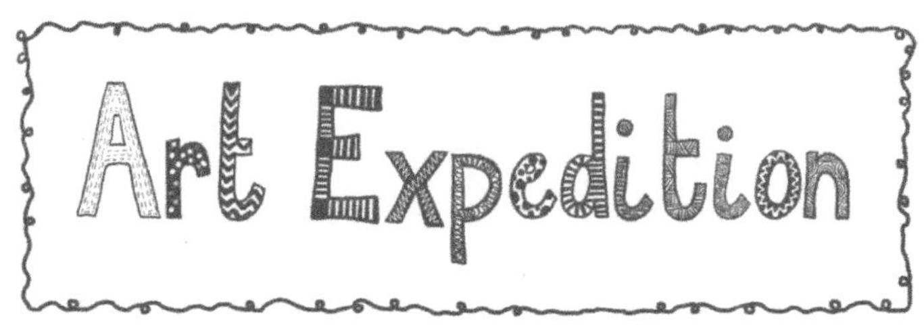

Utagawa Hiroshige • Key Stage 1
What can we learn about trees?

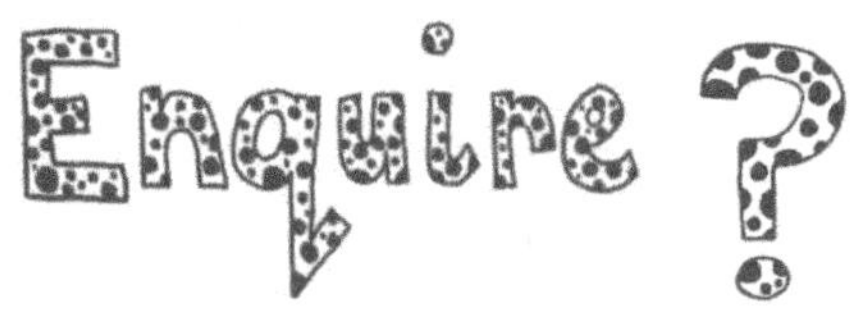

Ask children what they already know about trees. Do they know any names? Anything about the way they look or the way they grow? What kinds of things grow on trees or live in trees?

Signpost: Through this project, we will be creating our own mono-prints of trees using cardboard and other 'junk' materials.

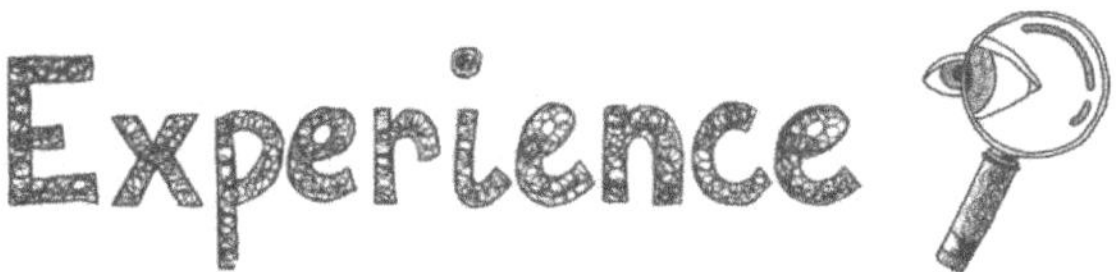

On a sketchbook page, see what else we can find out about trees.

Go outside and experience trees! Give children lots of art supplies to choose from and let them have free rein. There are so many ways that children could respond to this but if you feel that your class might require some prompts, here are some ideas.

- Draw the trees themselves or the shape of the leaves.
- Look for patterns in the bark, the branches or the veins of the leaves and make marks to represent these.
- Take rubbings (frottage) of the leaves and bark using wax crayons or oil pastels.
- Draw around the leaves.
- Look around the tree and draw things that might be living there, e.g. birds or bugs.
- Listen carefully and try to draw the sound the leaves make when the wind blows, or the pattern of the birdsong.
- Stick leaves directly into their sketchbooks and try to copy them.
- Mix colours using watercolours or oil pastels to try to create the right green for the leaves, or the right brown for the bark.

- Stand back from the tree and try to cut out the silhouette directly into paper.

Make sure that children explore multiple ideas to fill a sketchbook page with lots of wonderful responses.

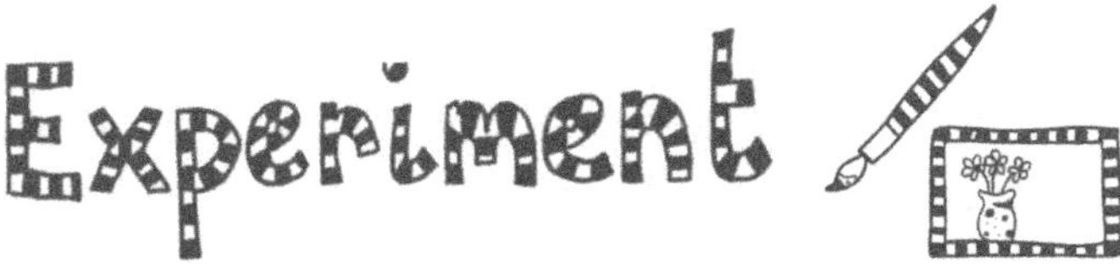

Look at the work of Utagawa Hiroshige, focusing on his prints of trees, blossoms and branches. Experiment with ways of printing.

Introduce children to Japanese wood block prints of trees, branches and blossom. Ask children how they think the images have been made. Explain how these prints were created by painstakingly carving into wood, and that although time-consuming, the beauty of this type of printing is that the print block can be used repeatedly.

Give children time to experiment with their own ideas of printing. Put out paper plates of paint. Then allow access to as many interesting objects and textures as you can and see what patterns the children are able to create on a large sketchbook page (or many pages!). Depending on the age of the children, try to encourage annotations so that they can remember how they made the marks that they did. Here are some easily sourced suggestions for exciting print making:

- corrugated card (encourage the children to try this whole and with one layer peeled off)
- bubble wrap
- LEGO®
- the rim of a paper plate
- fingers and hands
- leaves
- bark
- foam shapes
- toy car wheels
- any type of construction toy
- sponge
- corks
- string
- straws (whole or split at the end)
- forks.

Extend the children by encouraging them to try printing with the same object but with different paint colours each time.

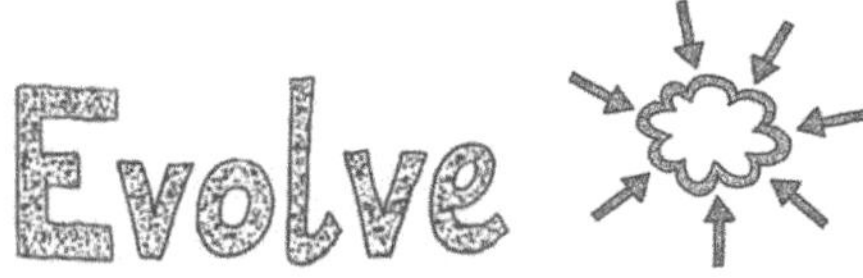

Show children what a collagraph is. Ask them to create their own, ready to print the branch of a tree.

Look back at Hiroshige's 'Plum Park in Kameido'.

Show children how to make a collagraph of a tree branch. A collagraph is a piece of corrugated card packaging that has different surfaces or textures stuck to it with PVA or glue gun. Once it is dry, the children can apply paint or ink in order to take prints.

Ask children to look back at the marks they made in the Experiment stage. Which materials would be appropriate to use to make a collagraph? The options that work best are corrugated card, bubble wrap, string, foam shapes and flat, thin LEGO® bricks. The other materials that the children experimented with can be used afterwards to embellish the collagraph branches. For example, they might decide to glue card and bubble wrap onto the collagraph to create branches and blossom, then use a fork to create thinner twigs directly onto the paper after the collagraph has been printed.

In the Evolve stage, children need to do two things: create their collagraph (don't forget that everything on the collagraph will be reversed when printed!) and choose a background. This could just be a piece of coloured paper, or a more effective alternative is to ask children to paint a graduated coloured or sky-style background ready to print on next time.

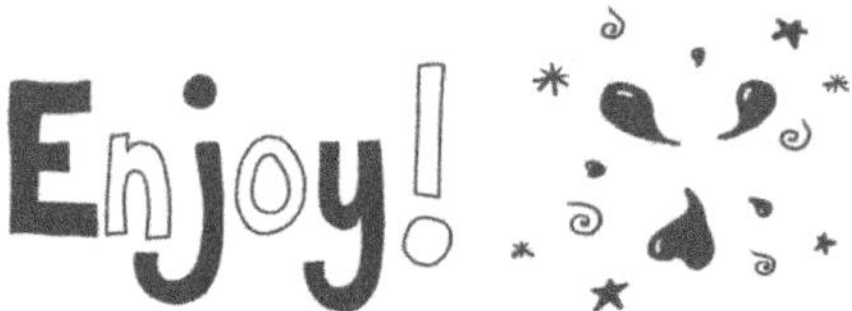

Create a final piece – print onto your background using your collagraph!

Use the collagraph to print onto the background in black paint or ink. Treat this as an iterative process. It is worth printing onto scrap paper first so you can make refinements to the collagraph in the moment. Have a glue gun on hand so if something needs adding to the collagraph it can be done there and then ready to print with. If a part of the collagraph does not work well, encourage children to evaluate and improve as they go. Make sure you keep the scrap paper attempts for the sketchbook as a brilliant way of demonstrating progression in artistic thinking!

Once this part is dry, encourage children to use some of the other printing techniques they learned in the Experiment stage to add any further blossom, birds or leaves to their branches!

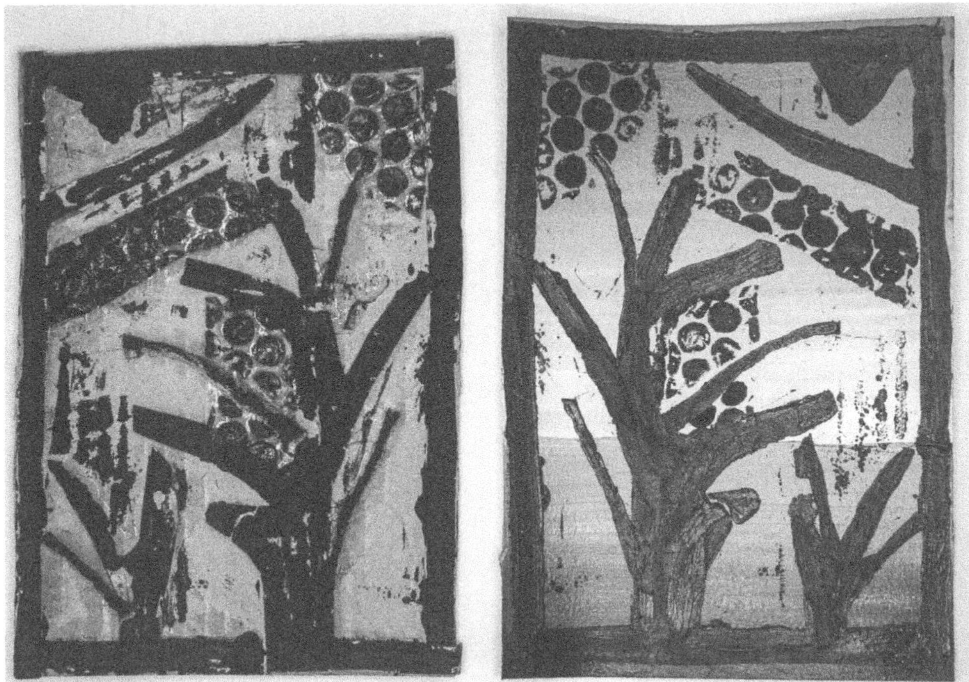

The image on the left is the original collagraph made with corrugated card and bubble wrap. The image on the right is the print transferred onto a pink and white gradient background using black printing ink.

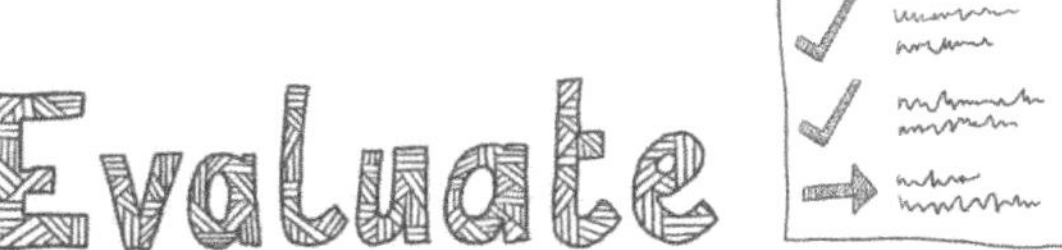

How did it go? Class and self-assessment

Class evaluation

As a class, discuss these questions:

- How were each of the printing marks made?
- Which textures are most effective?
- How could the picture have been improved further?

Self-evaluation

Ask children to annotate around their picture in their sketchbook.

- Which part of your collagraph worked best?
- Which part of your collagraph would you change, and how?
- How did your collagraph develop with every new part?

Lesson plan Lower Key Stage 2: How do colours work together?

Artist biography

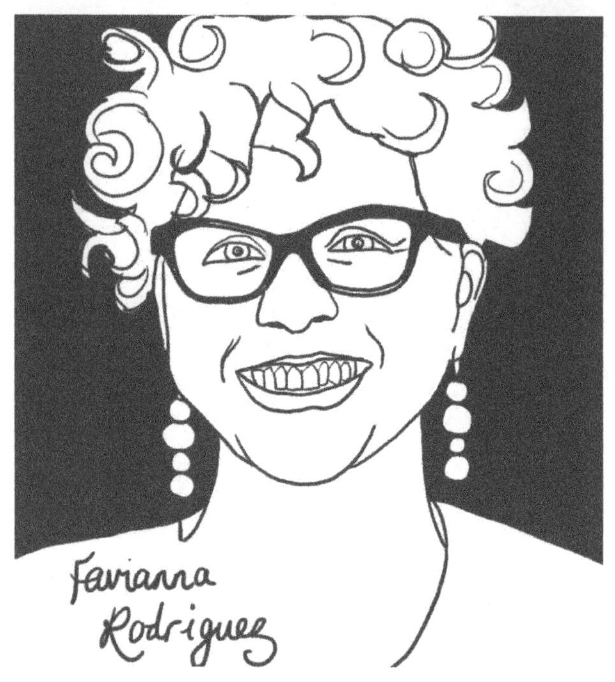

Favianna Rodriguez

Born:	1978
Died:	–
Birthplace:	California, USA
Discipline:	Printmaking, collage – social activism

Favianna Rodriguez was born in California to Peruvian parents. From a very early age it was obvious that Favianna had an artistic talent. She entered and won art competitions and even made TV appearances to share her work! She always wanted to pursue art as a career but she felt pressure from others to follow a more 'prestigious' career as a doctor or an engineer.

Much of Favianna's work is intertwined with her social and political activism, and she uses her art to send a message about injustice. This interest was born from growing up in a largely Latino neighbourhood and witnessing firsthand the prejudice and discrimination that existed towards her own community.

Favianna's first job in art was as a poster designer, and this bold, vibrant and punchy style is still highly visible in her work today. Her art still employs contrasting colours and strong shapes as she addresses a range of issues, including racism, immigration and women's rights.

Favianna is an activist and has founded many organisations that encourage artists to use their work to challenge the status quo and speak out against injustice.

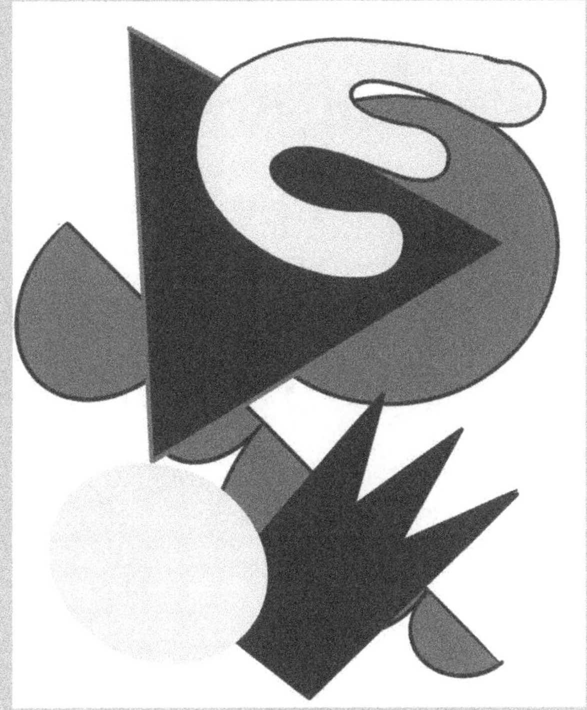

Find out more

Website: https://favianna.com/

Instagram: www.instagram.com/Favianna1

Images to inspire

Have a look at these series:

Intersectionality (2018)

Silence Breakers (2018)

Freedom (2017)

Lani Shaw (2017)

Other artist links

Karen Lederer: Karen uses bright vibrant colours to create pictures.

Benjie Torrado Cabrera: Benjie carves into his prints to create interesting fine lines and patterns.

Henri Matisse: The shapes included in Matisse's collages have similarities with the printed shapes used in Favianna's colourful work.

'Art is always an expression of a human experience.'

Favianna Rodriguez (Ben & Jerry's, 2018)

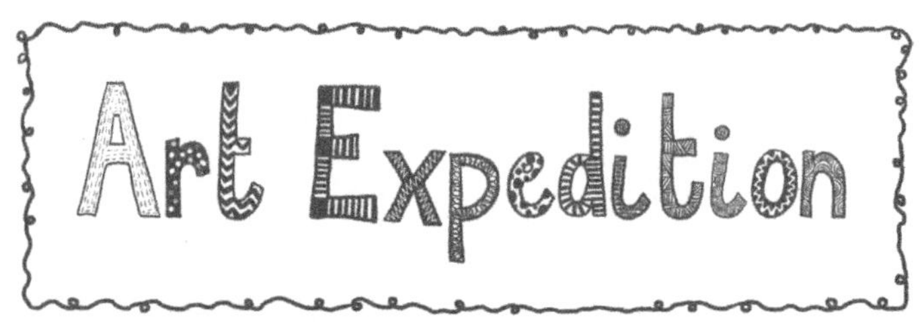

Favianna Rodriguez • Lower Key Stage 2
How do colours work together?

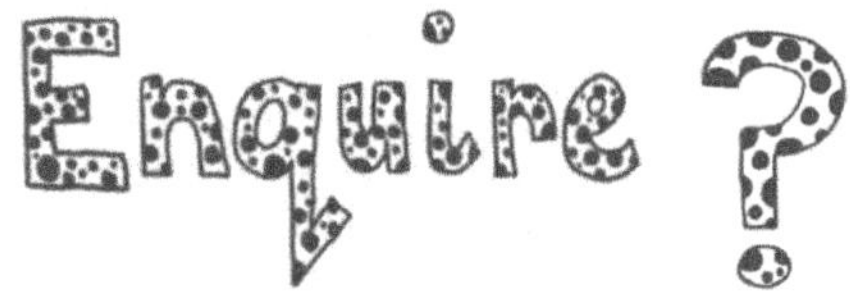

Do children have preconceived ideas of colours that 'go together'? Can they think of colour combinations in their own lives that they feel work effectively or otherwise? Can children identify any types of colour? For example, clashing, vibrant, pastel or iridescent. What are their favourite colours and why?

Signpost: Through this project, we will be experimenting with different colours and shapes to create vibrant, layered prints.

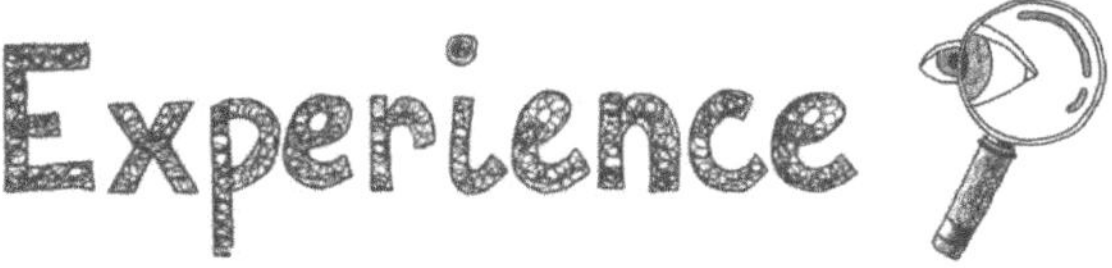

On a sketchbook page, encourage children to experiment with colour.

Show children a colour wheel and revise colour mixing. Show children how colours on opposite sides of the wheel are 'complementary' and work well to make each other stand out. The adjacent colours on the wheel are 'analogous' and work in harmony together.

Give children poster (or even better, acrylic) paints in primary colours. Encourage the children to mix the colours to create new colours of their own, which can be painted as swatches in their sketchbook. Ask them to annotate as they go, to record how they made each of the new colours. They could also try to use some of the colour wheel vocabulary above to further their understanding. Encourage the children to create lots of different colours on their palette. Using a piece of card as a palette that can be dried out, kept and stuck in sketchbooks as a record of their artistic process is a great idea, as well as saving on washing up!

Once lots of colours have been created, ask children to create colour combinations and comment on how well they work together. Children could make statements such as:

- These colours remind me of...
- This colour makes this colour look...
- I like this combination because...
- This combination doesn't work because....

The idea is to encourage children to create a collection of their own colours that they feel work well together as a set.

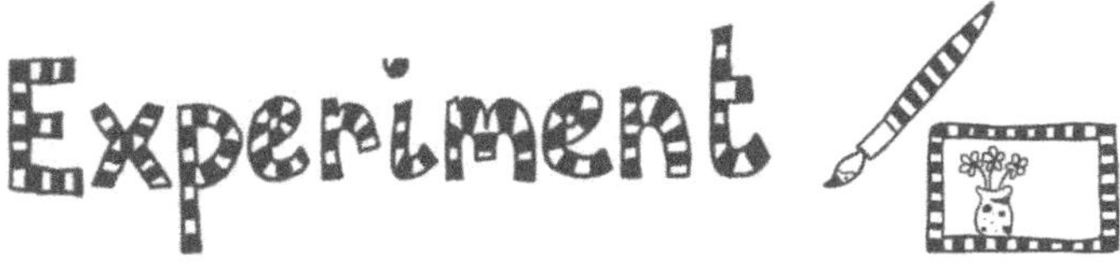

Look at the work of Favianna Rodriguez – learn how to create colourful monoprints.

Show children the colourful works of Favianna Rodriguez. Although some of her works are collages, the patterns and colours that she uses to create these are monoprints.

Give children time to experiment with their own prints as they learn how to create different effects. They could create posters exploring an issue that the children feel passionately about (see Favianna's protest art) or simply use the time to explore and enjoy a new technique. The ideal printing technique for this session is gelli printing, which involves taking prints from gelatine sheets. These can be quite expensive to buy (although they are amazing if you have the budget!), so here is an inexpensive alternative.

Laminate enough sheets of A4 card for the whole class to have one each. Use a roller to roll a thin layer of acrylic paint over the sheet and then place a piece of paper face down on top of the paint layer to remove the print. This will transfer the paint onto the paper. This basic technique can then be manipulated to create all sorts of interesting effects.

- Roll the layer of paint, then make marks into it using different tools before you print onto the paper.
- After rolling the paint layer, cut out paper stencils and place them on the paint. When you print onto the paper, the areas covered by the stencils will be left white.
- Press into the paint layer with interesting textures (bubble wrap, feathers, string, etc.) to create different patterns that will transfer when the paper is laid on top.
- Apply multiple colours and roll them together to create different paint effects.
- To create shapes like in Favianna's work, cut a stencil out of paper, so that only paint within the cut-out shape is transferred to the paper.

Because you are using such a thin layer of acrylic, the sheets will dry very quickly allowing you to apply multiple effects onto one sheet. Using the stencils to block the paint will allow you to see the different designs through each layer.

When all the papers are dry, encourage children to cut out small sections that best exemplify the effect they were trying to achieve, so that these can be stuck in sketchbooks with annotations. Make sure children reflect on the effectiveness of each attempt to inform the Evolve stage. Keep the offcuts for future collage projects!

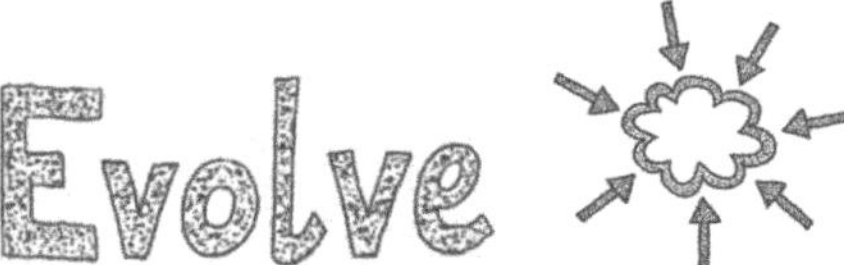

Children design their finished monoprint in the style of Favianna Rodriguez.

Look back at Favianna's work, in particular her 'Intersectionality' series where she layers colours and shapes on top of each other.

Ask children to plan their own print on one sheet of paper. This will require careful planning, thinking about the use of stencils so that layers underneath will still be exposed through subsequent applications of paint.

Give children a storyboard style sheet to plan each layer of their print. Look back at the initial sketchbook page and choose colours based on the decisions that were made during the colour mixing exploration. It is important to consider the order of the layers and how that will impact the paint coverage.

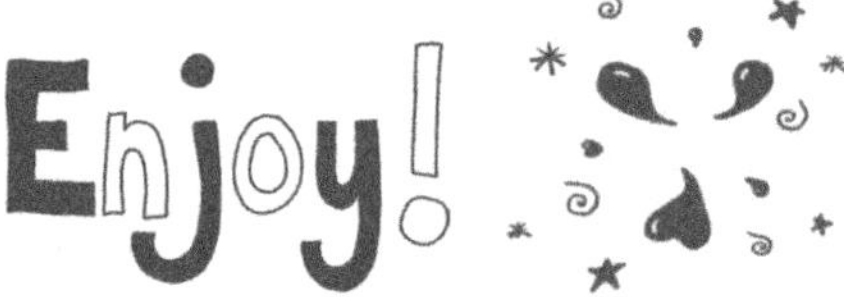

Create a final piece – print!

Children work through their design, completing each layer of print. This may need to be done over several sessions to ensure that each layer is dry, although if the acrylic paint is rolled thinly enough this should not be an issue. Having a hairdryer on hand is always a good idea for printing!

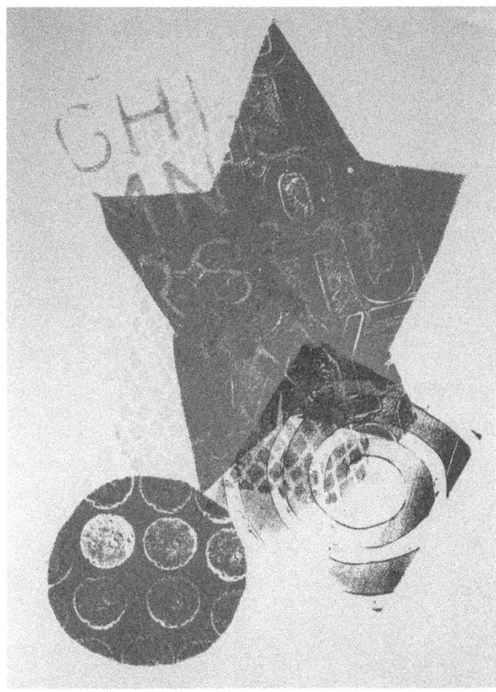

These shapes have been created by cutting stencils to leave only a specific shape of printing surface exposed. This surface was then given a pattern using bubble wrap, corks, net and letter stencils to create interesting textures to each layer.

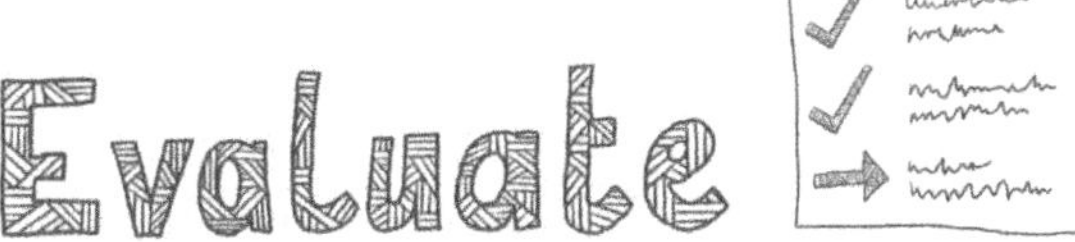

How did it go? Peer and self-assessment

Peer evaluation

Ask children to look at each other's work and deconstruct the process through discussion.

- Look carefully at the work. Can you describe the process the artist has gone through?
- Which layer was most effective?
- What tip would you give the artist for next time?

Self-evaluation

Ask children to annotate around their print in their sketchbook.

- Which layer worked best?
- Did any of the layers turn out differently than you expected?
- Look back at your design. How would you modify your plan?

Lesson plan Upper Key Stage 2: What does it mean to be free?

Artist biography

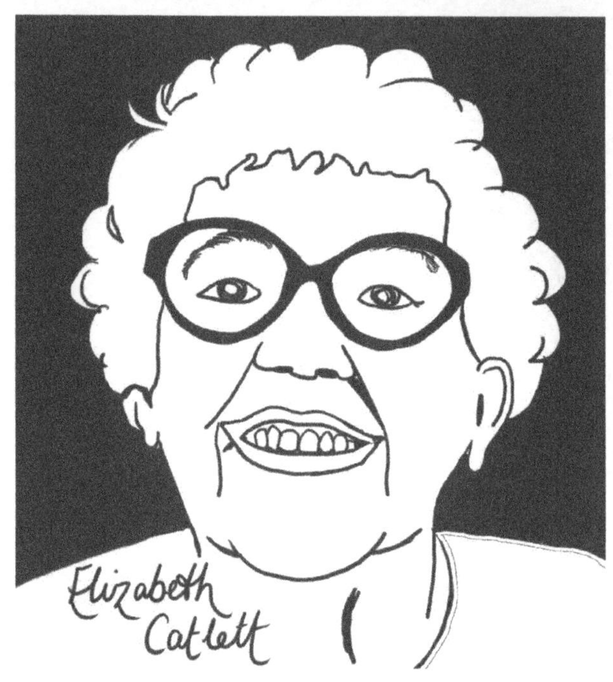

Elizabeth Catlett

Born:	1915
Died:	2012
Birthplace:	Washington DC, USA
Discipline:	Sculpture and printmaking – cubism

Elizabeth Catlett was a Black American artist whose grandparents were freed enslaved people. She grew up hearing stories from her grandmother about the oppression of her family and the atrocities endured by enslaved people. Elizabeth's mother had to work several jobs to provide for the family as her husband had died before Elizabeth was even born.

Elizabeth always showed an interest in art and was inspired by a wood carving that her father had left behind when he died. Although it was an unlikely career choice for a Black woman at the time, Elizabeth trained in art at university with a view to becoming a teacher. Whilst studying at university, Elizabeth was not permitted to live on campus due to the colour of her skin, so she had no choice but to rent a room and travel in for her studies each day.

For much of Elizabeth's life, she was a teacher, but in 1946 she was invited to Mexico to join a collective art and mural workshop. This is where her career really began.

Encouraged to create art about what she cared about, Elizabeth began portraying Black American people, including women, children and significant figures throughout history. Her prints often centre on the human struggle against poverty and the empowerment of women.

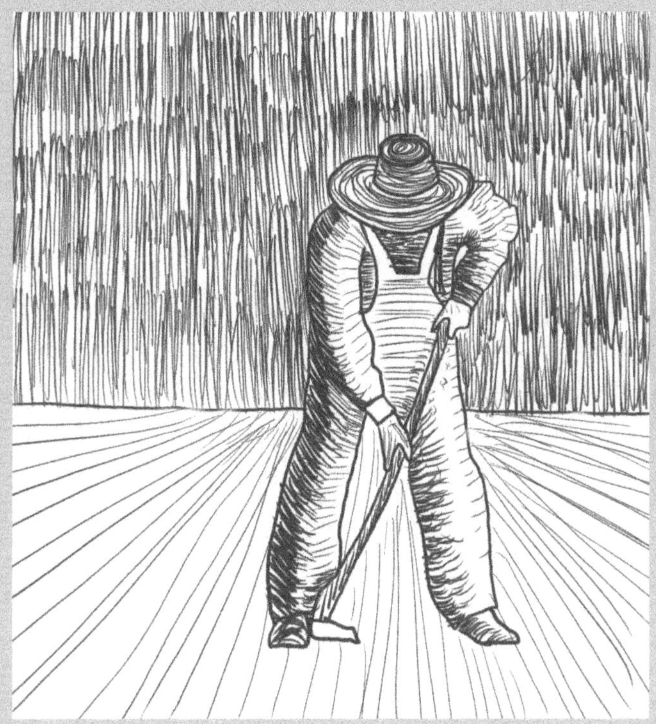

Find out more

Artnet: www.artnet.com/artists/elizabeth-catlett/

MOMA: www.moma.org/artists/1037

BBC: www.bbc.co.uk/programmes/b09tf0d8

Images to inspire

Chile 1 (1980)

Pan (1952)

Sharecropper (1952)

I Have Special Reservations (1946)

In Harriet Tubman I Helped Hundreds to Freedom (1946)

Other artist links

Henry Moore: Henry's images of sheep and the underground employ monochrome mark making to give depth to his images.

Charlie Mackesy: Charlie uses gestural mark making to create images of animals and people.

Vincent van Gogh: Vincent used mark making in his preparatory sketches which translated into his gestural brush strokes.

'Art is only important to the extent that it aids in the liberation of our people.'

Elizabeth Catlett (CHR, 2016)

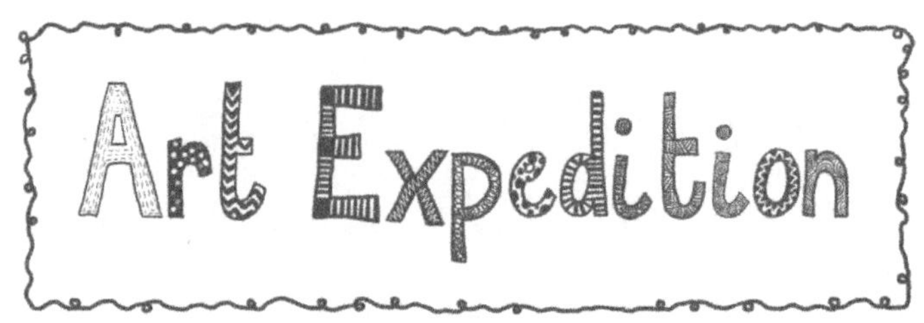

Elizabeth Catlett • Upper Key Stage 2
What does it mean to be free?

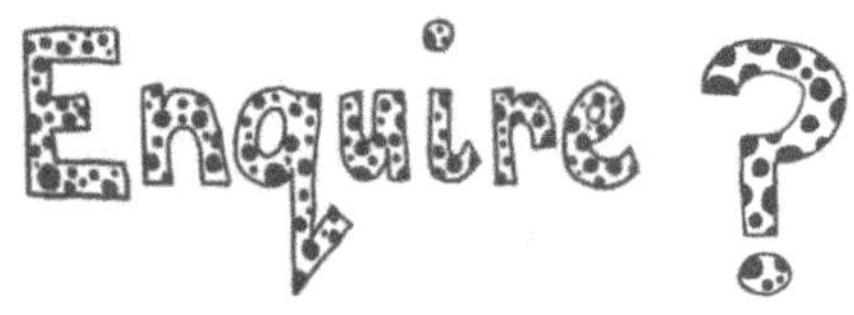

Can children define freedom? What does freedom mean in their own lives? What about on a global scale? How has access to 'freedom' changed throughout history? Is freedom always a positive thing?

Signpost: Through this project, we will be creating lino prints of important historical figures who have stood up for justice.

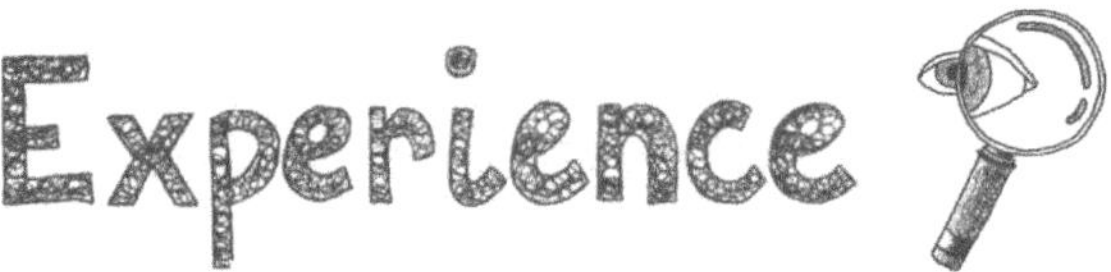

Ask children to research figures from history who have fought for freedom and represent them artistically.

Give children photos of a range of different historical figures who have fought for freedom and equality. Try to consider figures who have fought for a range of different causes. You can select your own, or even better, follow any threads that the children might have discussed in the Enquire phase. Some suggested famous people could be:

- Harriet Tubman
- Martin Luther King Jr.
- Nelson Mandela
- Emmeline Pankhurst
- Winston Churchill
- Chief Joseph

- Boudicca
- Olive Morris
- Claudia Jones
- Malala Yousafzai.

Give children photographs but no information. What can they deduce about the person just from looking closely?

In sketchbooks, choose one picture to stick in and encourage children to make multiple quick sketches of their chosen person using different media.

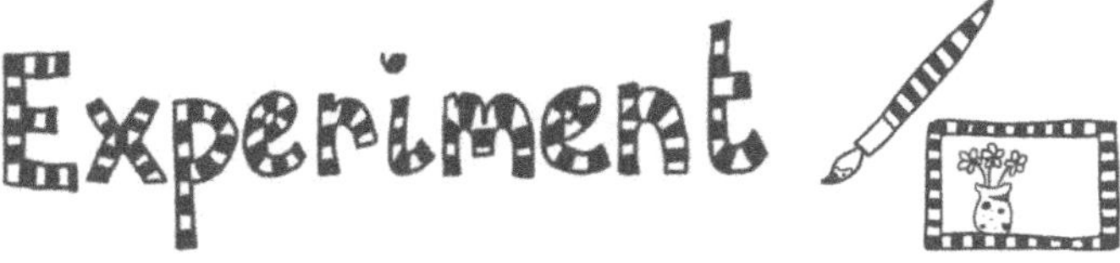

Look at the work of Elizabeth Catlett – how does she use mark making in her prints?

Show children a range of prints by Elizabeth Catlett. Look at the way that she makes marks to enhance her designs. Can the children deduce how these prints have been made from looking at the marks?

Encourage children to notice how the marks made as part of the lino cutting process have been purposely left as part of the finished image.

This learning expedition would ideally be done with lino, but could easily be achieved with polystyrene foam if you prefer. Upper Key Stage 2 children should be able to use soft lino safely, as long as they are taught to place their supporting hand behind the tool they are cutting with.

Give children a small piece of either lino or polystyrene foam (this needs to be whatever children will use to create their final piece). Encourage children to make different marks in the surface to practise their control of the different tools. Then print the marks into the sketchbook using black printing ink.

Encourage the children to make multiple prints so that they have a chance to experiment with different loads of paint to get a clear and crisp image.

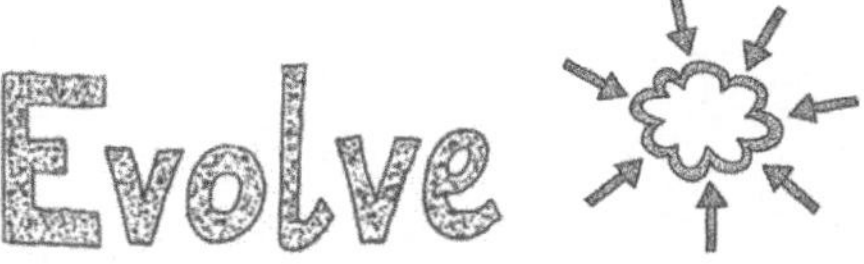

Children design their finished print in the style of Elizabeth Catlett.

Look back at Elizabeth Catlett's work. How does she use marks to accentuate the shape of her subject's faces and bodies? How does she use marks to make the backgrounds stand out? Make sure children recognise that the white marks are where the lino (polystyrene foam) has been cut away and the black marks are created by the surface left behind.

Children design their own print of their chosen historical figure from the Experience phase. Think about the marks that will be used to cut away each surface. Children should create their design on tracing paper or paper depending on how the image will be transferred to the lino. This could be done by tracing a photocopied image of the person's face and then adding the marks on, or it could be drawn from scratch.

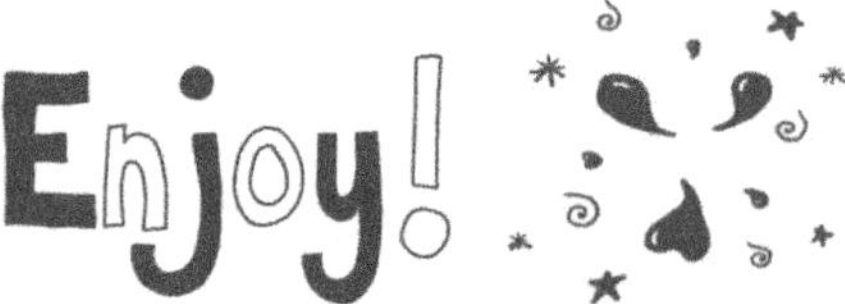

Print a final piece!

If you have used tracing paper, take the design from the Evolve phase and turn it face down onto the lino. Scribble on the back so that the image is transferred to the surface as a guide for cutting. If you have used paper, then use carbon paper to transfer.

If you are using polystyrene foam, then place the tracing paper design onto the polystyrene foams and carve straight through the paper onto the polystyrene foam with a sharp pencil.

Carve the design into the surface and add different marks to develop the contours of the face and the background.

Then roll on black ink and print the final design! Don't be afraid to print more than once to get the most effective outcome.

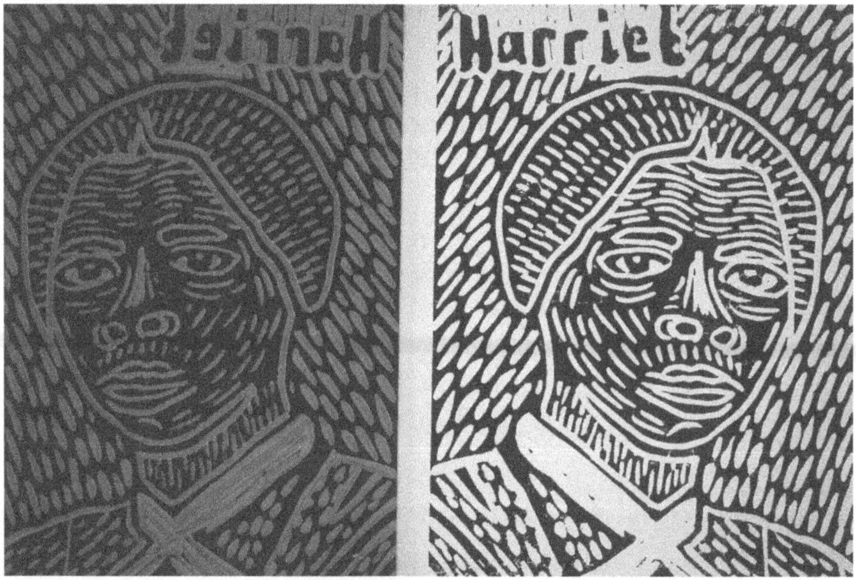

The image on the left is the original soft-lino cut of Harriet Tubman. This child then used simplistic marks to carve out the features of Harriet's face, which were then rolled with black printing ink and transferred to white cartridge paper (right image). Don't fear the lino – the results are well worth it!

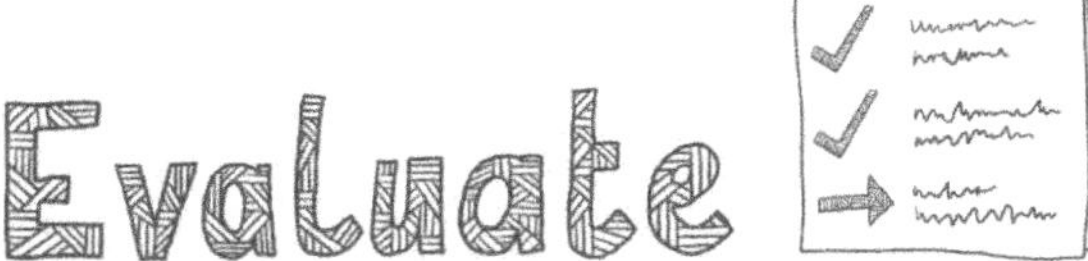

How did it go? Peer and self-assessment

Peer evaluation

Ask children to discuss their final piece, looking at both the paper prints and the original carving. Ask children to compare the way that the original carving has transferred in terms of the marks made and the effectiveness of the final print.

- How has the artist used mark making?
- Where does the carving work most effectively?
- Can you suggest any areas for future development?

Self-evaluation

Ask children to annotate around their print in their sketchbook.

- How well has the image printed?
- Where is the most effective use of marks?
- How could you develop your printing skills further?

Chapter 8
Textiles

Introduction to textiles

Incorporating textiles into your primary art curriculum is a fantastic way to challenge children's preconceptions of art and artists. Historically, textile art was seen as 'women's work' and carried a far lowlier status to that of 'fine art', which was typically the domain of White, Western men. This myth has also been perpetuated by our education system where girls used to learn sewing whilst boys learned woodwork. Even now, uptake for Textiles GCSE (if you are lucky enough to find a secondary school that still offers this) is overwhelmingly female.

Raising the profile of textiles is fundamental if we want to redress the gender imbalance that exists in art. Part of this is helping children recognise that there is so much more to fibre art than just sewing running stitch into binca squares (This is a core memory from my childhood – do you remember the colourful fabric with pre-prepared holes as part of the weave? I spent many dismal hours practising my cross stitch with embroidery thread in my Year 3 class at primary school. I am hoping that your experience of textile education was more dynamic!). Textile processes are colourful, exciting, unpredictable and fun: everything we want primary art to be! There are many pioneering male and female artists who have put their own unique take on textiles that are both contemporary and highly engaging for all children.

Textiles are also an incredible way to connect children to their own identities. The history of most cultures are illustrated in the colours, patterns and designs of their traditional fabrics, and yet the artists responsible for these are largely anonymous. Shining a light onto artists who create and use these designs, whether that be makers of traditional Nigerian Ankara fabric or the Persian-Scottish hybrid we now call paisley, creates deep connections with our own histories through pattern and colour.

One of the barriers to textiles work in primary school can be the cost of resources. It is always worth planning a project with plenty of time to see if donations can be sourced from the school community. Putting out an annual plea for unwanted sheets, old clothes and left-over yarn will usually give you a starting point for some interesting projects. If not, charity shops can be a treasure trove of items that can be repurposed for a textile activity at a fraction of the price it costs to buy from an educational supplier. In doing so, you can also keep your projects dynamic and open-ended. By restricting children's choices to what they already have access to, we allow them to creatively make decisions about how they want their art to be, rather than serving it on a plate.

Textile ideas to try

There are many different textile projects that work well in primary schools. Most of these can be adapted depending on the age of the children, your budget and the amount of time you have. Here are some of my favourites, with a few ideas about how they can be implemented to get the most out of your project.

Printing

Children can print directly onto any fabric using fabric paint or just using standard acrylics if you do not plan to wash the project. Have a look at Chapter 7 (Printing) for some ideas of ways that screen printing, polystyrene foam prints and collagraphs could be used to create designs on your fabric.

Weaving

There is much more to weaving than the cardboard looms that you can buy from educational suppliers (although these are brilliant too!). If you search online, there are many patterns where children weave to create different designs beyond the basic in-out-in-out weave, using both the warp and the weft to develop different surfaces. Have a look at the work of Anni Albers for inspiration here. So many different things can be used as looms to take weaving to a new level. Chicken wire, outdoor fencing, plastic crates and nails in wood can all provide the uprights to weave through. Also, sticks tied together at the centre, or circles of card with string threaded through slots cut in the edges can be used to create circular, radial weaves that look incredibly effective.

Batik

Batik is the process of using wax as a resist to fabric dyes. Traditionally, hot wax would be poured to create the lines, using a small tool called a tjanting. With supervision, this is a wonderful art activity to do with children as the results are stunning. You can buy wax pellets or just collect old candles and melt them in a bowl over a pan of hot water. Once the wax has set, apply the fabric paint, dye, ink or food colouring. When the whole thing is dry, the wax can be removed by sandwiching your project between pieces of newspaper and ironing them.

There are other ways in which the effect of batik can be achieved. You can buy cold batik fluid that can be used straight from the bottle, still getting the fun of using a tjanting but without the burn hazard. This can then be washed away with hot water after the colour has been applied.

You could also give children PVA glue in small bottles and allow them to pour the glue directly onto the fabric to provide the resist. This takes longer to dry but is a very cheap alternative. Most PVA glues wash away easily with hot water, but I would recommend trying a sample with your chosen brand of glue first before attempting this with a class of 30!

Silk painting

Silk painting is very similar to batik except it is guttering that is used to prevent the colours running together. This special paint comes in many beautiful colours such as gold and silver, and remains on the finished piece as part of the artwork.

Note: when painting both silk and batik, it is imperative that the fabric being painted is not in contact with anything, otherwise the colour will spread via the surface underneath the wax resist or the guttering. You can buy frames to remedy this or staple the fabric to an old picture frame. Another inexpensive hack is to secure the fabric with a rubber band over an ice cream tub so that the painting surface is suspended over a hollow area.

Felt

Wet felting is a really easy art discipline for children to learn where beautiful results can be achieved incredibly easily. Wool tops (the raw material from which the felt is created) can be bought in class sets for less than you think, and a little really does go a long way. Just lay a thin layer of wool onto a piece of bubble wrap and spray with a mix of water and washing up liquid. Then add layers with the threads at right angles to the previous layer each time. Keep spraying the layers and working them by kneading them together with your knuckles. Keep the fabric nice and wet with the soapy mixture. Once all the layers are added, roll up the bubble wrap with the felt still attached and roll to apply pressure. Plenty of this and soon you will have created a beautiful felt masterpiece that can be hung out to dry!

Tie dye

Tie dye is an old favourite but so much fun! This works best with natural fabrics, so a donation of a couple of white cotton bed sheets would be enough to make some incredibly beautiful designs. Experiment with string and rubber bands to provide the traditional white patterns. You can apply the dye from squeezy bottles or diluted in a bucket (you can get bottles pre-filled with dye for ease, or create your own). Leave the dye on the fabric as long as possible for the most vibrant results.

Make your own natural dyes

The majority of the projects listed here require some kind of fabric colouring, so a wonderful way to take a project to the next level is to involve the children in the process of making their own dyes. There are many natural dyes that are incredibly effective. Just chop vegetables (see examples that follow), bring them to the boil in water, simmer for an hour, then let the mixture cool. Then, the vegetable matter can be removed and the remaining liquid is your homemade dye! If you add a cup of white wine vinegar to every four cups of dye, you will create a more concentrated colour.

Here are some great ideas to try.

Vegetable dyes

- beetroot (purple and bright pink)
- red onion skins (pink)
- white onion skins (yellow)
- red cabbage (blue).

Spice dyes

Use roughly three tablespoons per cup of water.

- curry powder (orange)
- turmeric (yellow)
- chilli powder (red/orange).

With natural dyes, it is important to remember that they are unlikely to survive a machine wash in the same way as chemical dyes, but they will work brilliantly for purely aesthetic projects and can be used to great effect as fabric paints. Just give the dye as much time as possible in contact with the fabric and you will be able to create some incredible pieces with your class!

Lesson plans

All three of the artists in the following lesson plans use textiles in innovative ways. You can adapt each art expedition to work for you and your class. Hopefully the different techniques will also inspire you to create some exciting journeys of your own!

Lesson plan Key Stage 1: Can rubbish be beautiful?

Artist biography

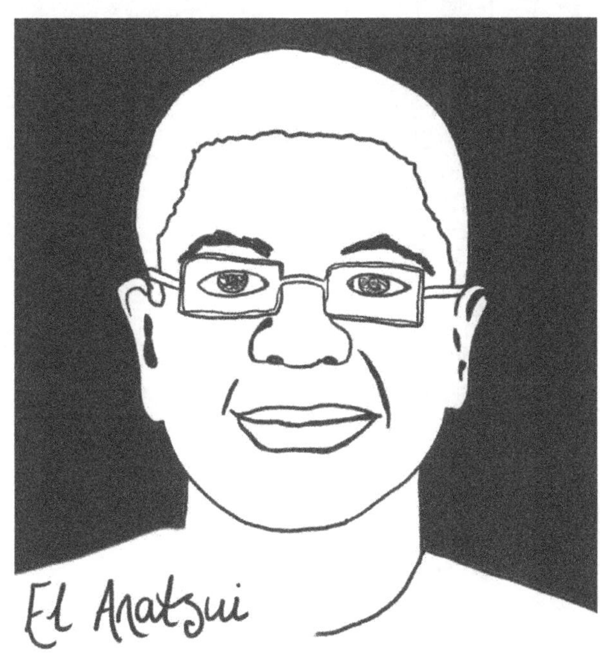

El Anatsui

Born:	1944
Died:	–
Birthplace:	Anyako, Ghana
Discipline:	Sculpture and textiles – contemporary

El Anatsui was born in Ghana, the youngest one of 32 brothers and sisters! He studied art at university where he specialised in producing wooden sculptures that were inspired by the cultural heritage of his home.

El Anatsui went on to achieve international fame for his iconic tapestries from found objects such as bottle caps. He explores the idea of bringing rubbish together to make something so beautiful that it suggests royalty. His enormous tapestries weave these found materials together with copper wire to create shimmering surfaces that catch the light.

Due to the mixture of materials used in El Anatsui's work, his work is hard to classify. His tapestries have many parallels with mosaics, painting and sculpture, as well as textiles.

The use of bottle caps goes beyond turning something perceived as rubbish into something beautiful. El Anatsui talks about recycling as something that for some communities is a necessity not a luxury. His work also suggests that human life itself is something that constantly evolves and changes, just like the pieces of El Anatsui's tapestries.

El Anatsui works with large teams of assistants who painstakingly sew the pieces of metal together to create panels that are then arranged and rearranged to create interesting patterns. Some of El Anatsui's tapestries are over 5 metres long!

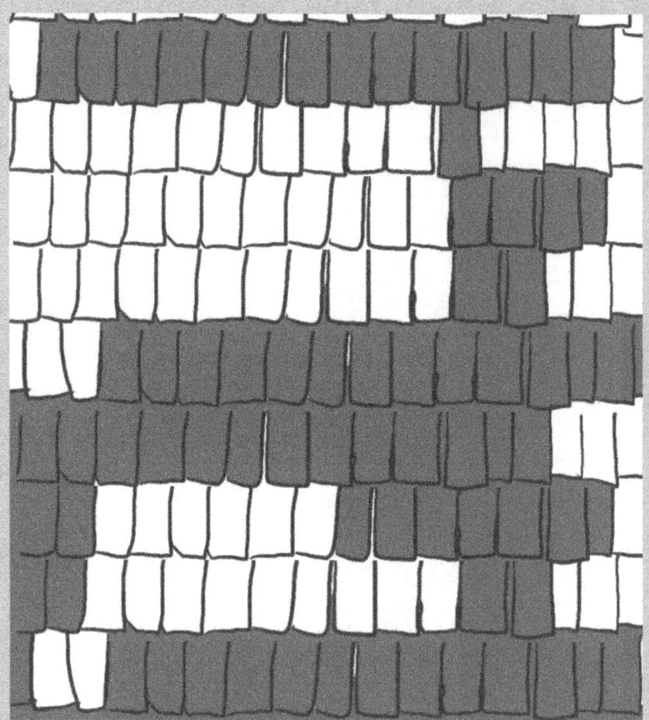

Find out more

Tate website: www.tate.org.uk/whats-on/tate-modern/el-anatsui

Website: https://elanatsui.art/

Images to inspire	**Other artist links**
Straying Continents (2010)	**Vanessa Barragão:** Vanessa creates beautiful, ocean-inspired tapestries using waste from the textile industries.
Bleeding Takari (2007)	**Jo Atherton:** Jo collects rubbish from rivers and combines found objects to create beautiful, colourful montages.
Many Came Back (2005)	**Guerra de la Paz:** Guerra collects discarded clothes and reassembles them to make large, three-dimensional sculptures.

'The poverty of the materials used in no way precludes the telling of rich and wonderful stories.'

El Anatsui (October Gallery, n.d.)

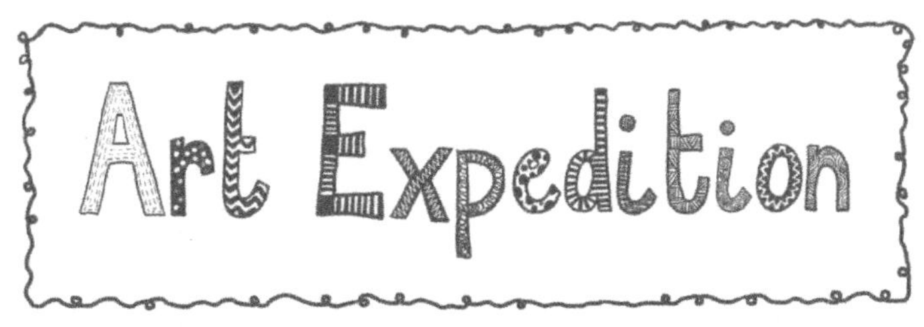

El Anatsui • Key Stage 1
Can rubbish be beautiful?

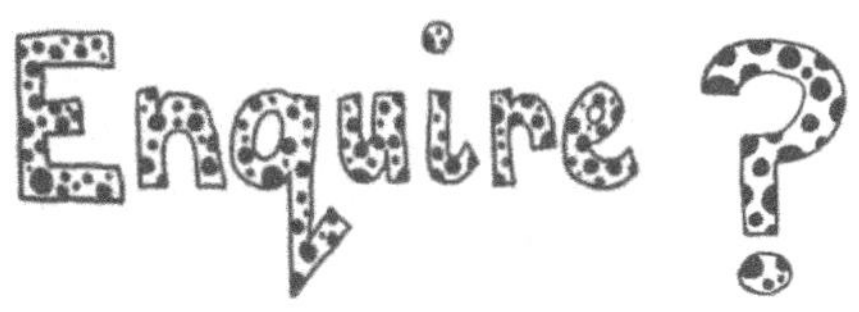

Ask the children to list the things that they consider to be beautiful. How do they know when they see something beautiful? How does it make them feel?

Signpost: Through this project, we will be using threading to turn rubbish into something beautiful.

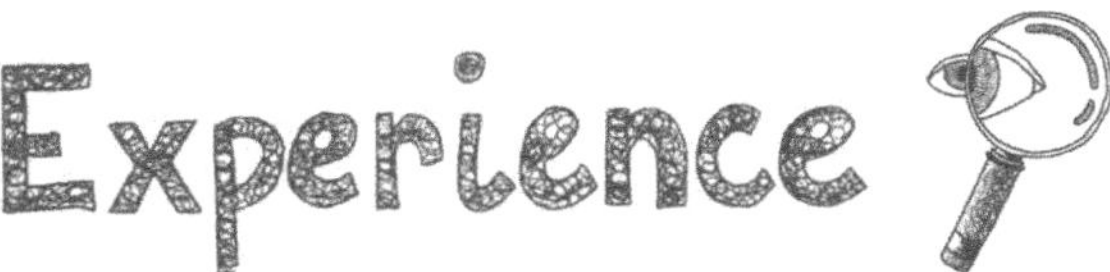

Give children pieces of packaging, recycling or rubbish to explore in their sketchbooks.

You might decide you want to have a consistent theme for children to explore, so that within the final piece, children are working with the same materials. Examples that work well with this project are:

- crisp packets
- fabric (ask children to donate old clothes)
- cereal boxes
- carrier bags.

Or you may decide to leave it open and let each child decide on the 'rubbish' they would like to explore.

Remind children of the question: Can they find aspects of the 'rubbish' that are beautiful or interesting? Encourage children to sketch and collage using the material as inspiration. It might be copying logos or looking for repeating patterns. They might also be able to use collage to create something new from the patterns and shapes that exist on the different surfaces. Maybe they could see how many different colours they can find and create a colour wheel from collaged materials?

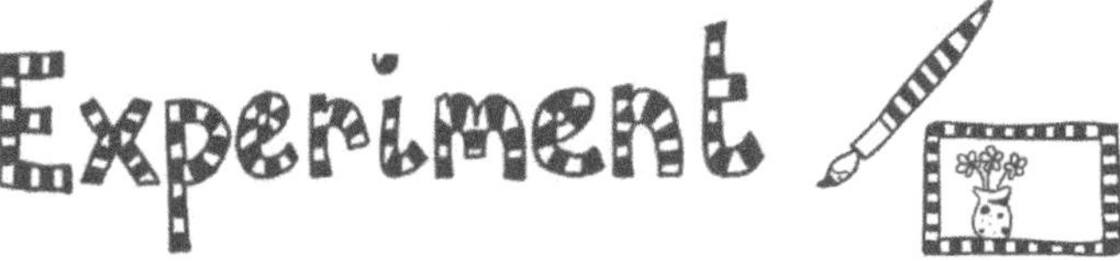

Experiment with ways of joining materials – give different options for 'sewing'.

Introduce children to the work of El Anatsui. Encourage them to look at his large-scale tapestries and suggest words to describe what they can see. Then ask children to look more closely at his work and the materials that he uses. Explain that you are going to 'sew' sections of the chosen 'rubbish' into a beautiful tapestry in the style of El Anatsui. These will be individual pieces that are then combined to create a whole class extravaganza – the perfect example of the sum being even greater than its parts!

What makes El Anatsui's work so interesting is the way he joins materials so that each piece can still move independently. This adds to the shimmering quality that is fundamental to his style.

Give children different materials and tools so that they can experiment with joining materials through threading. The aim is to thread sections of the material to create a line of 'bunting', which allows the materials some movement. Good options for threading could be:

- pipe cleaners
- embroidery thread and big-eyed needles
- hole punches
- wire
- string.

Encourage children to try different ways of joining two sections together and stick examples of each join into the sketchbook, annotating how effective the joining process was. This may be the point that children discover that some materials are easier to join when mounted onto paper or card first!

Note: an adaptation to this unit could be weaving. By wrapping string around a piece of card to create the warp, children could weave with strips of different found materials.

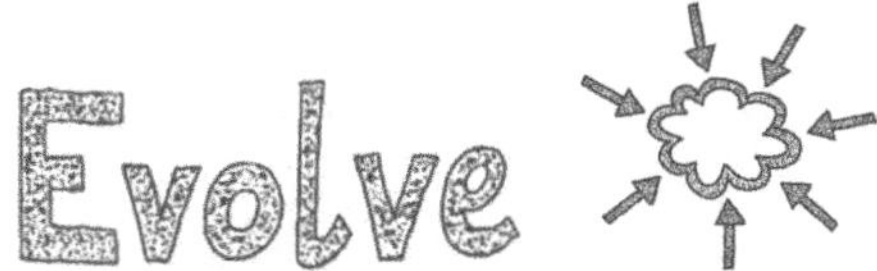

Create a collage, making choices about materials.

Begin to make decisions about the final piece. Using small sections of the materials that will be used, encourage children to make small collages that show how their line of panels will be arranged.

Encourage children to try out more than one idea. Will they use similar colours? A repeating pattern? How big will each panel be? (Children may wish to create a template so all sections are the same.) How will the sections be threaded? Include all this information on the sketchbook page.

Note: if you have chosen the weaving option, children could experiment with different weaving patterns as they choose the design of their final piece.

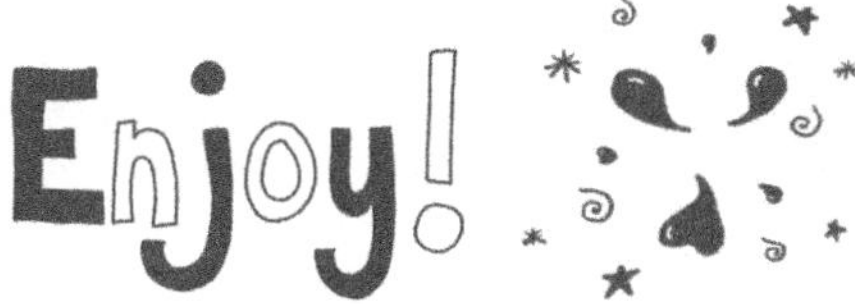

Create a final piece – a tapestry made from rubbish.

Children cut out their sections from the material and thread them onto lines to create interesting shapes and patterns from the 'rubbish' they have been given.

These lines of 'bunting' can then be displayed in parallel lines to create a class tapestry in the style of El Anatsui.

Take photos of the individual contributions and the class piece for sketchbooks.

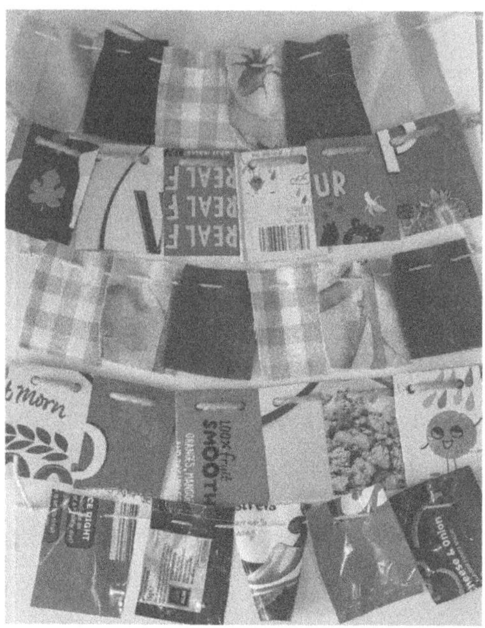

This piece has been created with a mixture of scraps of fabric, crisp packets and old packaging. Each piece has been woven onto thread in a repeating pattern to create a tapestry that is as interesting as it is beautiful!

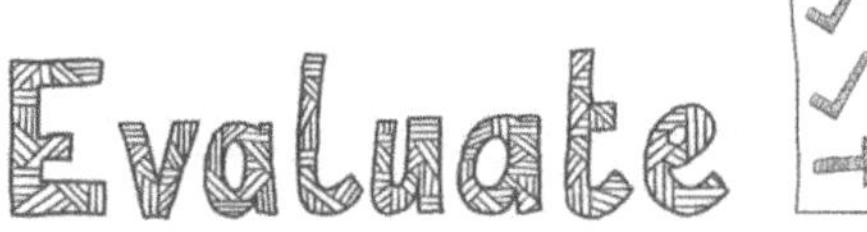

How did it go? Class and self-assessment

Class evaluation

As a class, discuss these questions:

- How do the individual final pieces work together?
- What other materials could we do this with?
- Have we created something beautiful?

Self-evaluation

Children could feedback the answers to these questions verbally to each other or an adult. Or they could form the basis of basic annotations in the sketchbook.

- What worked well about using this material?
- What was tricky about using this material?
- Can rubbish be beautiful?

Lesson plan Lower Key Stage 2: What can you do with a thread?

Artist biography

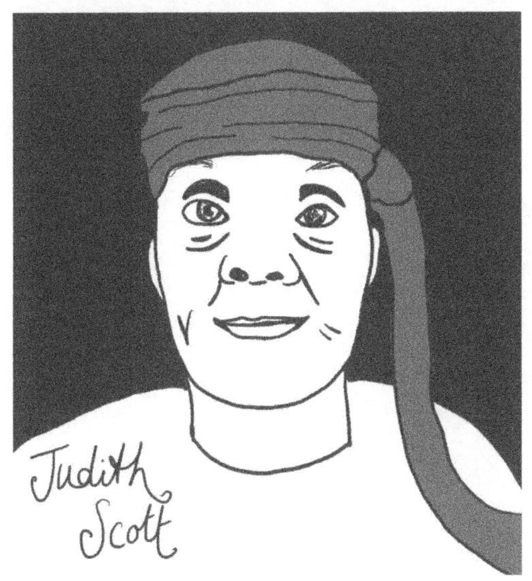

Judith Scott

Born:	1943
Died:	2005
Birthplace:	Cincinnati, USA
Discipline:	Fibre art and sculpture

Judith and Joyce Scott were twins, born to an American family in 1943. Unlike her sister, Judith was born with Down's syndrome and as a result of contracting scarlet fever as a child, Judith was also deaf.

Despite their parents trying to treat both girls equally, in 1950 it was advised that Judith was sent to an institution for people with learning disabilities when she failed to pass the entrance test required to attend her local school. Judith had been deemed 'uneducable', partly due to her deafness being undiagnosed. Judith's separation from her family was devastating for both children, who missed each other terribly.

In the institution, Judith was denied any kind of education. She became very withdrawn and her behaviour became increasingly erratic.

Despite this, Joyce never gave up on Judith and after 35 years, she became her legal guardian, bringing her home to live with her in California.

Judith showed little interest in the art classes she was enrolled in until she discovered fibre art. When the other students were sewing or embroidering, Judith instantly began winding and weaving the wool to create the sculptures she is best known for today.

During her lifetime, Judith received international recognition, working day in and day out to produce over 200 sculptures. Judith used a whole range of unusual materials to create these exciting and dynamic creations. Anything from shopping trolleys and tubing to bicycle wheels! Judith's work was considered so groundbreaking that she was given her own solo show at the Brooklyn Museum entitled 'Judith Scott: Bound and Unbound'.

Art became Judith's language and she used her pieces to communicate her imagination and creativity to the rest of the world.

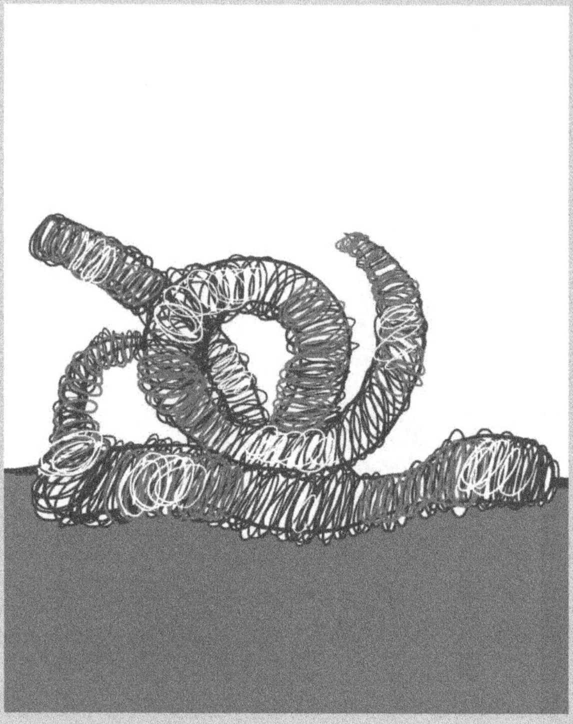

Find out more

Children's book:

Joyce Scott, Brie Spangler and Melissa Sweet, *Unbound: The Life + Art of Judith Scott*

More information:

www.textileartist.org/textile-artist-judith-scott-uncovering-innate-talent/

Images to inspire

Judith Scott's works are untitled, but here are a selection of her most famous ones:

www.artsy.net/artist/judith-scott

Other artist links

Eva Hesse: Eva created form by winding string around objects to suspend them and by tangling string into hanging forms like spiders' webs.

Sheila Hicks: Sheila winds wool and thread around fabric to create exciting, colourful sculptures.

Agata Oleksiak (Olek): Olek is a Polish-born fibre artist whose yarn bombing exploits are fantastic inspiration for children!

'Everything radiates its own beauty and an aliveness that seeks no approval, only celebrates itself.'

Joyce Scott (Scott, 2016)

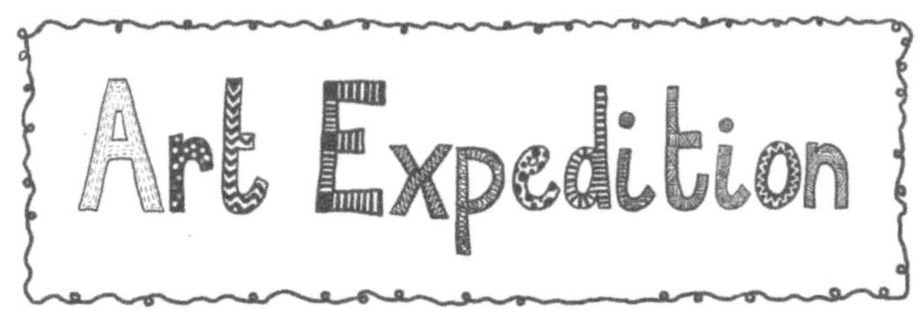

Judith Scott • Lower Key Stage 2
What can you do with a thread?

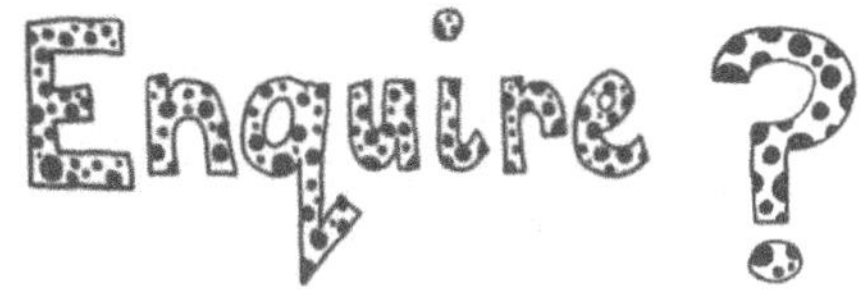

Ask the children to think about the different ways they have seen threads and string be used. Encourage them to think beyond art – when have they seen string and rope being used at home or in other situations?

Signpost: Through this project, we will be creating sculptures, experimenting with different threads.

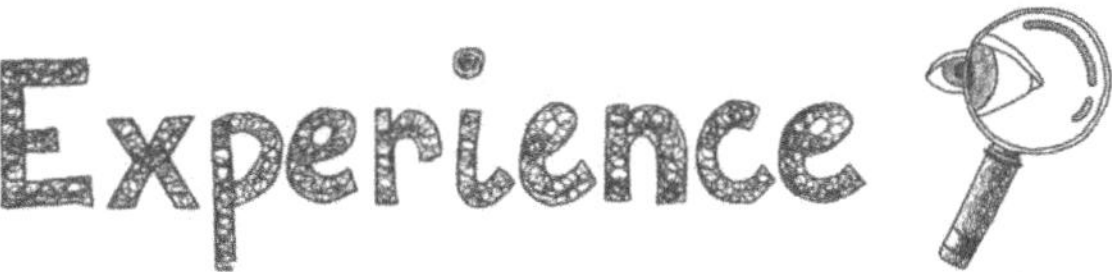

Give children a chance to experience and learn from each other using different kinds of fibre.

Give children a chance to share the skills that they may already have acquired when using thread. You may have some experts in knot-tying, you may have children who can crochet, finger-knit or knit. You may have children who can plait or make friendship bracelets. Give children time to share skills and teach each other new techniques. You may well learn something new too!

Put out lots of different threads for children to experiment with, for example:

- cotton
- elastic
- wool
- string
- rubber bands
- embroidery thread.

Encourage children to use the threads in as many ways as possible, and stick examples into sketchbooks with masking tape or PVA glue. Children might make different patterns with one thread, or combine different threads in different ways to make something new.

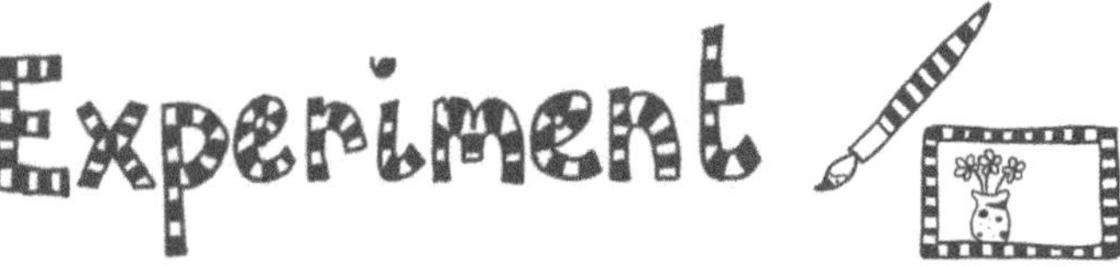

Experiment with wrapping and weaving inspired by Judith Scott.

Show children the work of Judith Scott, Eva Hesse, Olek and Sheila Hicks. Look at how they use fibre to wrap and weave to create 3D sculptures. Give the children a chance to experiment with this way of working. This will give them the opportunity to see how wrapping works with different types of thread – how easy it is to tie knots and how thick the threads work up when they are wrapped.

Also, give children access to things that they could incorporate into their wrappings, e.g. buttons, sequins, paper shapes.

Objects that might be fun to wrap at this stage could be:

- toy cars
- plastic animals or people
- dolls
- stationery, e.g. pencils, pencil sharpeners.

Make sure children realise that this stage is just experimentation, so try different ways of wrapping, photograph, unravel and try something new!

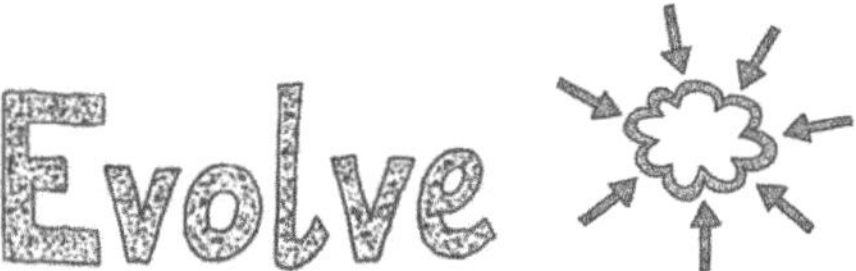

Design something original to be wrapped.

The frame for the children's final piece could be made from anything, just make sure that the maquette (small model) made at this stage is made from the same material as that used in the final piece. Children could plan to wrap shapes made from junk, clay or even LEGO®. I think wire works well for this and gives children opportunities to experiment with an often-new material. Copper wire is pliable with just fingers, but any wire will do if you have access to pliers.

Give children the wire and encourage them to design different shapes for their final piece in miniature. Encourage them to think about different angles and limbs that will create an interesting end shape, as well as giving plenty of options of places for the thread to be wrapped and secured.

Make sure that children have a chance to consider all aspects of their final piece by producing a maquette. This will equip them with the skills they need for the next stage.

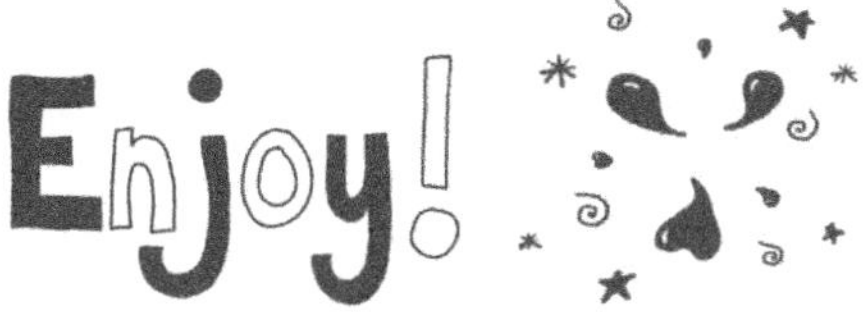

Create a final piece – a structure wrapped in thread.

Children create a structure from the medium rehearsed during the Evolve stage.

Then, using different threads in a selection of colours, encourage children to weave, twist and wrap to produce their own sculpture in the style of Judith Scott.

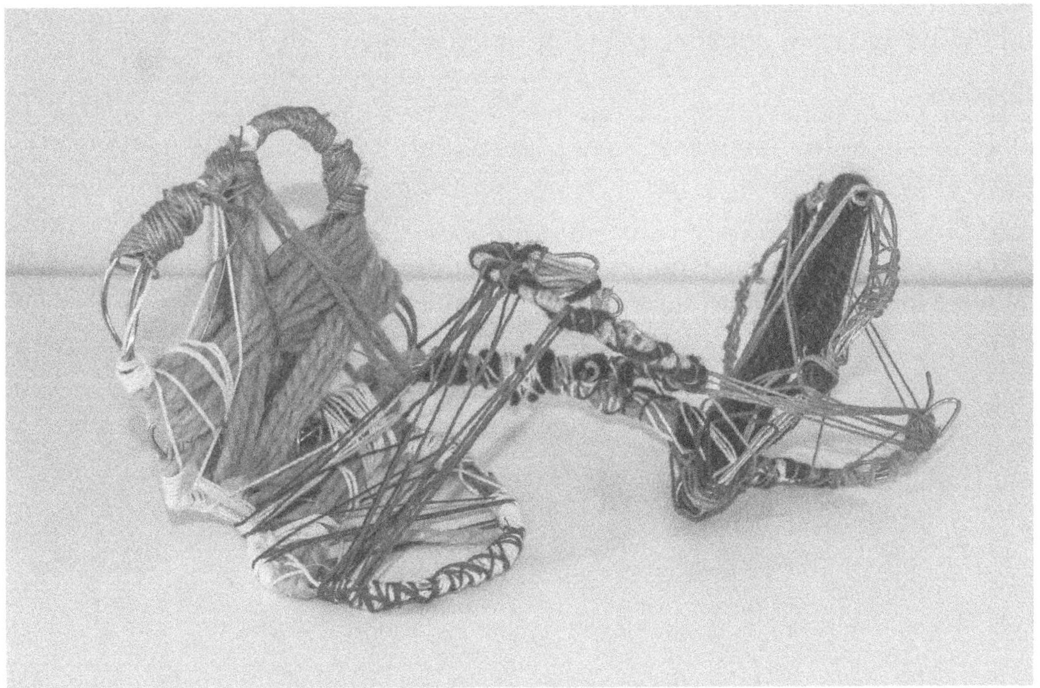

This sculpture was made from twisted wire which has been wrapped with wool, string and cotton. You will be amazed how therapeutic this process is – it is really difficult to know when to stop!

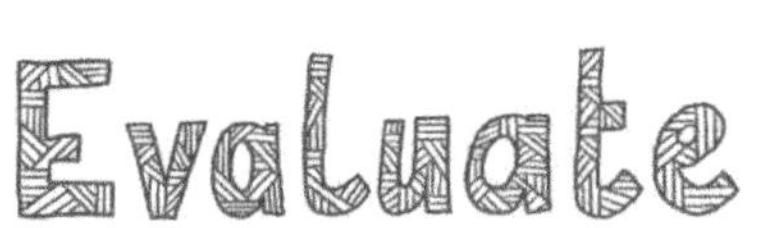

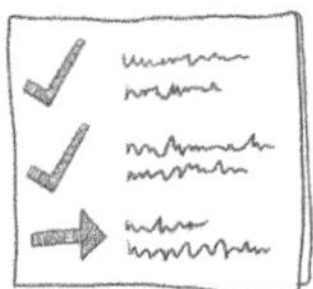

How did it go? Peer and self-assessment

Peer evaluation

Encourage the class to view all of the sculptures that have been produced and celebrate them with the artist. Here are some questions that might form the basis of some exciting conversation!

- Does the form of the sculpture remind you of anything?
- What works best about the sculpture?
- What could be added to enhance the sculpture further?

Self-evaluation

Ask children to add notes about their final piece as annotations around a photo of their final piece in their sketchbook.

- What did the initial structure of your sculpture look like?
- How did the sculpture evolve when thread was added?
- In what ways did the sculpture turn out as you expected?

Lesson plan Upper Key Stage 2: Why do we come together?

Artist biography

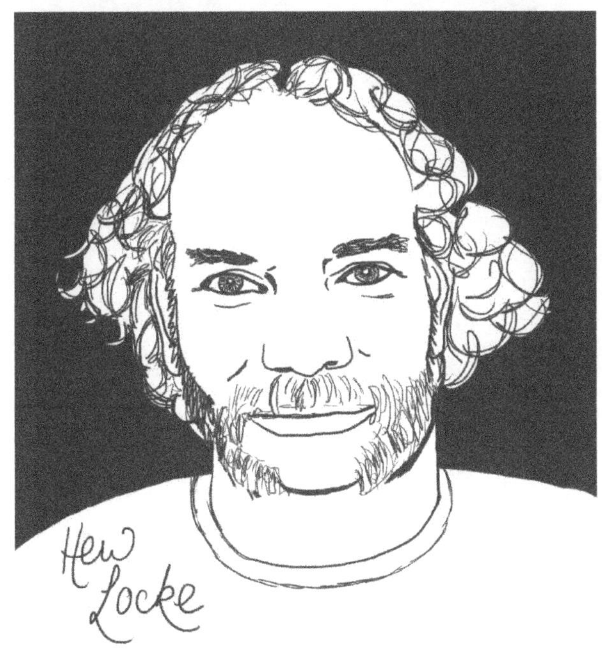

Hew Locke

Born:	1959
Died:	–
Birthplace:	Edinburgh, Scotland
Discipline:	Sculpture, textiles, found objects – contemporary

Hew Locke was born in Scotland but spent most of his childhood in Georgetown, Guyana, Guyana being the birthplace of Hew's father. Both Hew's parents are artists; his father is a sculptor and his mother is a painter.

Hew returned to England to study fine art at Falmouth University and there he began his career as an artist. There are many themes to Hew's work, one of which is royalty. In the series entitled 'House of Windsor', Hew creates images of members of the royal family, an ongoing piece of work where he explores ideas of nationalism and culture, using Queen Elizabeth II's face as a starting point.

Many of Hew's works begin with a found object from a market or charity shop, which he customises and embellishes to create a brand-new piece of art. In his work 'Armada', many boats are suspended from the ceiling, some of which Hew has made from scratch, and some of which have evolved from models Hew has acquired and improved.

His recent work 'The Procession' is a hugely ambitious piece, where 140 figures, each dressed in different costumes and carrying different artefacts, 'process' through the gallery of Tate Britain. This colourful sculpture explores the reasons that people 'come together' to move forward as part of the circle of life.

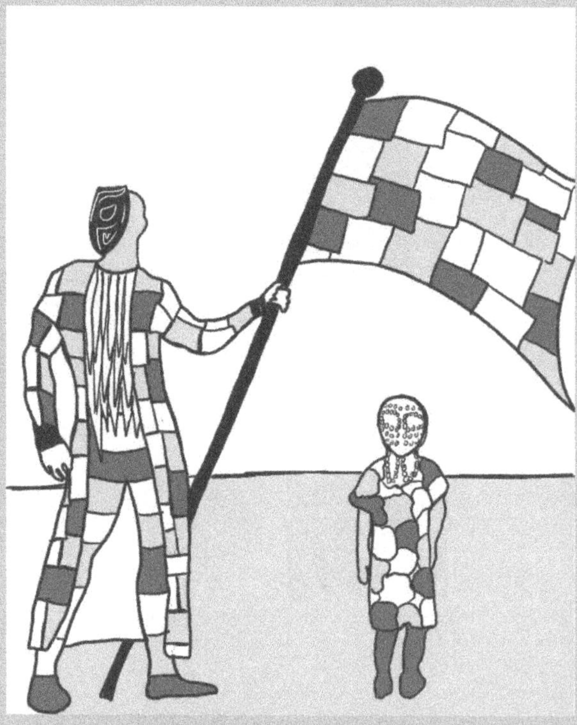

Find out more

Tate website: www.tate.org.uk/whats-on/tate-britain/hew-locke

Website: www.hewlocke.net/Homepage2ndsite.html

Images to inspire	**Other artist links**
The Procession (2022) Armada (2019)	**Nick Cave:** Nick creates soundsuits, elaborate and dynamic costumes that make a noise when they are worn. **Eileen Agar:** Eileen embellished plaster busts with feathers, fabric and other found objects. **Yinka Shonibare:** Yinka creates outfits for his faceless sculptures based on the colours and patterns of Ankara fabric. He explores identity and the impact of colonialism by combining the style of nineteenth-century Western dress with traditional African fabrics.

'What I try to do in my work is mix ideas of attraction and ideas of discomfort – colourful and attractive, but strangely, scarily surreal at the same time.'

Hew Locke (PPOW, n.d.)

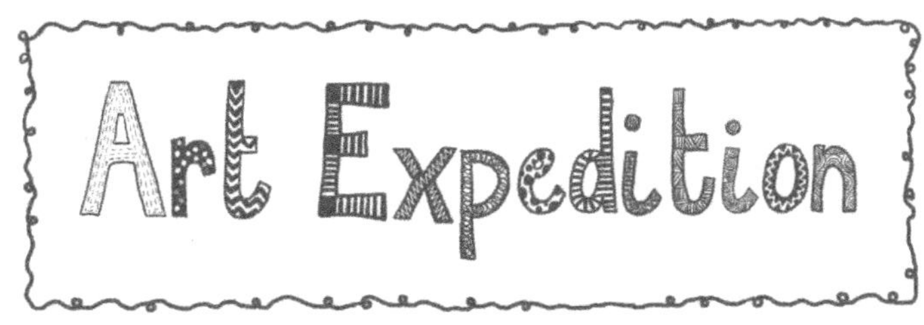

Hew Locke • Upper Key Stage 2
Why do we come together?

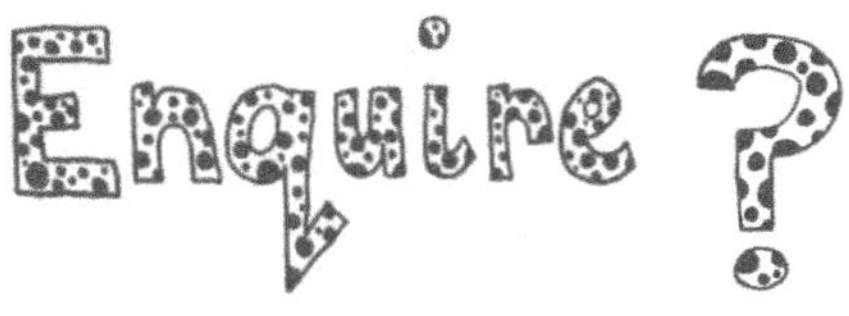

Ask children to consider the times in their life when they have gathered with others. Try to explore ideas beyond meeting in family groups. What festivals are celebrated where people come together? Where else might children be aware that crowds of people gather? Also encourage children to consider the reasons that people come together in protest, in celebration or because of shared ideals.

Signpost: Through this project, we will be using textiles to represent the celebrations that are important in our own lives.

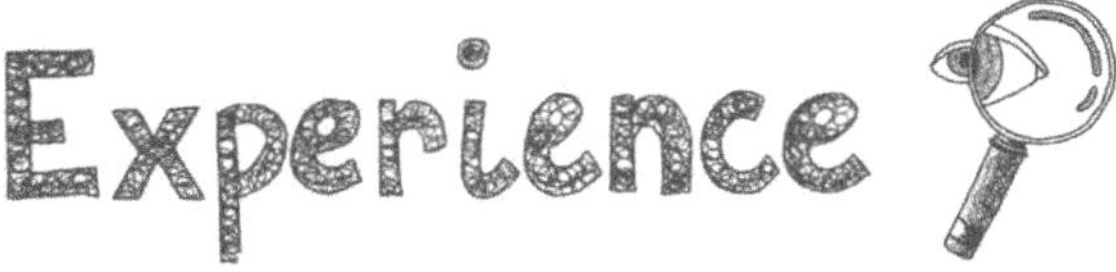

Collect symbols and imagery that represent the places and reasons why people come together.

Look at Hew Locke's 'The Procession'. Why do children think these figures have come together? Remember, there are 140 very different figures, so ensure children have the opportunity to really explore this work.

Give children images from 'The Procession' piece to cut out and stick into sketchbooks. What can they learn from the figures they can see? Encourage the children to annotate the images. Here are a few prompt questions that might promote some interesting responses.

- What might the colours represent?
- What could be the significance of what they are holding?

- How do the figures relate to each other? What do they have in common? What is different?
- What materials have been used?
- What might the figures stand for?
- What can we learn from the way the figure is standing?

Then, ask children to think about the gatherings they discussed in the Enquire stage. What colours or symbols might represent those occasions/ideas? Encourage children to draw a collection of images and marks in their sketchbooks without using words and see if a partner can guess what gathering they are trying to represent.

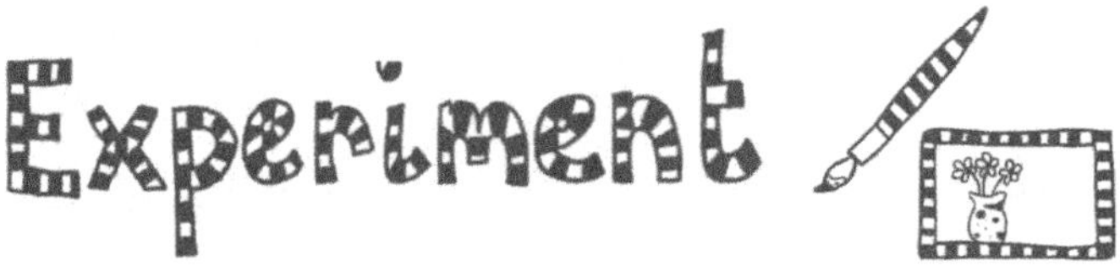

Experiment with different ways of combining, colouring or printing to create their own design on fabric.

This section of the art expedition could be as long or as short as you like – you can decide which technique you wish the children to develop as they move towards their final piece. You could teach the children multiple disciplines that they can select from, or you could focus on one. There is more information about each of these disciplines in the introduction to this chapter, but here are some suggestions of the skills you could choose to develop through this art expedition:

- screen printing
- printing
- weaving
- batik
- silk printing
- felt making
- tie dye.

Children will need an opportunity to experiment with whichever skill or skills you have selected, so that they have some proficiency in this area of textiles in order to be able to produce an achievable design at the next stage.

Children will also need to learn how to join and embellish fabric. Make sure that sessions are planned in advance to allow children to practise the skills they will need to join or applique the fabric to the finished project. This could be through practising a basic running stitch or using a sewing machine. Even if you decide to use glue or staples, make sure that children have had the opportunity to try this out, so they have the knowledge they need to realise their intentions.

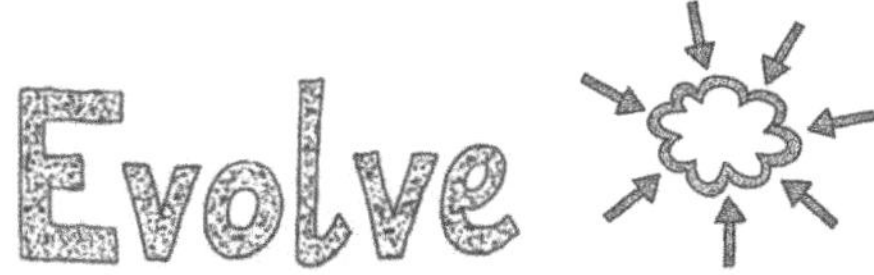

Begin the design process!

This is the stage where the children design how their final piece will look. The brief for this will depend on what you are hoping the outcome will be. Whatever you choose, children are designing a piece of textile that represents a chosen opportunity for people to come together, as explored in the Experience stage. Again, there are many ways in which you could evolve this idea, depending on how ambitious you would like to be.

1. You could ask children to bring in old clothes which they then embellish using the textiles discipline you have been learning. The aim is that children 'become' their own living procession, wearing the textiles they have created. You could create papier-mâché or cardboard masks if you wanted to really go for it!
2. All the children could work on an item for one person. The model could be a child from the class, or if you are lucky enough to be able to borrow a dress-maker's dummy or a mannequin, the children could embellish this using the pieces of fabric they have created.
3. Children could create a textile square to represent their chosen 'coming together' and the squares could be arranged together to create a blanket, a cape or even a flag.

Children should draw their design in their sketchbooks and think about the design of the fabric they will create, based on the ideas they generated during the Experience and Experiment stage. If the pieces of textile are going to be assembled, then children need to plan this carefully too!

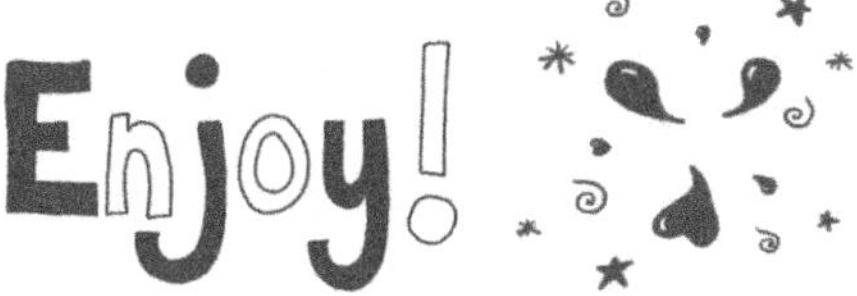

Create a final piece – a portrait, divided into squares, with text used to enhance the image.

Children create the fabric they need based on their design.

Turn this into the final piece that you have decided you want the class to create as their final outcome in collaboration with the children.

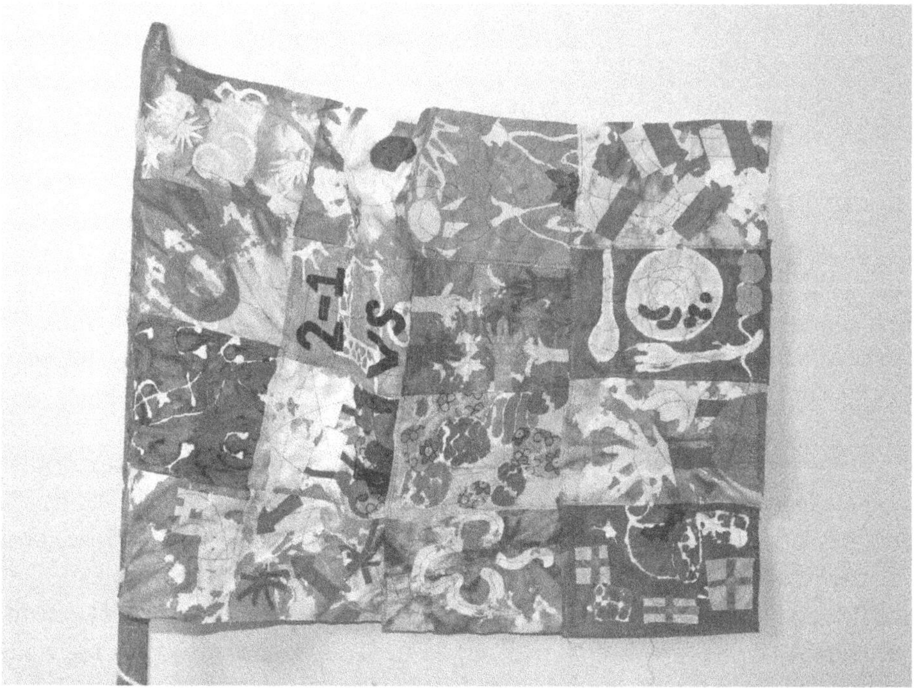

We created a flag and appliqued shapes and patterns to our fabric to represent the reasons why people come together. The backgrounds of each panel are either flour and water batik or tie dye.

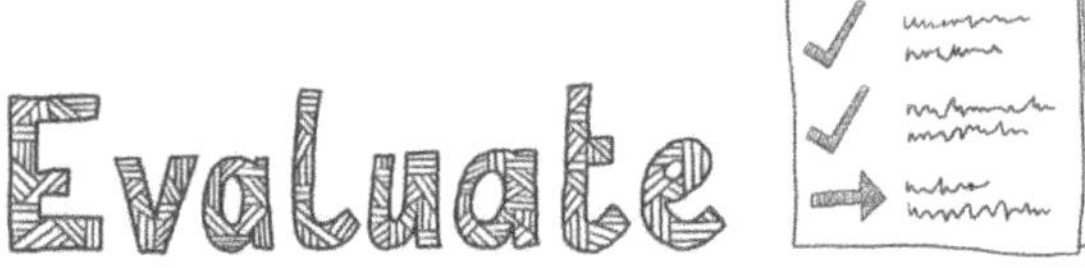

How did it go? Peer and self-assessment

Children in Upper Key Stage 2 should be given the opportunity to respond to these questions in their own way through their annotations. Peer assessment can be verbal or on a sticky note, so that children are not writing in each other's sketchbooks.

Self-evaluation

These questions could be answered as annotations around a photo of the finished 'Procession' in sketchbooks.

- What was your greatest success with this piece?
- What was your biggest challenge?
- What does this procession say about the class?

Peer evaluation

Discuss these prompts in partners.

- What is the impact of this piece?
- Is there anything you would do differently when working on a piece like this?
- If you were to design a piece of textile work for your partner to wear, what colours or techniques would you use to say something about them as an individual?

Chapter 9

Inspiring children to understand the world of art

The consequences of a lack of diversity in the primary art curriculum

One of the many problems with the lack of diversity in the primary art curriculum is the way that art originating outside of Western culture is 'othered'. The term 'other cultures', which is regularly used in primary schools to describe anything that is not White and European in origin, makes the incorrect assumption that all children identify as being White Europeans. For many children, these 'other cultures' might actually be the culture with which they most identify.

We also need to be aware of our use of generic and wide-reaching terms such as 'African art' to lump together the vast and varied artistic contribution of a continent. Showing children one image of a Ugandan ceremonial mask, without further exploration of the context of that piece in relation to Uganda's art history, implies that one piece of art is somehow able to encapsulate thousands of years of rich creativity that has originated from African countries. It narrows children's understanding of all that art can be in a way that does not usually apply to the study of Western art in schools. The equivalent would be showing children the work of van Gogh, labelling it 'European art' and never studying another European artist again. Obviously, children would then assume that the only European art that has ever existed could be personified by van Gogh's style of oil painting.

Another missed opportunity is when we look at the incredible art that the world has to offer without considering the links that exist between them. Historically, the art establishment held up sculptures such as those created by The Fang, who live in western equatorial Africa, as primitive. But it is only in recent times that we have come to understand how these elongated sculptures were actually early examples of abstract art that later inspired artists such as Picasso to take the idea and run with it. Yet another example in art history where an idea has only gained traction once pioneered by a White, European man.

How you can give children a broader understanding of the world of art

As primary school teachers, we shouldn't focus on traditional art from around the world without placing it into the context of when and how it was created. Henna patterns and mandalas are beautiful examples of Indian art that hold deep cultural significance, but we must be mindful not to reduce the huge wealth of creativity that has existed in India to these two, rather stereotypical, examples. To give children a better understanding of the world of art, it might be more enriching to show how art has evolved within a culture, comparing how traditional influences have paved the way for incredible modern and contemporary artists working today.

This is why it is important for children to have a basic understanding of the timeline of art, to recognise how influences have been shared between and within cultures to produce art that is ever evolving. We must be mindful not to allow children to think that only Europe and America have contributed to the fields of modern or contemporary art. In the examples below, it is also interesting for children to consider how contemporary artists often draw on or actively resist ideas from their ancestors, putting influences from traditional art at the forefront of what they do. Making these links may encourage your children to make connections of their own with their individual cultures and identities.

Inspirational art forms and artists

Here are just a few examples of how to use inspirational art forms and artists to get you started in demonstrating a broader overview of a country's art history. You could select a number of examples from within one country's art history and teach them sequentially to give children a very broad overview of the way that art has evolved within a culture. Or you could teach an individual art style in more depth but ensure that children are aware of where that activity fits within the timeline of a culture's artistic legacy. However you choose to approach this, it is important for children to make connections between what has come before and after artistically to see how inspiration and traditions are passed down through generations.

I have used the terms traditional, modern and contemporary to group artists as this is the current terminology favoured by Ofsted. However, art history does not fit into categories in this way, so there is much crossover in these paradigms that could see many of the artists fitting into multiple categories. I have also attempted to pick artists that are less well known, in the hope that you might discover some new favourites to add to your repertoire! There are infinite artists that could be chosen, but here are a few exciting examples that I feel lend themselves to study in the classroom, focusing particularly on cultures that often feature in primary art education.

Indian art	
Traditional	**Warli paintings:** Warli paintings originate from the North Sahyadri Range in Maharashtra and are often painted directly onto walls. All Warli paintings are created using a white paint made from rice flour, water and gum, applied using fine twigs. Perhaps children could make their own paint (substitute gum for PVA glue) and create images on coloured sugar paper? They could even make their own tools to paint with! Or children could draw directly onto the outside walls using white chalk. Encourage children to use Warli symbolism in their creations: circles represent the sun and moon, triangles represent trees and mountains, and squares represent human innovation – or they could come up with their own. **Tanjore paintings:** These beautiful, textured paintings originate in southern India and depict homely scenes inlaid with rich gold and jewels. Children could create relief images, building layers of corrugated card. These images could then be covered with tin foil or faux gold leaf to pick up the details in their work. You can purchase embossing foil from craft shops that could be carved into in order to create a similar textured surface.
Modern	**Amrita Sher-Gil:** Sher-Gil's use of colour and depictions of everyday life make her work stand out from the work of other artists. Encourage children to look at the way that Sher-Gil blocks out shadows and highlights in her pictures and see if they can identify these patches of light and dark in their own paintings. Or children could study Sher-Gil's paintings of the everyday and use this inspiration to paint scenes from their own daily lives. **Sayed Haider Raza:** Based on the bindu (Sanskrit for point or dot), Raza produces beautiful vibrant abstract patterns that usually centre around a black circle. Raza claims his interest in the dot as a motif stemmed from his teacher drawing a dot on the blackboard and telling him to stare at it in an effort to encourage him to concentrate! Children could create their own bindu-inspired work by drawing around different geometric shapes or cutting out shapes from paper and experimenting with tessellation to create intricate patterns.

Contemporary	**Mona Rai:** There is something fascinating about Mona Rai's images created from tiny squares. She uses found materials to create her collages and to explore interesting textures. Children could paint multiple sheets of paper in contrasting colours within which they explore different shades of their colour choice. Once dry, the sheets could be cut into small squares and children could reassemble them in different ways, exploring how the colours and shades work together in different combinations. **Jogen Chowdhury:** Zoom in on Jogen Chowdhury's incredible drawings and paintings, and you will find the most amazing inspiration for mark making and shading. The contrast in his images is made entirely from crosshatches, squiggles, lines and swirls that come together to provide the texture for his figurative drawings. Even just asking children to collect examples of different marks from within his images would demonstrate fantastic drawing development in sketchbooks.

Chinese art	
Traditional	**Jiǎn zhǐ – the chinese art of paper cutting:** These paper cuts, often constructed from red paper, are as intricate as they are beautiful. The designs often feature dragons, tigers, carp and the phoenix. They can also contain the animals of the 12 Chinese zodiac signs. Children could free cut animals from red paper, or for a more ambitious project, they could draw their designs first and then cut out the patterns using a craft knife. If you wanted to develop this further into a digital art project and you know someone with an electronic paper cutter like a Cricut® or Silhouette Cameo® machine, children could design their images on iPads and cut these out by uploading them to the cutter's software. **Silk painting:** Silk painting actually originates in China, so is an excellent art discipline through which to study the changing movements of art. Silk designs uncovered in the Mawangdui Han tombs make a fantastic comparison to the work of Wilson Shieh to show how the art of Chinese silk painting has evolved over time. Children could experiment with silk painting in a more traditional way using gutta and inks (gutta is a paint that can be used as an outline, once the gutta is dry, ink cannot permeate the barrier allowing the artist to keep colours separate and provide definition), or they could take inspiration from Wilson Shieh and paint with more controllable mediums such as gouache and acryli (paints that are more permanently applied and less likely to bleed).

<table>
<tr><td>Modern</td><td> Qi Baishi: Qi Baishi employs the traditional ink and brush style of Chinese art but with a more fluid, dynamic touch. I particularly like the way that Baishi creates depth by layering undiluted ink on top of lighter, watered-down marks. Encourage children to paint leaves or flowers using a brush dipped in very watery ink or watercolour paints, using quick marks and gestural strokes. Once this is dry, give the children undiluted ink and let them work over the top to create a clear definition between foreground and background. Pan Yuliang: Pan Yuliang was a post-impressionist artist who combined traditional Chinese water and ink painting techniques with a European expressionist style. Look closely at her work and you will see the loose way that she applies paint in patches of colour. Reading her story, we learn that she overcame the considerable odds faced by women artists of the time to forge a career as a painter. It would develop children's painting style to encourage them to experiment with this way of applying paint using different brushes, or even tools such as spatulas or palette knives. Not with a view to copying Pan Yuliang's paintings as a whole, but as a way of understanding her technique. </td></tr>
<tr><td>Contemporary</td><td> Yin Xiuzhen: Yin Xiuzhen's landscapes within a suitcase are exactly as they sound. An open suitcase brimming with skyscrapers, parks, buildings and roads. You could either recreate this as a class project within an old suitcase you have managed to source, or children could work individually to fill a small box with their own city. This could be using junk, mixed media, clay or even construction bricks such as LEGO®! Huang Yuxing: Huang Yuxing creates mesmorising, colourful landscapes that look like something from a psychedelic dream! Children could quite simply go for it with coloured oil pastels on bright coloured paper. Or, you could create your own scratchboards by covering a piece of card in thick oil pastel and then applying a thin layer of acrylic paint over the top. Traditionally this paint is black but to draw on Yuxing's style it might be more impactful to choose another bright colour of acrylic. Once the scratchboards are dry, carve into the paint with a cocktail stick, a needle or a scraper tool to create a colourful, translucent world full of dynamic shapes and marks. </td></tr>
</table>

Japanese art	
Traditional	**Daruma:** Daruma are traditional Japanese dolls that are named after the Chinese monk, Bodhidharma, who brought Zen Buddhism to Japan. These small round dolls are made of painted papier-mâché. Using an underinflated balloon, children could papier-mâché their own daruma and then paint them using the traditional red, black and gold design, leaving the eyes blank. Legend says that when you set a goal, you colour in one of the Daruma's eyes. Once the goal has been achieved, the other eye can be coloured, giving the Daruma 'full sight', a step towards the Buddhist ideal of self-actualisation. **Katsushika Ōi**: Ōi, the daughter of Katsushika Hokusai (best known for his iconic 'The Great Wave off Kanagawa'), has long been missing from the history of art. However, recent evidence suggests that she may have been responsible for supporting, or even producing entirely, some of Hokusai's Ukiyo-e masterpieces. Certainly, the few pieces directly attributed to Ōi stand up in their own right against the masters of the Ukiyo-e art form. Have a look at her sketches to inspire clean-lined, figurative drawings. And yes, Ōi means the same translated in Japanese as it does in English. It was Hokusai's rather charming nickname for his daughter!
Modern	**Yatsuo No Tsubaki:** Tsubaki progresses the traditional art of woodblock print to a more modern place, creating simplified designs that are often printed in just two colours. These two-tone images are the perfect inspiration for a project using polystyrene foam to create prints. Many of Tsubaki's prints are of flowers or leaves, so encourage children to work from direct observation to press a print into polystyrene foam that can then be printed onto coloured paper or card. **Yamada Hikaru:** Have a look at Hikaru's ceramics, in particular his constellations collection. Hikaru creates slabs of clay and prints into the surface using different tools to create interesting marks and effects. Children could roll out clay tiles and use found objects to press patterns into the surface of their slab. Or you could use modelling paste on thick card, which could be pushed through stencils or carved into before being left to dry.

Contemporary	**Yayoi Kusama:** No discussion around Japanese artists would be complete without reference to the mighty Yayoi Kusama, empress of polka dots. It is difficult to limit the inspiration from this artist to just a few ideas, but painting spots on pumpkins in Early Years is a great start. This could progress to modelling vegetables from clay to be painted in two colours, with a contrasting background and spots. Creating stuffed forms from spotty textiles to create a class sculpture would also be incredibly effective, and covering anything in spotted stickers in the style of Kusama's 'Obliteration Room' would be lots of fun. **Takashi Murakami:** Takashi Murakami is a contemporary artist famous for his happy flowers! His vibrant, cartoonish, simplified forms are extremely accessible and highly appealing to children. Murakami works with many different disciplines, so children could create their own flowers out of textiles, clay, collage, paint, or even digitally produced designs. Just make sure the children's creations feature Murakami's iconic smile!

African art	
Traditional	**Basket weaving:** Weaving baskets from palm raffia around banana leaf stalks is an art form that has been prevalent throughout the history of Uganda. These skilled craftspeople are able to create baskets in a multitude of intricate shapes and patterns. Raffia can be bought inexpensively for children to use and can be wrapped around a cardboard template to create a basket. If you want to focus more on the intricate designs and patterns that can be created by weaving, children could weave on a cardboard loom or using bamboo plant stakes tied at the centre to create a radial weave. Have a look online for the many weaving patterns that you can easily print and download, or see if the children can compose their own! **Batik:** Batik is an art discipline that exists in many cultures, but there are lots of fine examples of Ugandan batik work. Using melted wax to resist the dyes or inks you are using, children can create their own images. Traditionally, Ugandan batik would feature scenes of everyday life: hunting, cooking, homelife or celebrations, but more modern pieces can include pretty much anything!

Modern	**Theresa Musoke:** Theresa Musoke's beautiful images of Ugandan and Kenyan wildlife would be the perfect inspiration for an art project celebrating the continent of Africa's beautiful animals. Black silhouetted animals in front of a sunset sky is a standard art project in primary schools, so taking inspiration from Musoke would add an authentic twist to an old favourite. Perhaps children could sketch their animal, then choose a few lines to accentuate in black ink. The background could be created using bright watercolours, allowing the paint to drip down the page to create the movement that exists in Musoke's work. **Francis Nnaggenda:** Ugandan artist Francis Nnaggenda is arguably one of the greatest sculptors that the African continent has produced. His sculptures often feature smooth, abstract figures and are the perfect inspiration for experimentation with surfaces and edges when using clay with children. Children could create their own clay sculptures by observing and sketching their classmates, and then attempt to reduce their figures down to simple shapes and lines.
Contemporary	**Donald Wasswa:** Ugandan artist Donald Wasswa's drawings are an amazing way to introduce pattern and mark making. His work centres around extra-terrestrial beings, and his black and white images evoke alien figures constructed from geometric shapes. Children could experiment with continuous line drawings, which could be completed blind, to develop the level of abstraction featured in Wasswa's work. They could also draw around their own geometric shapes and fill them with patterns. Children could create their own patterns, take inspiration from Wasswa or look for patterns around them to create new ideas. **Lilian Nabulime:** In Lilian's series entitled 'Children, wood, metal and nails', she dresses wooden figures in clothes made from found materials which are suspended from string in rows like bunting. The lines of figures are reminiscent of paper dolls, which would be a fantastic way to access this work with children. Encourage your class to 'dress' their own cardboard figures with scraps of textiles or paper. The children could think about their own style of dress or consider the patterns and colours that they feel represent their own identity or culture.

Australian art	
Traditional	The traditional art of Australia was created by the indigenous Aboriginal and Torres Strait Islander communities. Only those who have permission from them are allowed to recreate the stories of their culture, so it is disrespectful to copy the symbols and images that appear in traditional dot paintings. Adopting this style of art in primary school would be considered cultural appropriation, although that does not mean that children cannot look at or enjoy the beauty of this art form and the stories that it tells. **Dot painting:** Although it is considered disrespectful to copy elements of a dot painting, there are really interesting aspects of this work that can inspire children to create their own art. One unique idea that exists in Aboriginal and Torres Strait Islander communities art is the perspective that is used to denote its subject. Most images that exist in traditional Australian art are viewed from an aerial perspective. Children could create scenes of their own using toys or natural found objects, and practise sketching or drawing these items from above to develop their observation skills. **Rock painting:** The Aboriginal and Torres Strait Islander communities of Australia used 'natural galleries' to display their artwork on rocks, walls, tree trunks, or any other surface where paint could be applied. These images were used to tell stories and record events. Although the content of such art is not to be recreated, children can still be inspired by the methods and techniques. Perhaps children could mix their own paints from ground-up chalk, mud or soft stone, and use available surfaces in the school grounds to tell their stories, using their own symbolism to represent people and events.
Modern	**Albert Namatjira:** Albert Namatjira is considered to be one of the most prolific and successful Australian artists ever. His watercolour paintings employ vibrant colours and awesome perspective that exemplify the great open spaces of the Australian landscape. Over several sessions, children could build up watercolour images of their environment, working from light to dark, building layers of colour to create an image with similar perspective. **Ethel Carrick:** Ethel Carrick's impressionist style makes her a worthy candidate to be held up against her more well-known male counterparts like Monet or Renoir. The bright colours and loose brushstrokes of her work are perfect inspiration for children to experiment with a more exploratory style of painting.

	The application of her paint is apparent: encourage children to use different tools to apply paint in a similar style, and to use unmixed colours together to create different effects where the individual colours are still visible.
Contemporary	**Sidney Nolan:** Sidney Nolan is famous for his paintings depicting the life of the infamous outlaw, Ned Kelly. Not only is this story incredibly engaging for children, but the stylised image of Ned that appears as a motif in many of Nolan's paintings makes him a perfect starting point to further children's understanding of Australian history. Children could paint a favourite part of Ned Kelly's story and then add his figure in black paint or collage to bring the image to life. **Nonggirrnga Marawili:** This artist draws on the art from her ancestors to produce beautiful, vibrant images that speak to the work of traditional Aboriginal art. Marawili's work is not to be copied as the patterns she chooses are steeped in the history of her people, but her use of pattern is still incredibly inspiring. Children could create their own patterns that could be painted onto sticks or tubes of card to create free-standing sculptures, such as Marawili's series of 'Lightning' sculptures.

British art	
Traditional	**Illuminated lettering:** Illuminated lettering was often painstakingly completed by monks who would write and illustrate texts, often the Bible, by hand. These beautiful letters are works of art in themselves and are usually themed to represent the meaning of the text. Children could create their own illuminated letters; it could be their initials decorated with symbols important in their own lives, or the letter could be at the beginning of a poem or story, decorated with images to signpost the reader to the content of the upcoming text. **Celtic knots:** Celtic knots can be recreated in the classroom in many ways. Children can experiment with circles of string, adding twists and loops to create their own symmetrical patterns. These can then be stuck down and sprayed silver or gold. Celtic knots can be carved into tin foil on cardboard or embossing foil to create a more authentic design. Copper wire can even be purchased reasonably cheaply that can be bent by hand and then hammered flat to create brooches, bracelets or other interesting designs.

Modern	**Eileen Agar:** Eileen Agar was fascinated by found objects. As a surrealist, she enjoyed putting objects together to create new forms and experimenting with the relationship between unlikely things. Agar is an excellent catalyst for 'assemblage', the process of putting objects together to make something new. Agar spent lots of time outside collecting her materials, particularly at the beach. She also enjoyed making hats with flamboyant and exciting themes; definitely an exciting project to recreate in the classroom! Perhaps children could collect objects from their own environment and practise arranging them in different ways to create interesting sculptures. This would also be a great opportunity for a photography unit, using different angles and cropping to turn everyday objects into something new and exciting. **Sonia Delaunay:** Sonia Delaunay's use of circles makes her work extremely accessible to children. The way that her concentric forms are deconstructed and offset against each other opens up a world of inspiration for paintings as well as collage. Kandinsky's circles (which are so often studied in school) could be evolved by cutting and reassembling them to create a whole new masterpiece inspired by Delaunay. Children could create their own circles using collage or paint, experimenting with different combinations of complementary colours.
Contemporary	**Banksy:** If ever there is an artist that will capture children's imaginations, it is the illusive Banksy! And he is the perfect opportunity to encourage children to have a go at stenciling. Stencils can easily be made from card, or from plastic dividers from folders if you need something more robust. To create Banksy's iconic black and white images, children will need to create two stencils, one with the dark areas cut out and one with the light areas cut out. Start with a very simple black and white image where the distinction between light and dark has a high contrast. Then, you can either sponge on the paint one layer at a time, or you can spray using either a hand pump full of ink or an actual aerosol. This project takes a bit of thinking about, but the results are well worth it! **Frank Bowling:** Frank Bowling's paintings are as much concerned with the paint itself as with the subject of the painting. Underneath the many layers of colourful paint, there may be hidden surprises that are deliberately obscured from the viewer. Some paintings include shells, objects and images that cannot be seen in the final image. Children could think about things they would like to hide within their paintings before they apply and experiment with the way that the paint moves across their page. Encourage children to use different tools to move the paint around and see how the colours react when they are mixed and smeared together.

Final thoughts

The purpose of this book is not to provide a curriculum to be delivered verbatim, but rather to inspire a different way of thinking around the content and delivery of your personal art curriculum.

Personalising your curriculum is hugely important. Only you know your class, its demographics, and the interests and passions of your children. You have the freedom to take all these things into account through the design of your art sessions. Your school should have developed a roster of skills and processes to focus on, but the inspiration behind your teaching should always be open to flexibility.

Local living artists

An area that I was unable to cover in this book is the wealth of possibilities that exist within local, living artists that might exist in your community. There is nothing in the National Curriculum that says that the artists you learn from must be famous on an international or historical scale. In fact, the guidance is left deliberately vague to give you the option to choose artists that are specific to you and your class. There is nothing more inspirational for children than to work with real-life artists who can share their unique perspective on their art process and show children how ideas can be generated and evolved.

Look around your local area. Check social media and ask amongst parents. Local artists are often delighted to be asked to come into school to share their expertise. These artists do not need to be famous – it might be a parent with a talent for a particular craft, or a painter from the community who enjoys responding to the local area. Anything that supports children in the recognition that art is something that real people do, as either a job or a hobby, is hugely beneficial.

Support for your curriculum as a whole

There are many online resources to support the teaching of artists from diverse backgrounds, but there are some areas of your curriculum that need a more holistic approach to ensure that the art you deliver is as inclusive as possible. There is no better resource for this than the National Society for Education in Art and Design's (NSEAD) Anti-racist Curriculum Checklist, which can be freely downloaded from the NSEAD website.

This incredibly user-friendly checklist supports you in looking at your curriculum with a critical eye. It also provides advice on how to consider colonial legacy and correct terminology within your teaching.

Find out more

I hope that this book will support you on your journey to discovering the incredible artists that have been overlooked by art history, so that you can bring your own ideas into the classroom and teach from artists that inspire you, or deal with themes that you know your class will enjoy.

If you wish to find out more, there are plenty of places to look.

Instagram

@kaytieholdstockart: This is me! Daily primary art inspiration from diverse artists.

@amazingblackartists: A fabulous Instagram account celebrating the work of Black artists.

@thegreatwomenartists: The wonderful Katy Hessel celebrating women artists. There is also a podcast of the same name which is well worth a listen.

Books

The Story of Art without Men (2022): Katy Hessel's incredible book that takes its inspiration from the famous art textbook *The Story of Art* by E.H. Gombrich, which didn't featured a single female artist.

Black Artists Shaping the World (2021): Sharna Jackson has written this beautifully accessible book which would be perfect in your book corner for your children to enjoy.

The Art Book (1994) and *The 20th Century Art Book* (2014): These new editions of the Phaidon classics have been updated to feature a greater range of diversity within the featured artists. Really lovely visual guides.

Great Women Artists (2019): Another Phaidon reference book. This time, solely dedicated to women artists.

Online resources

The Visualise report provides a crucial insight into the diversity crisis in art education. The report is based in secondary education but I am sure you will see that its findings are highly relevant to primary education also:

www.runnymedetrust.org/visualise

The NSEAD's Anti-Racist Art Education (ARAE) page contains a wealth or resources to support you on your journey to a diverse and inclusive art curriculum:

www.nsead.org/resources/anti-racist-art-education/

Enjoy creating your own diverse art curriculum

As you discover more amazing artists, you may be inspired to create art expeditions of your own. The six-part structure of the expedition has been deliberately designed to be replicated so that you can build your own journey using a starting point that you think will inspire your class. It might be the work of an artist that excites you, or it might be a theme that fits in with another curriculum area that you are hoping to explore. If this is the case, you might find this resource incredibly useful: www.artuk.org. This website is the online collection of public art in Britain and can be searched by key words. Simply type in the theme you wish to explore and the website will suggest artwork that fits with it. You can also access free lesson plans and resources through the site.

I hope this book is a supportive resource on your quest to diversify your primary art curriculum. I also hope that it reaffirms your commitment to the importance of an arts-rich education for all. The future prosperity of our country is dependent on the innovation and creativity of our young people, so it is imperative that we place a high value on the subjects through which these skills are explicitly taught.

Art is undeniably a vehicle for social mobility, for community engagement and for happier, healthier lives. Our children deserve an education that is as unique and diverse as they are.

Bibliography

Arts WA. (n.d.). 'Jacob Lawrence.' Available at: https://www.arts.wa.gov/artist-collection/?request=record;id=2092;type=701 (Accessed: 6 Dec 2023)

Ben & Jerry's. (2018). 'The Art of Pecan Resist: A Q&A with Favianna Rodriguez.' Available at: https://www.benjerry.com/whats-new/2018/10/qa-favianna-rodriguez (Accessed: 13 Dec 2023)

Blair, I.F. (2021). 'What exists at the edge of our perception? Artist Kenturah Davis is here to show you.' *Los Angeles Times*. Available at: https://www.latimes.com/lifestyle/image/story/2021-05-26/kenturah-davis-interview-on-black-art-and-the-world-of-los-angeles-that-cannot-be-known (Accessed: 5 Dec 2023)

Briggs, P. (2022). 'How do non-specialist teachers teach art?' (Online Video). *Vimeo*. Available at: https://vimeo.com/679902070?embedded=true&source=vimeo_logo&owner=9888868 (Accessed: 23 Nov 2022)

CHR. (2016). ELIZABETH CATLETT: (1915–2012). Callaloo, 39(5), 999–1080. Available at: https://www.jstor.org/stable/26776259 (Accessed 13 Dec 2023)

Crafts Council. (2022). 'Make First: Dive straight into making with Make First, our craft education pedagogy.' Available at: https://www.craftscouncil.org.uk/learning/make-first (Accessed: 19 Dec 2022)

Cultural Learning Alliance. (2017). 'Key Research Findings: The Case for Cultural Learning.' Available at: https://culturallearningalliance.org.uk/wp-content/uploads/2017/08/CLA-key-findings-2017.pdf (Accessed: 21 Nov 2022)

Department for Education, (DFE). (2014). 'Art and design programmes of study: key stages 1 and 2 National curriculum in England.' Available at: https://assets.publishing.service.gov.uk/government/uploads/system/uploads/attachment_data/file/239018/PRIMARY_national_curriculum_-_Art_and_design.pdf (Accessed: 23 Nov 2022)

DuBois Shaw, G. (2005). '"Moses Williams, Cutter of Profiles": Silhouettes and African American Identity in the Early Republic.' Proceedings of the American Philosophical Society, 149(1), 22–39. Available at: http://www.jstor.org/stable/4598906 (Accessed 12 Dec 2023)

Eisner, E. (2002). 'The Arts and the Creation of Mind.' *What the Arts Teach and How It Shows*. (pp. 70–92). Yale University Press. Available at: https://www.arteducators.org/advocacy-policy/articles/116-10-lessons-the-arts-teach (Accessed: 18 Dec 2023)

Graham, L. (n.d.). 'Zaha Hadid: The Story of an Architectural Genius.' *Elysian*. Available at: https://readelysian.com/zaha-hadid-the-story-of-an-architectural-genius/ (Accessed: 4 Dec 2023)

Higgins, C. (2017). 'Turner prize winner Lubaina Himid: "I have more things to say – this gives me the chance."' *The Guardian*. Available at: https://www.theguardian.com/artanddesign/2017/dec/06/turner-prize-winner-lubaina-himid-interview (Accessed: 12 Dec 2023)

Hunt, T. (2023). 'Sarah Biffin: the Incredible 19th-Century Artist You Probably Haven't Heard Of'. *ArtRKL*. Available at: https://artrkl.com/blogs/news/sarah-biffin-the-incredible-19th-century-artist-you-probably-havent-heard-of (Accessed: 6 Dec 2023)

Jay, L. (2018). 'Shini-e and Art of Japan: "I leave my brush in the East."' *Modern Tokyo Times*. Available at: https://moderntokyotimes.com/shini-e-and-art-of-japan-i-leave-my-brush-in-the-east/ (Accessed: 13 Dec 2023)

Jean-Michel Basquiat.org (n.d.) 'Jean-Michel Basquiat Quotes.' Available at: https://www.jean-michel-basquiat.org/quotes/ (Accessed: 5 Dec 2023)

Moderna Museet. (n.d.). 'Topics and central works.' Available at: https://www.modernamuseet.se/stockholm/en/exhibitions/hilma-af-klint-2013/topics/ (Accessed 5 Dec 2023)

MOMA. (n.d.). 'Cindy Sherman Untitled Film Still #84 1978.' Available at: https://www.moma.org/collection/works/57236 (Accessed: 13 Dec 2023)

October Gallery. (n.d.). *El Anatsui, OCTOBER GALLERY | EL ANATSUI | ART | BIOGRAPHY* Available at: https://octobergallery.co.uk/artists/anatsui (Accessed: 19 Dec 2023)

Ofsted. (2023). Research Review Series: Art and Design. Available at: https://www.gov.uk/government/publications/research-review-series-art-and-design/research-review-series-art-and-design (Accessed: 17 May 2023)

PPOW. (n.d.). 'Hew Locke: The Procession.' Available at: https://www.ppowgallery.com/exhibitions/hew-locke-the-procession2#tab:slideshow (Accessed: 18 Dec 2023)

Robinson, M. (2018). 'The Mexican Street Artist Destroying Male Stereotypes.' *The Book of Man*. Available at: https://thebookofman.com/mind/culture/victoria-villasana-street-artist/ (Accessed: 13 Dec 2023)

Ryzin, J.C. van. (2022). *Deborah Roberts sues another artist, gallery for copyright infringement, Sightlines*. Available at: https://sightlinesmag.org/deborah-roberts-sues-another-artist-and-her-gallery-for-copyright-infringement (Accessed: 19 Dec 2023)

Schorske, Carina del Valle. (2022). 'Cecilia Vicuña's Desire Lines.' *The New York Times*. Available at: https://www.nytimes.com/2022/08/25/magazine/cecilia-vicuna-art.html (Accessed: 11 Dec 2023)

Scott, J. (2016). *Entwined: Sisters and secrets in the silent world of artist Judith Scott*. Boston: Beacon Press.

Tate Kids. (n.d). 'Who is Chila Kumari Singh Burman?' Available at: https://www.tate.org.uk/kids/explore/who-is/who-chila-kumari-singh-burman (Accessed: 12 Dec 2023)

The All-Party Parliamentary Group for Art, Craft and Design in Education. (2023). 'Art Now Inquiry'. Available at: https://www.nsead.org/community-activism/policy-and-research/all-party-parliamentary-group/artnow-inquiry-2023/ (Accessed: 10 April 2024)

The Cut. (2016). 'Jerry Saltz and Kehinde Wiley Explain How Art Invents New Ways of Seeing.' Available at: https://www.thecut.com/2016/11/jerry-saltz-tiff any-new-ways-of-seeing-whitneybiennial-video-series.html (Accessed: 6 Dec 2023)

Weiwei, A. (2011). *Ai Weiwei's blog: Writings, interviews, and Digital Rants, 2006-2009 (the MIT Press Writing Art Series)*. Lee Ambrozy. Translated by L. Ambrozy. MIT Press.

Wiltshire, S. (n.d.). *An artist who draws buildings and Skylines, Stephen Wiltshire*. Available at: https://www.stephenwiltshire.co.uk/ (Accessed: 19 Dec 2023)

Wu, M. (2018). 'Mitchel Wu Toy Photography Behind the Scenes.' Available at: https://www.mitchelwutoyphotography.com/post/mitchel-wu-toy-photography-behind-the-scenes-brainwashing-with-dr-finkelstein (Accessed: 13 Dec 2023)

Index